37th Infantry Division

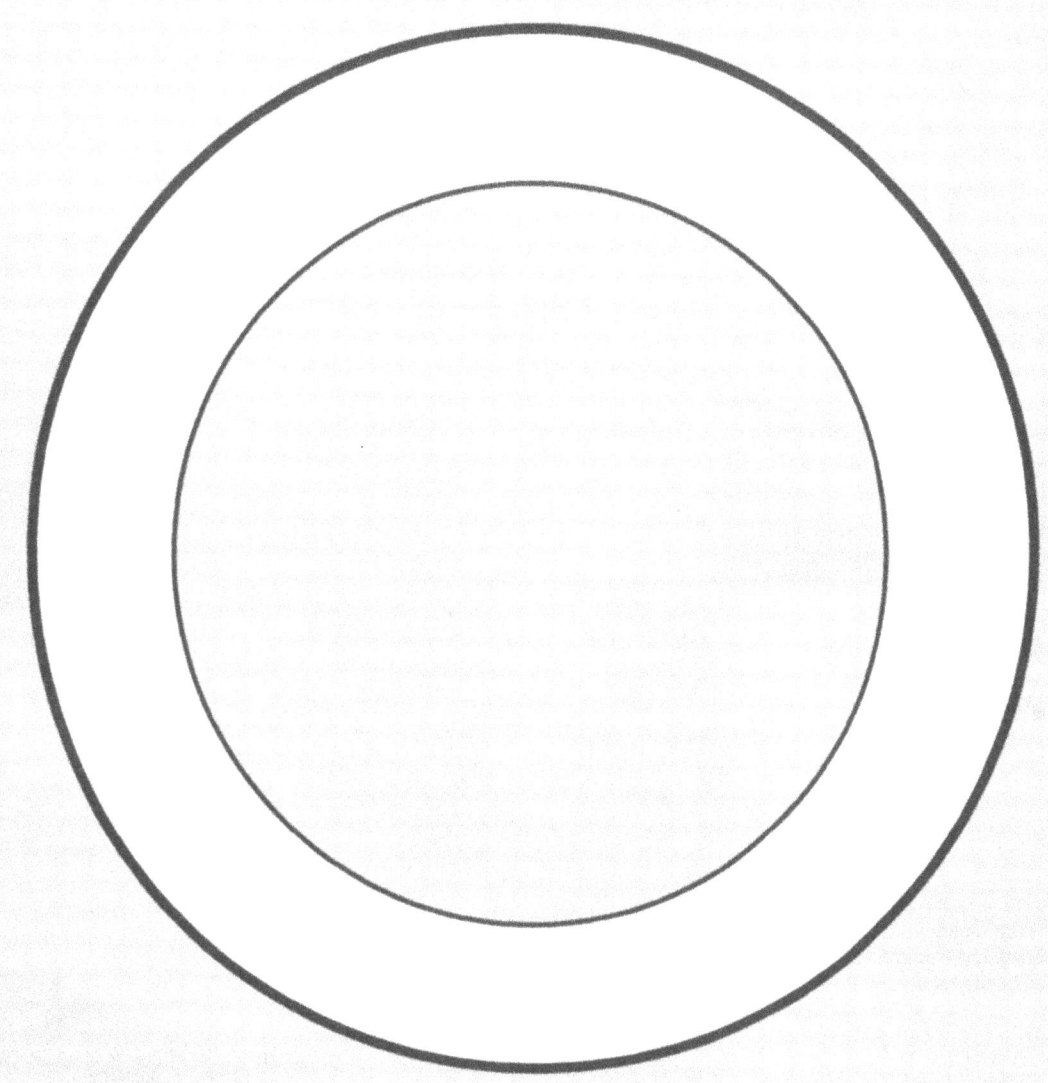

"Buckeye Division"

TURNER PUBLISHING COMPANY

Left, Maj. Gen. Robert S. Beightler, Commanding Officer of the 37th Infantry Division throughout WWII. (Courtesy Chaney)

Below, New Caledonia, 1944-45. The sea coast at sundown. (Courtesy Chaney)

37th Infantry Division Association Book Chairman: William Marshal Chaney
Coordinated and Designed by: David Hurst

Copyright©1995 37th Infantry Division Association
Publishing Rights: Turner Publishing Company

This book or any part thereof may not be reproduced without the written consent of the publisher and author.

This book was compiled and written with available and submitted materials. Turner Publishing Company and the 37th Infantry Division Association regret they cannot be responsible for errors or omissions.

Library of Congress Catalog Card No.: 95-060088
ISBN: 978-1-68162-290-3

Limited Edition: additional copies may be available directly from the publisher.

37th Infantry Division

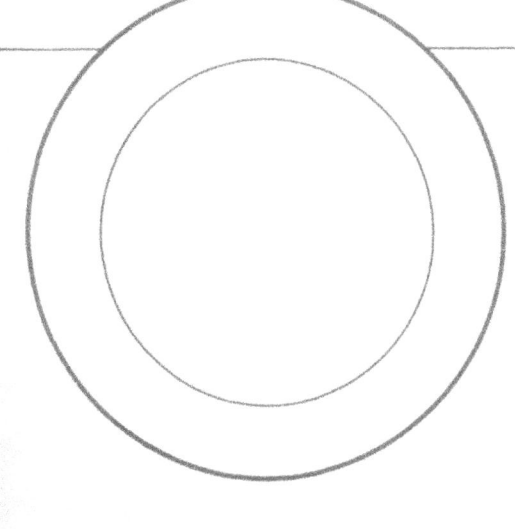

CONTENTS

Preface 4
History of the 37th Infantry Division 8
    Casualties 18
    Camp Shelby 20
    Indiantwon Gap 24
    Memories of Service 28
    Guadalcanal 35
    Serving God and Country 47
37th Infantry Division Association 61
37th Veterans 66
Index 95

As I write my first article as President of the 37th Division Veterans' Association, I am truly honored to serve as the 77th President of this great Association. Those who came before me have all served with distinction. I will do my utmost to follow suit.

On behalf of all the members of the 37th Division Veterans' Association, I extend my congratulations to all involved in the publication of this book about the 37th Buckeye Division and many of the individuals who served therein.

From its initial inception the 37th Buckeye Division, which evolved from the Militia established in 1760, the members of this great Division constantly strive to mold this organization into a combat unit to be reckoned with. The outstanding heroism of its members during WWI, II, and Korea, made it one of the most outstanding peacetime organizations in the United States.

Through the trenches in France, the swamps and jungles in Guadalcanal, New Georgia, Bougainville, Emirau, Iwo Jima, Saipan, Tinian, Okinawa and the Philippines; the men of the 37th faced the enemy in many different battles with their courage and determination to bring the enemy to his knees. Although great losses were inflicted on the enemy on all occasions, the organization also suffered the loss of many very brave men...at times displaying individual feats of heroism. During World War I, the 148th Infantry had one recipient of the Medal of Honor, who under fire distinguished himself "above and beyond the call of duty." During World War II, the 145th Infantry had one recipient of the Medal of Honor, and the 148th Infantry had six recipients of the MOH, in the Asiatic-Pacific Theater, whose names are engraved on the 37th Division Monument at Camp Shelby, Mississippi.

May this history book be a tribute to the brave heroes who gave their lives for God and Country to help preserve a free America.

Frank B. Niehaus
President
37th Division Veterans' Association

Admiral William F. "Bull" Halsey Jr.

The tide of Japanese Imperial aggression was rolled back at Guadalcanal. The hitherto victorious Japanese first tasted the bitter fruits of defeat, here on this island that they preferred to call "The Island of Death" or "Starvation Island."

The Commander of the South Pacific Forces, "Admiral William F. "Bull" Halsey Jr., perhaps best portrayed "The Spirit of Guadalcanal" as he wrote in 1944, "The successes of the South Pacific Forces" were not the achievements of separate services or individuals but the result of whole-hearted subordination of self-interest by all in order that one successful 'fighting team' could be created."

Admiral Halsey as "the man of the hour" was admired and respected by all those under his command, and equally feared by the enemy. It would behoove we veterans of the Guadalcanal Campaign to be ever mindful of the Admiral's words of admonition, as the victory won at Guadalcanal can be understood only by an appreciation of the contribution of the role of each service.

Let each combatant of the campaign take pride in the fact, that it was eight months to the day after Pearl Harbor, that we Americans met the Japanese at Guadalcanal, on their chosen fields of battle, and they were ours.

Let us strive to perpetuate "The Spirit of Guadalcanal," by being ever ready to fly to the relief of our country, and to advance the bonds of brotherhood among our former Comrades-of-Arms.

                                      Yours in Comradeship,
                                      William Marshal Chaney, Chairman
                                      37th Infantry Division History Book Committee

Right, U.S. Navy ships off the coast of Emirau Island waiting for the 147th Infantry Regt. to come aboard, July 9, 1944. (Courtesy Chaney) Below, American Military and Naval Cemetery, Bougainville Island, 1943-1944. (Courtesy Chaney) Bottom, Sunday service in the jungles of Bougainville. (Courtesy Hochwald)

Left, 117th Combat Eng. Bat. (Courtesy Muller) Below, (Courtesy Atkins) Bottom, British Samoa maidens show influence of western missionaries. They are wearing halters. (Courtesy Chaney)

A Brief Highlighted History of the 37th Infantry Division

by Stanley A. Frankel, official historian of the 37th Div. in WWII

Although the 37th Division did not receive its formal designation and authorization until July 18, 1917, the troops who were to comprise the 37th had already seen service along the Mexican border. For nine months, during 1916 and 1917, elements of what was then the Ohio National guard, were stationed at Camp Pershing, near El Paso, patrolling the border in that sector.

However, the fathers and grandfathers of the soldiers who later manned the infantry, the artillery, and the other components reflected the military tradition of Ohio's fighting men by their hand-to-hand combat in dense woods and trackless forests against the Indians before the Revolutionary War. The exploits of Ohioans George Rogers Clark and Simon Kenton in jungle-like terrain against a primitive but brave foe set the stage for WWII jungle warfare in Guadalcanal, New Georgia and Bougainville.

After clearing their enemy out of forested Ohio, the famed Minute Men next matched rifles and wits with British-organized Indians in the Revolutionary War. Those Minute Men were farmer-soldiers, prepared to work the fields or to fight the British and their mercenaries. Out of this citizen-soldier tradition came the institution of the National Guard, prepared to leave home and hearth on short notice to defend the new nation.

Next, in the War of 1812, Ohio found itself on the front lines, deep in the conflict on both water and land. The state of Ohio with a population of 230,000 furnished the men who fought the battle of Lake Erie, and the gallant defense of Fort Meigs by William Henry Harrison's soldiers stopped the forces of Britain's General Hulk which had just conquered Detroit and then moved against the Ohio territory. In the Mexican War, Ohio sent 7,000 men, or about one-eighth of the total land forces used by the U.S. in that war. In the following Civil War, Ohio's manpower made a heavy contribution in both fighting forces and leadership to the Union armies. In the Spanish-American War, the State furnished 15,000 troops, a proportion far greater than its percentage of U.S. population. These were the precursors of a long slow movement toward an Ohio-only unit which finally came to fruition in World War I, officially named the 37th Infantry Division, and drawing men only within the state of Ohio. When World War I broke out, after a frustrating series of political moves aimed at incorporating Ohio troops into other regional units, Ohio Governor Cox pled with President Woodrow Wilson for this Ohio - only authorization. On July 18, 1917, the internecine political battle was won and the 37th Division was established. Ohio troops were sent to Camp Sheridan, Alabama, to prepare for the ensuing world war. Though several of the components were split off to fight under other divisional jurisdictions, the 37th Division itself was shipped overseas and directed to the Baccarat sector of the Western Front in France, fighting in the stalemated trench warfare while readying for the great offensive which eventually ended the war.

The Division played a starring role in the Meuse-Argonne, and was one of the first

En route to Indiantown Gap, February 1942. Jenkins, Gardiner, Charlton. (Courtesy Pierce)

Indiantown Gap Military Reservation, 1942, 37th Cavalry Reconnaissance Troop. (Courtesy Lawless)

American divisions, with Verdun in telescopic sight, to participate in the last, great offensive. The Division fought bravely at Pannes, part of the St. Mihiel sector; then, after a rest, shifted to Flanders in Belgium, taking up positions along the Lys and Escaut River. The river was crossed under heavy fire on November 2, and the Division pushed on to the Synghem sector, remaining there until November 11 when the Germans surrendered.

After the Armistice, famed German General Von Rundstedt specifically named the 37th as among the best divisions the German troops had faced. The 37th was brought back to the States and demobilized in April 1919.

The National Defense Act of 1920 set up the rebuilding of the Division, a peacetime effort which led to federal reorganization in 1923 whereby the 37th was reshaped into a "square division." This included two brigades of infantry, each with two regiments; one brigade of artillery with three regiments and a full complement of service regiments. These units were organized at "peace" strength, about one half of full, war strength, and consisting of a total of 10,000 men.

During the 20 year period between world wars, various units engaged in summer maneuvers at different sites, including Ohio's Camp Perry and Camp Knox, and the state of Ohio provided generally first-rate armories as centers for meeting and training. Enlistment was strictly voluntary, but the 37th remained strong and fit, until the formal European conflict led to the Guard being federally mobilized in October 1940. The just passed military draft eventually added 10,000 Ohio conscripts who were shipped to the training base at Camp Shelby, Mississippi.

Fully manned at last, the Division shifted into a 24 hour a day plan of physical and mental discipline to ready the 37th for war fitness, which included massive maneuvers in Louisiana. Basic training consisted of putting up tents, digging trenches, night hiking, range firing, saluting, keeping weapons clean and usable. And quick start and stop troop movements via jeep-trucks and feet. The war was exploding all over Europe, with the Germans pushing their adversaries around, and the Japanese had launched their invasion of China. Despite general feeling in the nation that we should stay out of this one, the knowledgeable men in Washington believed our entrance was inevitable. The Japanese attack at Pearl Harbor on December 7 surprised most everyone, but as if in anticipation of some unknown event, the military draft had been extended and the draftees had their tour of duty lengthened in August 1941. When the nation was precipitated into the War on December 8, 1941, the 37th soldiers may not have been willing, but they were ready, to get at it. Mass furloughs were awarded to the soldiers because it was now clear that within a few months, the 37th would be moved into one of the two war zones—Europe or the Pacific.

Several division units, including the 166th Infantry Regiment, were detached from the Division, and the "new" 37th Division consisted of the 145th, 147th and 148th Infantry Regiment; the 134th, 135th, 136th and 140th Field Artillery Battalions, the 112th QM Battalion, the 112th Medical Battalion, the 37th Signal Company and Headquarters and MP companies, plus a motorized cavalry reconnaissance troop, destined to win a Presidential Unit Citation later in Bougainville.

In February 1942, the Division was moved to Indiantown Gap, Pennsylvania, ostensibly to be reshipped to the European Theater, and warm woolen clothes were issued. However, in April, the 147th less one battalion was detached and shipped to the Pacific Theater, to be followed on May 24 by the rest of the divisions on...to the Pacific Theater via San Francisco...where the wool uniforms were exchanged for more tropical garb. The 145th was dropped off in New Zealand, and most of the remaining units of the Division sailed to the Fiji Islands a strategic portion of the South Pacific, thought to be the next Japanese objective after it had digested Guadalcanal, a Solomon Island relatively close to the Fijis.

The Fiji Islands were the last and hardest training grounds for the 37th while the Marines were bloodily retaking Guadalcanal. In March 1943, the 37th was shifted to Guadalcanal for relatively easy daytime mopping up plus experiencing a

37th Division landing at Guadalcanal. (Courtesy Knipp)

number of uneasy nights when the Japanese bombers hit Henderson Airfield.

Only lightly scathed in Guadalcanal, the 37th moved in July 1943 to New Georgia, the next Solomon Island up the chain, and faced their first real test of mud and blood and eventual victory over well-entrenched and trained Japanese forces protecting their Munda air strip. The 148th's 3rd Battalion had its own mission of circling behind the Japanese, while the main force of the 37th met the Japanese head on. Fighting their way through almost impenetrable jungles which reduced tactics to their most primitive, the 37th captured Munda in a month and drove the Japanese literally into the sea by August 5, 1943. Nineteen officers and 217 enlisted men were killed in the New Georgia Campaign, including Private Rodger Young, the second 37th Infantry hero was awarded a posthumous Congressional Medal of Honor. This action was immortalized by songwriter Frank Loesser in his Ballad of Rodger Young and the ballad became the official U.S. Infantry anthem. The Japanese suffered 1,426 dead and 20 prisoners who did not surrender without putting up an almost suicidal fight. After New Georgia and its prize jewel, the Munda air strip, were secured, the 37th was shipped back to Guadalcanal for so-called R and R (rest and recreation). There was little rest as the soldiers were soon in training for the next combat mission—that up the Solomon Island chain to Bougainville; and the recreation consisted of movies, volley ball games and swimming off the lovely sand beaches, only sporadically spoiled by rotting hulks of ships and cargo.

Bougainville was chosen as the next objective because it could furnish an airbase to neutralize major Japanese air bases at Rabaul and pave the seaway for our return to the Philippines. This was the strategy, but the tactics were decidedly different from the Guadalcanal and New Georgia fighting painfully through the jungle to clear the islands. With Bougainville, the plan was to move inland only a few miles, secure perhaps 5% of the island on which to build our own airfield; set up a defensive perimeter, and defend it against the 25,000 Japanese on Bougainville. This tactic would force the Japanese to come to us, against well defended positions, supported by artillery and air. It proved to be a brilliant and relatively bloodless maneuver, and on November 6, the first elements of the 37th and the 3rd Marine Divisions landed at Empress Augusta Bay against minimal resistance, and began expanding and building the perimeter. By November 25, the final "offensive-defensive" line had been reached, and the digging in phase began with fields of fire cleared in front of the lines, sophisticated trenches and artillery positions honeycombed the friendly area, and the airfield was completed...all with minor casualties sustained in ineffectual bombing raids and pinpricking patrols.

It took the Japanese several months to deduce that we were not going to fight our way through the jungles to eliminate them; if they wanted action, they had to come and get us. On March 8, the Japanese did move in for their attack which continued up and down the perimeter as the Japanese felt out our lines for a soft spot. They thought they had located it at Hill 700 which overlooked the lines, and they proceeded to assemble most of their troops just beyond the Hill. Aided by information from a captured Japanese lieutenant, their assembly area was hit heavy by air and artillery for six hours; some of the Japanese units moved forward to get under the cover, of the incoming shells, and managed to capture Hill 700. Immediately their positions were counterattacked by 148th Infantry troops and driven off the Hill, an action for which two of the 148th units received Presidential Citations.

However, the bulk of the Japanese forces which had assembled for the attack were literally chopped up in the aerial and artillery bombardment; several thousand of the shell-shocked remnants fled back to their base on the other side of the island, never again to offer much of a fight. The dismembered 2,000 Japanese bodies, were buried by bulldozers and rear echelon personnel, who resorted to wearing gas masks for the first and last time in the South Pacific because of the horrendous and pervasive odor of this chopped-up flesh rotting under the tropical sun.

During the following months there was little fighting, the Japanese tended their farms on their side of the island and the 37th Division patrolled and surveilled from their fortress-perimeter and readied for the invasion of the Philippines. These months were spent preparing the 37th for a different kind of fighting than the jungle variety, or even the offensive-defensive plan of Bougainville. The Philippines were generally clear and flat, and the American firepower, the air support and heavy artillery, plus the armored vehicles and tanks, could finally be brought into "play." The next battle would resemble more closely the European Theater...along roads, through farmland, and often house-to-house combat in the cities and villages. On December 14, 1944, the Division was loaded on troop transports along with other U.S. and Australian units and the armada sailed toward Luzon on the Lingayen Gulf. The smaller island of Leyte had been hit a month before and MacArthur's return to the Philippines was featured in that invasion. However, Leyte was a sideshow compared to the vast array of troops and materials which were on the move toward Luzon...a convoy of all kinds of Navy vessels perhaps in size and strength second only to the D-day invasion of the coast of France across the English Channel which had taken place

The weary road to Bougainville. (Courtesy Hochwald)

Radio Section, Headquarters Co., 1st. Batt., 145th Inf. Sept. 1945, Northern Luzon. (Courtesy Morr)

the preceding June. Six hundred vessels of every description participated in the Luzon landing which began at dawn January 9, 1945, climaxing the largest single amphibious operation of the Pacific War. The landing was noisy but fairly bloodless, and the 37th along with companion troops quickly unloaded the jeeps, artillery and ammunition, and began moving across the broad, flat plains of the Philippines on a direct line to the main objective, Manila, about 110 miles from the landing site. In the first 17 days of the campaign, the 37th Division had advanced almost 70 miles. At that point, there was suddenly heavy resistance in the Clark Field-Fort Stotsenburg area which had been completely mined. The 129th eliminated that resistance which cost the enemy almost 800 dead against the three officers and 67 enlisted men of the 129th killed.

The race to Manila proceeded, and the Tulihan River just in front of the Manila outskirts, was reached, but not before the famous and bloodless Battle of Balintawak Brewery occurred. The Brewery was located at the River Bank, flowing over with brewing beer, presenting an unforeseen obstacle which slowed down the crossing of the River long enough for thirsty soldiers to drink their fill and replace the water in their canteen with green brew.

Engineer-built foot bridges to replace those blown by the Japanese were rapidly constructed. However, hours before the bridges somehow were completed, the order came from Army HQ to cross the river, even without heavy equipment and transportation, and rescue the 2,000 military prisoners at Bilibid, in the northern section of downtown Manila. The liberation was effected by 148th units without serious casualties. Malacanan Palace was next occupied, and on February 7, the crossing of the Pasig River which bisected Manila, was accomplished under heavy fire as the 15,000 Japanese holed up in buildings for a last ditch defense.

Building by building, section by section, the 37th relentlessly rooted out an enemy determined to stop our soldiers or die in the effort. Storied names like Intramuros, the Post Office Building, the Gas Works, the Police Stations, the English Club, the Steinberg General Hospital, the Library were all cleansed of the enemy...with both the attackers and the defenders taking severe losses. Then the Philippines General Hospital, with its adjoining Medical School and Nurses Home, the University of the Philippines, the National Sweepstakes Building, the Municipal Theater, the Ice Plant, City Hall, Ft. Santiago, the age-old fortress in the Walled City, Santa Rosa College....each one with its own bloody tale story and its own heroes. Finally the last Japanese died in the Finance Building the morning of February 3, and the battle for Manila was over. The 37th Division had killed 13,006 enemy of the total 16,655 who had died in its defense.

Three weeks of recuperation, rest and relaxation, were rudely interrupted by orders to take Baguio, the summer capital of the Philippines, and the Division units on March 29 began moving up the winding, twisting mountain road to Baguio, practically every bend in the road defended by rear guard and suicidal enemy. Americans fought their way slowly and painfully up mountain Highway 9 and in one typical incident, two Japanese tanks loaded with ready-to-die Japanese, turned into the lead American troops just as Colonel L.K. White and his adjutant were attempting to speed up the attack. Colonel White was badly wounded; the CO of the lead American company was killed, but the tanks were finally eliminated. By May 4, all resistance leading to and inside Baguio were destroyed.

There was little rest or souvenir hunting in the cool and rich city of Baguio, as 37th Division elements were ordered to move into the last bastion of the Japanese in the Philippines: the hills of northern Luzon, with the objective of taking Japanese positions around Baguio, Cagayan Valley and Ballette Pass. This entire portion of Northern Luzon was isolated by the Japanese defense of Ballette Pass. After several months of fighting, the Division took this pass and was next assigned the mission of spearheading the drive through the north central Luzon plains to Aparri at its northern most tip. This 250 mile route was defended by approximately 50,000 Japanese troops, but Aparri was reached in 25 days and the Division was linked up with the 11th Airborne. The Cagayan Valley was the final receptacle for all Japanese forces in the Philippines. Mortorized 37th Division patrols continued to the mountain areas, running into small units of unrelenting Japanese forces, up and down the valley until by June 27, the Japanese were shooting only when found and shot at. A kind of unspoken truce ensued until the news reached Headquarters of the dropping of the A bomb on August 5 on Hiroshima Japan, and days later, on Nagasaki. Then came the glorious declaration of the Japanese surrender on August 10, news which was loudspeakered up and down the valley. The Japanese, forlorn, hungry, and battered, were now ready to give up and POW camps were organized as they drifted down the hills and into 37th Division controlled areas.

A humorous sidebar to the August 10 surrender occurred when the writer of this sketch who had been on patrol during the day, reported into Division Headquarters that evening, unaware of the surrender. Unable to find his regimental commander, Frankel went into a three hole latrine and noticed someone sitting down next to him. Thinking it was a fellow American, Frankel

Remains of Hotel Manila after driving out the enemy. (Courtesy Hochwald)

37mm Gun Crew, A.T. Co., 145th Inf., February 1945, Manila. Standing, SSgt. Herb Thompson, Unk., Feldhouser, Tex. Essery, Marsh. Sitting, Unk., Cheche, Woody, Ransdell, Unk., Buck Sgt. Bowman. (Courtesy Ransdell)

began to talk to his seatmate, and when the response came back to him in pure Japanese, Frankel leaped from his toilet, ran out of the latrine screaming, "There are Japanese in there." To which a sergeant standing nearby coolly informed Frankel that he had just met the Japanese General who had come in that afternoon to surrender his troops.

The 37th waited in the Cabanatuan area for orders to go home; orders which seemed dreadfully slow in coming and which had stimulated a mass petition to the President insisting on being brought home now. Finally, on November 15 after two heartbreaking delays, the Division began loading on ships including the first group on USS *Weltevreden*. This initial shipment arrived at San Pedro, California on December 4 and by Christmas, all of the Division was home. On December 18, 1945, the 37th Division had been completely demobilized and ceased to exist legally. But...as the Division Historian wound up his history of World War II: "Among its friends (and its former enemies) the 37th Buckeye Division of World War II had achieved monumental immortality."

The 37th "Buckeye" Division had spent more than 592 days in combat in the Southwest Pacific. During the entire three and one half years in this theater, the 37th served without much relief for rest or recuperation; fought both offensively and defensively; was constantly in disease and insect infested jungles; engaged in amphibious landings, mountain fighting and the fiercest of street fighting. It obtained every assigned objective. The Division was never defeated. It was responsible for 33,500 casualties and took 2,180 prisoners of war. For heroism in battle, proud wearers of the Buckeye Division Insignia earned seven Medals of Honor, 109 Distinguished Service Crosses, four Distinguished Service Medals, 939 Silver Stars, 61 Legions of Merit, 94 Soldier's Medals, 6,366 Bronze Stars, and more than 9,800 Purple Hearts.

KOREAN CONFLICT: The 37th Division reorganized and rebuilt in 1946 and 1947 under the leadership of Major General Leo M. Kreber, who commanded the Division Artillery throughout the entire Pacific Campaign. In September 1951, the Division was alerted for induction into federal service on January 15, 1952. This induction was accomplished and the 37th moved to Camp Polk, Louisiana for training. It was one of the few National Guard Divisions called up during the Korean War.

By September 1952 the Division was assessed as combat ready. However, the 37th was not destined to see service as a Division. Practically all of the officers and men of the 37th were sent overseas as individual replacements and the Division was given the mission of training further replacements for our units in Korea. After training the equivalent of an entire division, the 37th was completely rebuilt from replacements. On January 14, 1954, when the 37th's two years of active duty was at an end, a well organized and highly trained division was turned over to the U.S. Army.

Immediately upon return to its 56 home stations in Ohio, the Buckeye Division was again reorganized and once again combat experienced officers and noncommissioned officers began rebuilding units. Within two and a half years, the 37th numbered more than 6,500 officers and enlisted personnel.

The current status of the 37th was best summed up at a ceremony on August 29, 1993 at the fittingly named Major General Robert S. Beightler Armory in Columbus, Ohio. This was the Reorganization Ceremony that officially changed the 37th Infantry Brigade (Separate) into the 37th Armor Brigade. The designation of the 73rd Brigade was changed to the 37th Brigade after annual training in 1992, in order to preserve the lineage and honors of the 37th (Buckeye) Division. The new organization will combine the 37th Infantry Brigade (Separate) and some elements of the 107th Armored Cavalry Regiment. The new 37th Armor Brigade will then be the only major combat arms command left in the state of Ohio. The new Brigade will consist of the Headquarters and Headquarters Company, 1st Battalion 148th Infantry (MECII). 1st Battalion 147th Armor, 1st Battalion 107th Cavalry, 1st Battalion 134th Field Artillery (SP), and the 237th Forward Support Battalion. This organization alone will carry the heritage of the old 37th Division into the future. This ceremony marked the beginning of another proud era in the evolution of the Ohio Army National Guard.

EDITOR'S NOTE ABOUT THE AUTHOR: The writer of this brief history, Stanley A. Frankel, was the official historian of the 37th Division in World War II, served with that Division for five and a half years, including the last three and a half years in the South Pacific. His official history was published in 1947 by the *Infantry Journal Press*; and he has recently had published his highly personal memoirs *Frankel-y Speaking About WWII in the South Pacific*.

Medal of Honor Recipients

Achieved by members of the 37th Division, mostly posthumously.

WWI

2/LT Albert E. Baesel, Co. B, 148th Inf. Regt., 37th Div., September 27, 1918

WWII

PFC Rodger W. Young, Co. B, 148th Inf. Regt., 37th Inf. Div., July 31, 1943

PFC Frank J. Petrarca, Medical Detachment, 145th Inf. Regt., 37th Inf. Div., July 31, 1943

2/LT Robert M. Viale, Co. K, 148th Inf. Regt., 37th Inf. Div., February 5, 1945

PFC Joseph J. Ciccetti, Co. A, 148th Inf. Regt., 37th Inf. Div., February 9, 1945

PFC John N. Reese Jr., Co. A, 148th Inf. Regt., 37th Inf. Div., February 9, 1945

T/SGT Cleto Rodriquez, Co. B, 148th Inf. Regt., 37th Inf. Div., February 9, 1945

PFC Anthony L. Krotiak, Co. I, 148th Inf. Regt., 37th Inf. Div., May 8, 1945

Maj. Gen. Robert S. Beightler, seated at desk, announces selection of Col. Russell A. Ramsey, far right, to be commander of 83rd Reserve Division. Beightler was Commanding General of the Ohio 37th National Guard Division throughout WWII. Ramsey was his chief of staff in 1945. Beightler became Chief Army Mobilization. Ramsey rose to major general and commanded the 83rd into the mid 1960s. (Courtesy Ramsey)

History of 37th Division

This article was written by Colonel G. Fred Graf. He passed away July 4, 1994, as BG G. Fred Graf. He was Past National President of the 37th Division Veterans Association.

The history of the 37th Division has already been written. The story has been told through the actions of its members over a span of two world wars. The sons have proven worthy successors to their fathers. This is just a brief account of the story as it has been told so many times in the past. Out of the past grows the present and so we pause now as the Division stands on the threshold of a third period of active duty to take a quick glimpse of the past.

Actually the history of the 37th Division starts long before World War I and the actual organization of a Buckeye Division. Ohio has a long tradition of military prowess that began in the days of the Indian Wars and has come down through the years in later battles. During the Revolutionary War the Indians of Ohio were organized by the British with the intent of attacking sea board colonies. Those were the days of the minute men. These early pioneers were citizens who were also soldiers. Out of this tradition came our institution of the National Guard. Such were the soldiers who fought the Indian Wars, the Revolution, and as volunteers, have been in every war since. They have afforded that storehouse of manpower upon which the country has depended in its difficulties. They have provided that defense of nations, which in time of peace occasions only a minimum of interference with their productive powers and in the time of war supplies manpower for a maximum effort.

In the War of 1812, Ohio found itself on the battle front, and deep in the conflict on both sea and land. The battle of Lake Erie is forever memorable in the annals of the State. The state of Ohio by this time had a population of over 230,000. The surrender of Detroit by General Hull left this rich territory open to invasion. The gallant defense of Fort Meigs by William Henry Harrison stopped that, and Perry's victory removed the threat.

To the Mexican War, Ohio sent about seven thousand men, or about one-eighth of the total land force used by our government in that war.

In the Civil War, Ohio was noted not only for the number of men which it contributed, but for the brilliance of leadership which it afforded to the Union armies.

In the Spanish-American War the State furnished 15,000 troops out of the 200,000 called by the national government.

These historical facts explain a movement that had long been under way and which, with World War I, came to fruition in a Division that could be called Ohio's own. The 37th Infantry Division was not the artificial product of arbitrary action of the War Department, but a child of grace that had been long asked for and at last granted.

The 37th Division received its original designation and authorization on July 18, 1917. Its troops had already seen service along the Mexican border. For nine months during the years 1916 and 1917, the Ohio National Guard, with the exception of the 1st and 7th Regiments of Infantry and the 9th Battalion, was on the border. During this time the Guard was stationed at Camp Pershing, near El Paso, Texas, patrolling the border in that sector. It then returned home. By March 17, 1917, all but the 3rd and 6th Infantry Regiments, the artillery, the engineers and the signal unit, had been mustered out of federal service.

On March 27, 1917, units of the Ohio National Guard had their first call to active duty in World War I. Units were sent to guard the State arsenal, viaducts, bridges, docks and other vital points within the State. It was not until July 15 that the Guard was diverted from State control into the service of the United States. On July 13, 1917, the War Department announced that the Ohio troops were to encamp and train at Camp Sheridan, Alabama, which was at that time nothing more than an open expanse of cotton fields and wasteland. Actual construction of the camp started on July 24, but was not completed until the end of the year. However, the first Ohio troops began to converge on the new site by August 25. Construction work and training proceeded concurrently. Familiarity with new arms and new methods of fighting were stressed as the 37th prepared itself for battle.

World War I 1917-1919

Courtesy of Findlay Daily Courier

The 37th Division, Ohio's own, saw service on five different fronts, the Baccarat sector, Meuse-Argonne, Saint Mihiel, Belgium, first phase, and Belgium, second phase, after they were mobilized for duty in response to the call of the President of the United States in July 1917, which fixed the mobilization date as July 15, 1917.

At this time the 3rd and 6th Ohio regiments and 1st Ohio Field Cavalry were already mobilized and had returned from duty on the Mexican border, being on duty in the state at the time of the call.

Besides the above regiments the 1st to 8th inclusive and 10th Ohio Infantry regiments, the 9th Battalion ONG (a battalion of colored troops) the 1st Ohio Field Artillery, 1st Ohio Cavalry, Ohio Signal Battalion and the 1st Ohio Engineers, were mobilized at this time, July 15. All of the above troops were of the Ohio National Guard.

In the month of August, a detachment of 16 men from each company of the regiments, was on order of the Adjutant General of Ohio, ordered to assemble at Camp Perry, where they were merged with the 42nd Division, which was a portion of the Rainbow Division and were designated for immediate service overseas.

At Camp Sheridan, Montgomery, Alabama, the first troops of the Ohio Guard began to arrive early in August 1917, and in October of that year all were assembled, the troops forming the 37th Division. Here all of the former units and regimental numbers of the old Ohio National Guard were lost.

The completed organization (with the exception of the 9th Battalion, colored) was combined into Division Headquarters, comprised of Headquarters troops and the 134th Machine Gun Battalion, the 73rd Infantry Brigade, which included the 145th, 146th Infantry and the 135th Machine Gun Battalion, the 74th Infantry Brigade, comprising the 147th and 148th Infantry and the 135th Machine Gun Battalion, the 62nd Field Artillery Brigade, which included the 134th, 135th and 136th Field Artillery and the 112th Trench Motor Battery, comprising the 112th Engineers, the 112th Engineer train, 114th Mobile Veterinary Unit, 112th Field Signal Battalion, 112th Ammunition Train, 112th Supply Train, 112th Sanitary Train and the 112th Military Police.

For 10 long months the division went through training under the leadership of Major General Charles G. Treat. On April 24, 1918, General Treat was relieved of his command. Major General Charles S. Farnsworth was assigned to command the division May 8, 1918.

On the date May 20, 1918, Division Headquarters, Headquarters Troop, Infantry Regiments, Machine Gun Battallions, Engineers and Train and Field Signal Battalion began to entrain for Camp Lee, Virginia. Two weeks were spent at this camp, during the time intensive war training and filling of the division to war strength occupied the attention of the men. Men filling in the Division were drafted from Camps Meade, Mills, Lee, Upton and Jackson.

The Division was broken up when on June 11, 1918, Division Headquarters, Headquarters Troop, 134th Machine Gun Battalion and 137th Infantry Brigade began to move to Hoboken, New Jersey, the port of embarking. They sailed June 15, on the USS *Leviathan*, and arrived at Brest, France, on June 22, having a safe passage across. Three days the troops rested at Pontanezen barracks at Brest, France, then entrained for the front, detraining June 29, in the Bourmont area.

The 74th Brigade and the Engineers followed on three ships, the *Susquehanna, Caserta* and *Pocahontas*, which were joined by four freight steamers besides submarine chasers, with battleships forming a convoy for protection of the troops at the time when submarines were roaming the seas near England and France in quest of human lives.

On July 5, they arrived in Brest and proceeded by the way of box cars which took them to the Division Headquarters and the 73rd Brigade stationed in the Bourmont (Haute Marne) area. This happened July 12, 1918.

The Field Artillery Brigade, Trench Mortar Battery, Sanitary Train, Military Police and 114th Mobile Veterinary Section followed, but first entrained at Camp Sheridan, Alabama, June 14, for Camp Upton, New York, where they stayed 10 days, embarking at Brooklyn, New York, on the steamships *Nestor, Plassy, Saxton, Titan, Phesus, Hororatia* and one tanker for overseas.

Then the 136th Field Artillery, less Battery E and F were sent to Montreal, Quebec, Canada, from which port they embarked on the steamer *Victoria*, this ship joining the rest, making 13 ships in the convoy. For protection the ships were scattered near the coast of England, the vessels bearing the Trench Mortar and Sanitary Train proceeded to Glasgow, Scotland, and the remainder to Liverpool, England.

The *Victoria* was rammed by a submarine, the alarm sounded soon after the crash and destroyers succeeded in destroying the undersea craft, leaving a scum of oil on the surface of the water in mute testimony of what became of the sea scavenger.

After railway journeys across England and the English Channel the 114th Mobile Veterinary Unit, Sanitary Train, Military Police, and Supply Train joined the rest of the outfits in the Division Headquarters at Bourmont area on July 15-18.

Now the Division was completed with the exception of the Field Artillery Brigade and Ammunition Train which were separated from the rest of the troops entirely and sent to Camp de Souge, France, after a training course in firing the French 75 and 155mm cannon.

The training course there lasted seven weeks and at the end the highest rating in average was given to the Brigade. After being equipped with these guns the outfits were assigned to the 1st American Army, on September 26, the opening day of the great Meuse-Argonne offensive. They served successfully with the 4th American Corps, 2nd American Army, 2nd Colonial Army Corps, French, and the 17th French Army Corps. At one time the Brigade was split into three regiments serving with as many different divisions, the 28th, 33rd and 92nd American.

On August 4, the 37th Division took over the trenches in the Barcarat sector after a lengthy intensive training in the Bourmont area, ending in July 1918.

The Baccarat sector, which was in the Vosges mountains, was taken over by the troops of this Division. The sector extended 15 kilometers from the Forest deu Elieux on the north to the southern edge of the Bois des Petres on the south. The sector, while not considered active, was such that at all times it had to be held securely.

At this place the troops received first training under fire and though continually under observation they trained unceasingly. Airplane attacks were numerous. Two being heavy, in which much damage resulted. The Division completed a successful gas attack, destroying enemy ammunition dumps and evening up the score with the Germans.

Not a long time after two patrol raids were staged which were very daring, the men penetrating the German line for over a kilometer, each time returning with prisoners without loss of a single man. They were so aggressive with the night patrols that at all times after occupation of the sector they virtually controlled No Man's Land.

General Duport was in command of the French Artillery which supported the troops in this sector and commended the Division after it was relieved September 16, 1918.

Next the Division was assigned to the Meuse-Argonne front, at which sector Verdun was plainly to be seen to the southeast. It was the first American Division to be honored as one which started the offensive at this point. It was given credit of being one of the main factors in the huge movement of troops that gave the final impetus to that large offensive which contributed so greatly towards the final victory. Here the 37th Division covered itself with glory.

On September 24, 25 and 26, artillery fire kept up incessantly, all making toward the drive which went down in history as one of the most brilliant of all times. Conditions of the field at this point were so adverse that at times the infantrymen advanced without the aid of artillery fire. Added to the conditions, a steady rain fell 12 or more days, making the field in No Man's Land one of mud continually. Lack of sufficient artillery fire made the road to victory harder for the men, but they advanced and clung to their advances with force that was amazing, while advancing continually.

For four long years this sector had been the strongpoint of the German Crown Prince. From a tower he directed the movements of the enemy supported by elite German troops commanded by Hindenburg. During the days of September 28 and 29, the difficulties of advancing became more and more difficult, through shell holes filled with mud, unprotected without sufficient artillery fire the Division made mile after mile, sweeping all ahead of it. Wall after wall of shock troops of the Germans fell before the relentless advance and more were rushed in from other German lines.

The Division was relieved from this sector October 1, after having fought for four days against great odds and against various forms of warfare, of which the enemy was using at that time.

After the 37th left, the other regiments carried on with the fight and when the armistice was signed the line had advanced to the city of Sedan, making one of the farthest advances through the shock German troops that was made in the World War.

In the first two sectors of the 37th Division was a total of 3,238 officers or men

Maj. Gen. Charles S. Farnsworth, commanding 37th Division, A.E.F., WWI

Belgium. (Courtesy Chaney)

killed, wounded or missing, the wounded amounting to more than 2,500, and the missing approximately 150. The total advance in the Meuse-Argonne sector was 9.8 kilometers.

The next sector that the Division saw duty on was the old St. Mihiel one. Here the lines of the troops extended from Boise de Jaulny along the northern edges to Bois de Charey on the southern edge. Many villages were in sight of the trenches some devastated by artillery fire of the enemy and some in the lines of the Germans.

At the time when the 37th Division took over the front there was very little real activity there, although at all times the enemy continued the heavy artillery fire, shelling all portions of the sector night and day. Airplanes paid nightly visits and dropped their terrorizing bombs in large numbers, inflicting heavy losses and causing everybody vigilance on the part of the aircraft guns. The clatter of machine guns was continually ringing in the ears of the troopers.

Here by fate's hand the Artillery Brigade of the Division was serving nearby at the same time and every effort was made to hunt the troops to the organization, but all efforts were met with failure. On the ninth day of activity of lesser nature the Division was withdrawn to the former camp, Pagny-sur Meuse. The casualties in the Saint Mihiel sectors were 11 killed, 180 wounded, six missing, making a total of 197.

At Pagny-sur Meuse two days of bustling activity were spent making ready the Division for a move to where no one knew. The little French box cars rattled away October 18 for an unknown destination, to the men. Then the train, after three days of travel, stopped at what the soldiers discovered was St. Jean and Wieltje, Belgium. Over where the villages formerly were was nothing but desolation as far as the eye could see, only signs marked where the two villages formerly were.

Division headquarters of the 37th was established at a distance of 20 miles from where the train stopped. This was on October 22. At this time the Division was attached to the French Army in Belgium and placed at the disposal of King Albert of Belgium.

Here was to be the sight of a great battle on October 31, at which time the 37th Division covered itself with glory. On this date, after five minutes' artillery fire, the men went over the top. The enemy answered the attack with every known method of warfare, using gas with terrible effect, but the tide of onrushing men could not be stemmed and the enemy finally withdrew to the Cruyshauten Ridge. Here on a slight rise between the Lys and Escaut Rivers a reorganization of the enemy began, and he prepared to stop the ever moving khaki line. But the Germans were routed with the aid of the French artillery fire and the American troops gained their objective, Crysshauten Ridge.

Then driving the Boche before them they went on to the Escaut River. It was on this river that the Division held one of the greatest battles in history. The headquarters were moved up November 1, and plans were made to cross the river.

Early in the morning of November 2, soldiers of the 37th crossed the river, swimming under heavy artillery and machine gun fire and working from both banks under the continual hail of lead, they constructed a temporary bridge over which late that afternoon 52 men had succeeded in crossing. At Heurne, nearby, efforts were made to construct a pontoon bridge, but all efforts were disbanded when the enemy rained shells continually on the workers. Further south a bridge was completed late that evening and the troops crossed over, fighting the Boche throughout the night to hold their hard gained position.

German airplanes shelled the troops incessantly, the whir of his plane could always be heard above and his work of dropping bombs inflicted much disaster on the men, but they did not falter in their task.

Against the elite of the German army the 37th made their greatest objective and victory at this point, and when headquarters and the position on the other side of the river was firmly established, they had been the first and only allied division to take and establish a position on the other side of Escaut River, or Scheldt River as it was known to some.

November 4 and 5 the troops were relieved by the French and returned to Thielt for a few days earned rest. The total number of prisoners captured was 366 besides much of the enemy cannons and weapons. The total advance was 14.56 kilometers. Casualties in this sector amounted to 1,612 (222 men being killed in one of the most notable battles and advances on the sector). After the relief of the troops, General H. Penet, of the French troops, issued a general order commending the Division and lauding the Division for its bulldog tactics of holding on against all odds and winning a great victory for the allies.

At Thielt, Belgium, where the Division stayed for four days re-equipping the outfits, they entrained to Chateau de Huysse and were assigned to the 34th French Corps. At Chateau de Huysse the objective was to force another crossing over the river, this time at a place about 15 kilometers south of Ghent.

Here, when they were about to engage in battle for their objective rumors of Germany's acceptance of Armistice terms began to circulate. All activities were speeded up in preparation for the advance and every plan was made to keep the German army on the run.

On November 10, at 8:00 a.m., the leading troops arrived in the advanced area. On their way at the village of Syngem, they were met with a volley of machine bullets and artillery fire and again the 37th Division was in the midst of the thickest of the fight.

The Escaut River for the length of the sector formed a U bent front with the bottom of the U toward the enemy. The ground

Cemetery. (Courtesy Chaney)

Cathedral ruin. (Courtesy Chaney)

at this point on the allied side was low and in a flooded condition, and the approach for a distance of two to three hundred meters was marshy, a sea of mud, with the enemy having the best advantage of the sector and holding it with well equipped forces and entrenchments.

Where the Division was to force its way, artillery fire from the enemy came from three sides. In gaining the advance the men were forced to crawl and slide forward in the mud, taking advantage of all the irregularities of the terrain. One by one the men made their way up the river bank, working in and entrenching, holding on with a vice-like grip to the ground gained.

The infantry crossed on a bridge constructed near the village of Heubel, on the extreme southern limit of the sector. The entire night was spent in feverish activity in obtaining a foothold across the river and on the morning of November 11, with Armistice rumors flying thick and fast, the Division was holding the eastern bank of the river with a secured hold.

The fight was pushed up to the last minute, and so fast did the troops advance, that at eleven o'clock when the advance was ordered stopped, the 37th Division was holding the line east of the village of Dickele, Zwartenbroek, Kerrken and Hundlegem.

The war was over and on the afternoon of November 11, the stillness was so intense that it was oppressing to the men. After the continuous rattle of machine guns and artillery fire, the calm was severe on the men and overshadowed the fact that the war was over and the Germans had run up the white flag denoting surrender.

A strange story is told of an American baseball rolling out from somewhere and being tossed about by the members of the Division, much to the amazement of the French and German soldiers on the front.

Casualties of the last battle were nine killed.

On termination of the Belgian offensive, a general order issued from the headquarters of General Degoutte, commander of the 6th French Army, commending the work of the officers and men of the 37th Division. In this commendation, the General praised the work of the men, their instantaneous carrying out of orders and their method of gaining objectives in the face of obstacles of magnitude which would falter and stop ordinary divisions.

The 37th was selected as one of the divisions to follow the German retreat to the Rhine and started on its last task by following in easy stages the retreats towards Brussels.

Not far from this city the Division was recalled and retraced its steps back through Belgium to Hondschoote, France, where headquarters was established on December 7.

Some of the detachments of the Division took part in the triumphant entry of King Albert into Brussels and Aix-la Chapelle. For the work in Belgium the 37th gained the respect of the whole nation of Belgium. Many of the soldiers proudly wore the Belgium Citation, war crosses. More than 200 of these medals besides nearly 2,550 of the French citations adorned the uniforms of members of the notable 37th Division. This was besides medals from the United States. The number of citations to the men is not known.

From Hondschoote the Division moved to Wormhoudt, France, its task completed and scheduled to return home with honor and glory.

On February 21, having been joined by the 62nd Field Artillery Brigade, united at last the Division encamped in the Le Mans area cleaning and reconditioning for the triumphant return to America. The Division sailed for home in March.

Taking part in three large offensives and engaging in other sectors, the Division gained distinction of being in the hottest battles along the entire front, never faltering on the battle line, and making huge advances on the various fronts that contributed greatly to the final surrender of the enemy. The 37th was always ready for action and never was surprised at a sudden move to where its services were needed.

World War II—1940-1945

The 37th Infantry Division sailed under the Golden Gate on May 26, 1942 for a tour of duty in the Pacific which was to last for more than 43 long, dirty, hard-fighting months. One of the first units to be sent to the South Pacific, the 37th, throughout its stay, saw little besides fighting and training for more fighting. While other units were sent to New Zealand and Australia for rest after campaigns, the Buckeye Division jumped from one operation almost directly into another. General Krueger called the 37th his "trouble shooters" and *Yank Magazine* referred to it as the "Heavyweight." The 37th Division was good. That might be considered one of its faults, because there was always plenty for a good outfit to do.

After leaving San Francisco, most of the Division, with the exception of the 145th Infantry Regiment and several other units which spent a month in New Zealand, went directly to the island of Viti Levu in the Fijis. Here, for 10 months, the Division garrisoned the Fijis and trained for the fighting which awaited it in the north. In the spring of 1943, the 37th Division moved to Guadalcanal as a preparation for jumping into the mud and blood of New Georgia. Third Battalions, 145th and 148th Infantry, went in with the Marines on July 5 and by the end of the month the entire Division was in action on New Georgia striving to take Munda Airfield. This was the baptism of fire which two and one-half years of training had prepared the 37th for. There is an amazing contrast between what was available to the Division for the attack on New Georgia and what the Division had when it tackled the Philippines a year and one-half later. The invasion of New Georgia was accomplished with LSTs accompanied by a naval force consisting mostly of four-stacker destroyers of World War I vintage; AirForce strength was numbered in scores of planes, compared to hundreds later on. The Japanese did not lack confidence in those early days: For them the war was won and the Americans were impudent interlopers on their private domains. It was on New Georgia that the 37th Division proved the feasibility of using artillery as a major weapon in jungle warfare. The tricks developed by the 37th for employing the full potency of artillery in the jungles were quickly picked up by other divisions and eventually proved to be one of the main causes behind the Japanese defeat.

In September 1943, the 37th Division was shipped back to Guadalcanal for a period of rest and rehabilitation. New equipment had to be issued to replace that destroyed and lost in combat and replacements were necessary to fill the gaps the New Georgia fighting had knocked in the Division. The 37th Division lost 206 men killed in action and 928 wounded on New Georgia while destroying 1,426 of the enemy; 20 Japanese were captured. After this fracas, the Division was ready for a long rest in some more civilized place than Guadalcanal, but with the Bougainville operation only about six weeks off, the 37th was booked for more action. One thing that should never be forgotten about the fighting in the Solomons is that the whole job was done by four Army and two Marine divisions plus attached combat teams. When the New Georgia battle was finished, three Army and one Marine Division were in rest areas. This left the 37th Bougainville-bound, and the Division hit the beaches on November 8, 1943, one week after the 3rd Marine Division had made the initial assault. By this time, the 37th Division was no longer strictly an Ohio organization, but rather an All American Division with men from every state in the Union and from all of the territories swelling its ranks. The invasion of Bougainville was an outstanding success, mainly because astute advance planning put the American troops ashore where the Japs least expected them, in the Empress Augusta Bay sector.

The 37th had it comparatively easy, aside from the continual, fierce air attacks during the first few weeks. The Marines started to pull out on Christmas Day, 1943, and were replaced by the Americal Division. The Japs had been driven across the mountain range which divided the island, a perimeter was set up, and all went well until March 1944 when the Nipponese made a desperate counter-attack in an attempt to drive the Americans into the sea. They lugged cannons over the mountains and through the jungles and pounded Hill 700 which overlooked the two airstrips so vital to the Americans in the Southwest Pacific. This was the big battle of Bougainville staged by the Japanese 17th area army, including the infamous 6th Division of the Rape of Nanking fame. The enemy slashed at Hill 700 again and again leaving their dead heaped 10 feet high in places. Finally, by sheer superiority of numbers and by crawling over their own dead and dying, the Japanese took the Hill. Never before had more frightful or bloody fighting taken place in the Pacific. But the 37th came back. In two days of fierce fighting, they smashed the Jap positions, broke the back of the campaign, and sent the enemy back over the mountains, never to come back again. The 37th killed 7,335 Japs and took 60 prisoners on Bougainville with a loss of only 185 killed and 1,426 wounded: a ratio of better than 75-1.

For all practical purposes, the battle of Bougainville was over and the 37th Division started to plan for a rest in New Zealand. But the American offensive in the Pacific had proceeded too far and was already several months ahead of schedule, so the Buckeyes, griping furiously, settled down to hold Bougainville and trained for the Philippine operation. The men were further infuriated when they received no Battle Star for the Bougainville Campaign. From April until November, the Division trained. In two campaigns the men had become the best of jungle fighters, but the next operation was to be over open terrain and this necessitated learning European style tactics. First came amphibious landing practice, then open ground fighting, and finally street-to-street combat. Much of it had to be simulated because Bougainville was not civilization.

By December 1944 everything was ready, the ships were loaded, and the Division was on its way to make the beachhead at Lingayen Gulf, Luzon, Philippine Islands. Christmas was spent at Manus in the Admiralty Islands and New Years on the high seas. When the convoy was about abreast of Manila Bay, the Japanese launched aggressive suicide air attacks which failed to stop the convoy, although one suicide plane crashed into the water about 20 yards astern of one of the ships carrying 37th Division men. The landing at Lingayen Gulf was effected on January 9, 1945 and the 37th Division, against only slight opposition, headed straight down the central plains for Manila. The first main Jap force was met in the Clark Field-Fort Stotsenberg section when the 129th Infantry Regiment had to swing to the right to wipe out the Japs there so that the Division flank would be protected. The Division continued to race southward, wiping out an enemy battalion holding Plaridel, the last defensive point north of Manila, and sweeping on into the city itself on February 4. Fires set by the Japanese were raging in Manila, destroying most of the business section of the Pearl of the Orient. The 37th Division pushed directly into the heart of Manila, crushing enemy holding forces and picking off snipers who tried to disrupt the advance. Old Bilibid Prison was taken and hundreds of American prisoners were rescued. The fires temporarily blocked the advance but the 37th went on and reached the Pasig River which split the city into two parts. On February 7, the 148th Infantry Regiment spanned the Pasig River in engineer assault boats and amphibious tractors and the hardest and most costly battle of the war for the 37th Division started. Fighting became a house-to-house struggle and in many cases a floor-to-floor and room-to-room affair. The Japs were bottled up south of the Pasig; they knew they were going to die; they chose to do it the hard way. For three weeks the fight south of the Pasig raged until, on March 4, the last Jap stronghold in the government buildings of the Wallace Field section was eliminated and the battle of Manila was declared over. In their fanatical attempt to hold the city, the Japanese lost almost 25,000 men, more than 13,000 of whom were killed by the 37th Division.

After this bloody task, the men thought they surely must get a long rest. Three weeks after the end of the battle of Manila, the 37th Division was fighting along the mountain highway leading to Baguio, the summer capital of the Philippines. The 145th Infantry Regiment did not go to Baguio, but instead was sent to the mountains east of Manila to take Mount Pacawagan, a bitter, bloody struggle.

After Baguio there was still no rest in sight for the 37th Division. Within 24 hours after being withdrawn from the lines at Baguio, the 148th Infantry was on trucks bouncing towards Balete Pass to help the 37th Division break the Jap resistance so that the drive up the Cagayan Valley could be started.

By the end of May the Jap force holding Balete Pass had been smashed and the entire 37th Division started its headlong race up the Cagayan Valley: a race which covered nearly 240 miles in 26 days. More than 50,000 Japanese troops, the last major organized force the enemy had on Luzon, held the Valley. The 37th Division, with about 15,000 men plus attachments of diverse kinds, was given the single-handed task of taking this section. By employing a maximum of close-in air support, artillery, and heavy weapons of every kind, the 37th completely routed the Japs. The 37th had long been known as the most "wasteful" division in the Pacific as far as the expenditure of artillery ammunition was concerned, but the practice paid off with the Division losing fewer men than any other division with comparable fighting time. After steam-rolling to within 35 miles of Appari, on the northern coast of Luzon, where it met the 11th Airborne Division which had parachuted in, the Division moved into the foothills to pursue the Jap remnants who were hiding there.

Finally, after more than two years of almost continual fighting, the 37th Division got the rest it had been waiting for. The war had ended and there was no place to go. The 37th killed 24,957 Japanese on Luzon and captured 17,531 while losing only 736 killed and 5,076 wounded. For its heroism during more than 592 days of combat in the Pacific War, the 37th Division was awarded seven Medals of Honor, 109 Distinguished Service Crosses, one Navy Cross, four Distinguished Service Medals, 61 Legion of Merits, 939 Silver Stars, 94 Soldiers Medals, 6,366 Bronze Stars, 49 Air Medals, 9,150 Purple Hearts and nine Presidential Unit Citations.

With the end of the war, all thoughts turned toward home, but it was two and a half months before the ships arrived to carry the battle-weary 37th Infantry Division back to the United States it had left 43 months before.

The record of the 37th Infantry Division has few equals. The men who fought and died and the achievements of the organization attest to that. No eulogizing is necessary. *John K. Macdonald, assistant editor, 37th Division History.*

Co. H, 148th Inf., 81 mm Mortar Platoon, 1943. (Courtesy Malandrino)

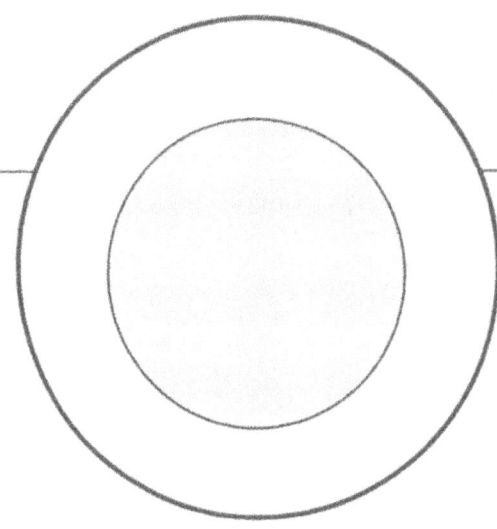

37th Division Casualties—World War II—Major Campaigns

	NEW GEORGIA	BOUGAINVILLE	LUZON
Killed in Action	206	185	736
Wounded in Action	928	1,388	5,076
Missing in Action	2	4	2
Died of Wounds	29	57	132
Injured in Action			155
Non-Battle Deaths	42		
Total - Killed in Action	1,834		
Wounded in Action	8,218		
Missing in Action	18		
	10,070		

Enemy Casualties

	KILLED	PRISONERS
Solomon Islands	9,087	65
Manila	13,006	459
Baguio	3,132	116
Cagayan Valley	7,746	1,528
145-148	1,609	12
Totals	33,580	2,180
Surrendered		15,351

Summary of Awards

	New Georgia	Bou-gainville	Luzon	By Other Units	Total
Medal of Honor	2		5		7
Distinguished Service Cross	13	31	65		109
Distinguished Service Medal	2	2			4
Silver Star Medal	161	169	609		939
Legion of Merit	17	29	15		61
Soldier's Medal	8	34	52		94
Bronze Star Medal	1,440		4,926		6,366
Purple Heart	1,083	1,630	3,917	2,520	9,150
Combat Infantryman Badge					15,690

Dedication of Regimental Chapel
147th Infantry
Camp Shelby, Mississippi
December 7, 1941

Order of Service

Assembly of Troops
Parade of Colors...Call: "To the Colors"
Invocation
Hymn *America*..No. 144
Responsive Reading..led by Lt. Col. Edwin Woellner (CO, 1st Bn.)
Scripture Lesson..read by Lt. Col. James Glore (Executive Officer)
Solo *The Lord's Prayer*..Sgt. William Nimmo
Presentation of Chapel Keys..Maj. Henry A. Ratterman (Regimental S-4)
Acceptance of Chapel Keys..Col. John A. Blount (CO, 147th Inf.)
Representing Men of Regiment..Mr. Sgt. Charles C. Daniels (Regimental Sgt. Maj.)
Hymn *Onward Christian Soldiers*.. No. 86
Sermon..Capt. Clifford Chadwick (Chaplain 147th Inf.)
Dedicatory Prayer..Maj. Frederick Kirker (Asst. Div. Chaplain, 37th Div.)
Benediction
Recessional

Dedicatory Prayer
Book of Common Prayer

"O Eternal God, mighty in power, and of great majesty, whom the heavens cannot contain, much less the walls of temples made with hands; and who yet hast been graciously pleased to promise thy especial presence wherever thy faithful servants shall assemble in thy Name; Vouchsafe, O Lord, to be present with us who are gathered together with all humility and readiness of heart, to consecrate this place to the honor of they great Name, and dedicate it to thy service, for reading thy Holy Word, for celebrating thy holy sacraments, for offering to thy glorious Majesty the sacrifices of prayer and thanksgiving, for blessing thy people in thy Name, and for all other holy offices. And grant, we beseech thee, blessed Lord, that whoever shall draw near to thee in this place, to give thee thanks for the benefits which they have received at thy hands, to set forth thy most worthy praise, to confess their sins unto thee, and to ask such things as are requisite and necessary, as well for the body as for the soul, may do it with such steadiness of faith and with such seriousness, affection, and devotion of mind that thou mayest accept their bounden duty and service and vouchsafe to give whatever in thy infinite wisdom thou shalt see to be most expedient for them. All which we beg for Jesus Christ's sake, our most blessed Lord and Saviour. Amen."

Prayer for the Army
"Oh Lord God of Hosts, stretch forth, we pray thee, thine almighty arm to strengthen and protect the soldiers of our country. Support them in the day of battle, and in the time of peace keep them safe from all evil; endue them with courage and loyalty; and grant them in all things they may serve thee without reproach; through Jesus Christ our Lord." Amen.

Camp Shelby Flag. (Courtesy Chaney)

Camp Shelby, Mississippi

Submitted by William Marshal Chaney, B Co., 147th Inf., 37th Div.

"Where Boys Were Transformed into Men— pronto!"

Camp Shelby is a sprawling military reservation in the delta region of the magnolia state. It is located 10 miles south of Hattiesburg, Mississippi, on the northern edge of the De Sota National Forest. The camp is situated in the center of an excellent rail and highway communications net. It is approximately one hundred road miles to Mobile, Alabama, to the east; to Jackson, Mississippi, to the northwest; and to New Orleans, Louisiana, to the southwest. The Gulf of Mexico is only one hour's drive to the south. In comparison to many sections of the United States, the southern Mississippi climate is mild year-round. Perhaps the locale has more than its fair share of rain with occasional light snows. Due to the high humidity, a skiff of snow or a heavy frost will produce bone-chilling air. But even so, the camp is ideally located for a training area.

Camp Shelby was established in 1917 through the efforts of the Mississippi Congressional Delegation, the Forrest County and Hattiesburg civic leaders, and the local businessmen. All worked closely with General Leonard Wood in making the site selection.

On July 18, 1917, the War Department designated the U.S./National Guard troops of Indiana, Kentucky and West Virginia to form the 38th Infantry Division. On August 3, they began concentration of what was to become known as Camp Shelby. The Kentucky contingent were the first to arrive; and in honor to them, they were permitted to name the new camp. They called it Camp Shelby in honor of Colonel Isaac Shelby, who was Kentucky's first governor. He served from 1792-1796; and later he served a second term from 1812-1816.

Colonel Isaac Shelby was born at North Mountain, MD on December 11, 1750. He died at Travelers Rest, Lincoln County, Kentucky on July 18, 1826. He was a surveyor, a soldier, and a statesman. He performed many remarkable feats which testify to his courage and leadership ability. However, Colonel Shelby is best remembered as one of the officers who, with 2,000 frontiersmen of western North Carolina and Virginia as well as those of present Kentucky and Tennessee, gave the British army its defeat on Kings Mountain on October 7, 1780. The British were under the command of Major Patrick Ferguson, the Scotchman who invented the first breech-loading rifle ever used in warfare and who had 200 British 8th Infantrymen and 925 American (Tories) loyalists as his soldiers. The frontiersmen had long rifles (Deckards) and no bayonets. The British charged downhill with bayonets fixed, and the Americans picked them off. Major Ferguson, dressed in his checkered wool skirt, was found dead with seven bullet holes in him. He had had his right arm shattered at Brandywine. The Major's successor in command, Captain De Peyster, was overwhelmed and raised the white flag of surrender. Fiske says of Ferguson's 1,125 men that 389 were killed or wounded, 20 were missing, and the remaining 716 surrendered with 1,500 stand of arms. The total American losses were 28 killed and 60 wounded. Colonel Shelby's command in this battle was a yell (perhaps the origin of the Confederates' rebel yell), "Shout like hell and fight like devils," and this the frontiersmen had to do as their commissary rations consisted only of bags of parched corn mixed with maple syrup. They wanted food as well as the hides of the British and their cohorts.

Initially, Camp Shelby was built at a cost of 3.3 million dollars. Four thousand civilian laborers built the installation which eventually boasted 1,206 buildings, most of which were used for administration and logistics purposes. However, the 36,000 troops that were stationed and trained at this post during World War I were quartered in tents, as they have traditionally been through the years at Shelby.

Upon arrival, the 38th Infantry Division during its first tour of duty at Camp Shelby, took up the drill and studies of the Arts-of-the Soldier, which included military courtesy

Camp Shelby, Miss. Summer of 1941. Foreground, regimental area of the 147th Inf. Near background, HQ of the 74th Inf. Brigade. Rear background, center, HQ, 37th Inf. Div.. (Courtesy Chaney

November 1941, Camp Shelby, Co. B, 147th Inf Regt. passing in review.

Camp Shelby, reception area for selectees.

Camp Shelby, A Company Street.

Camp Shelby, Second Avenue. (All courtesy Chaney)

and discipline, Close and Extended Order drills, and Chemical and Trench Warfare. "As boys they were transformed into men or soldiers. Pronto!"

While at Camp Shelby the 38th Division area was hit by a cyclone and extensive damage was done to the existing facilities. As a result, then and there, the 38th Division became known as "The Cyclone Division." Their divisional triangle shoulder patch insignia bears an overlay of the abbreviation "CY" in commemoration of the Shelby Cyclone incident. But the cyclone incident didn't check the lightening pace of the division's training schedule.

The 38th Division was shipped to France in September-October 1918. There they occupied a quiet sector and continued training to keep them razor sharp for anticipated front-line duty. But the Kaiser crumbled on November 11, 1918 and by December 1918 the division was en route back to the States for demobilization at Camp Taylor, Kentucky, without ever seeing the front lines. Camp Shelby, of all the First World War training centers, achieved the second highest health record and was awarded a special commendation for discipline and efficiency.

Camp Shelby, since the date of its inception, has been like the magician's mystical rabbit—first you see it (its physical structure), and then you don't. It was constructed as a military training post in response to a national emergency: first, in World War I, then re-activated during World War II, and then again during the Korean Conflict. After the danger and threats have abated, it has traditionally been deactivated and demolished. Following World War I all but four of the buildings were torn down which were ammo storage magazines. Today (1986) one of them, Building 6981, still stands near the western edge of the main cantonment area.

Sporadically, Camp Shelby was used as a summer training center during the peacetime years between World Wars I and II, mainly by National Guard and Army Reserve units. In 1934 Mississippi acquired the camp for its National Guard use. An older post, Camp McClellan, was dismantled and the materials were used to construct the early wooden buildings at Shelby, starting in 1937. Today, the majority of these buildings are still in use.

Land in the De Sota National Forest was used for Army maneuvers in 1938. With the assistance of the Mississippi Congressional Delegation, the federal government negotiated for the lease of additional land. Federal funds were appropriated and in September 1940, the camp was reopened as a federal installation.

On September 24, 1940, Congress approved the Selective Service Training Act effecting the first peacetime draft in U.S. history. This was inspired by the same threats of war that caused the Congress in August 1940 to authorize the President of the United States to mobilize the National Guard, Army and Naval Reserve units for a limited period of training.

The famed 37th Buckeye Division of the U.S./Ohio National Guard was federalized on October 15, 1940, and assumed its place in the ranks of the Army of the United States. The advanced elements of 1,400 men detrained at McLaurin, Mississippi, and on Sunday, October 20, they marched into Camp Shelby. They were assigned to what was later known as "The Old Area," which was in an early stage of renovation. Squad tents with wooden platform floors were aligned along the ungraveled, grass-covered company streets. Drinking water was at a premium, and it was drawn from Lister-bags at the end of the company streets. Company mess halls were of single boxed construction with dirt floors covered with sawdust. Chow was cooked on World War I wood-burning field ranges with no bottoms, but placed on a wooden box-and-mud foundation. We had only one gang shower to the brigade and one PX, well stocked, but housed in another primitive building. Basic training commenced on arrival, and liberty wasn't given until basic was completed. Following basic came extended order drill, the rifle range, and night problems.

In late November or early December, the Buckeyes moved into their new quarters or "The New Area." This consisted of permanent-type mess halls with GI tables and coal ranges, company showers with plenty of water for all purposes, squad tents pitched over wooden frames with floors, sidewalls and screens and equipped with Sibley stoves placed in the center of the tents on a box of clay.

The stoves were built like an inverted funnel with a small door two-thirds of the way up on the slopping sidewalls and had no bottoms; they burned either coal or wood. Our regimental headquarters, PX, and regimental recreation center were housed in framed permanent-type buildings as were the brigade and divisional headquarters. Later, company day rooms and divisional and non-divisional service clubs were added as well as post theaters, all of which supplied the needs of the troops. New equipment was arriving on a daily basis.

Following basic, the bulk of the troops, the privates, were given a raise in pay from

Sgt. Edward T. Halsey, snake, Woodrow Wilson.

Ralph T. DiLullo

Sgt. John A. Russell and Corp. Frank Russell, Dayton, Ky. brothers at Camp Shelby. (Courtesy Chaney)

$21 monthly plus room, board, and medical care to $30 monthly; that is, except for the goof balls who were held at $21 indefinitely. Over Christmas many of the troops were given leaves. On New Years Day in 1941, a vast majority of the soldiers were sporting new or additional stripes (such as PFC, corporal and sergeant chevrons) in anticipation of an influx of draftees during the last of January.

The initial quota of draftees arrived on schedule still carrying with them letters from their local draft boards, which notified them that they had been selected by their friends and neighbors to serve a year in the Army of the United States. It goes without saying that many of them at that point and time held their friends and neighbors in low esteem. Ha! The echoes of "May God Bless 'em all" could be heard throughout the camp, long and loud.

On Washington's Birthday, the 38th Division arrived in force at Camp Shelby; and Corps troops were arriving almost daily to occupy their stations. The 37th Division had more than doubled in strength since its arrival due to the assignment of reserve officers and draftees. By March 1941, there were 60,000 troops at Camp Shelby, making it the second largest military post in the United States, exceeded only by Fort Bragg, North Carolina; 14,000 tents had been erected on the base to house them.

Hattiesburg, Mississippi, the county seat of Forrest County and the nearest town of any size to Camp Shelby, had a population of 20,000, which was somewhat augmented by Camp Shelby construction workers. With 60,000 troops to choose from (many of whom were in their late teens and early twenties), the local girls were choosy and drove hard bargains. However, there were always such places as the houses on Hattiesburg's Southern Avenue where the girls and women (mostly the latter) would entertain the troops for the usual three-dollar fee. But for the GIs to go off the beaten paths to patronize these houses, they had to adopt the sailor's attitude—"Any Olde Port During A Storm."

The units of the 37th Division, due to the influx of draftees, went through another cycle of basic and extended order training. Most of the draftees committed themselves to the task at hand. By far and large they had more formal education than those who had earlier enlisted through the National Guard. As a result, those draftees with the proper attitude were soon wearing chevrons and in commanding positions; in fact, many of them went on to OCS and were commissioned.

The commanding general of the 37th Division, Major General Robert S. Beightler, believed in an equally balanced program of work and play—and that we got in its proper perspective. The General's unspoken motto was "If one doesn't soldier, he sure as hell doesn't play." The Camp Shelby of World War II contained 360,000 acres (an area slightly larger than the currently available land) plus an additional 400,000 acres leased for maneuver space. In all, over 1,000 square miles were in use for training, and the infantrymen covered every inch of it either on foot or on their bellies.

In addition to the tents erected in World War II, 17,000 construction workers plus Army engineer units built over 1,800 buildings and 250 miles of improved roads at a cost of 24 million dollars.

In June the 37th Division was trucked to Louisiana for Corps maneuvers. There they were given a practice session to prepare the division for the big 2nd and 3rd Armies' maneuvers which were scheduled for August, September and the first week of October 1941. Officers were to learn the details of commanding troops in the field and the chain-of-command functions, other than under garrison conditions, as well as movement of troops over long distances. To the rank-and-file soldier, especially the infantrymen, it more vividly meant thirsty, forced marches on empty stomachs, blistered feet, iodine swabs, band-aides, dripping shelter halves, clothing steeped in semi-tropical rain and mud for a week at a time; and, for good measure, chiggers (or were they rebel jig-roes that buried into the flesh and left red knots like ripened dogwood berries). The 37th Division was pitted against the 32nd Infantry Division. Success and shortcomings were noted. The 37th Division was returned to Shelby on July 3 to address and correct its inefficiencies and failures.

In August, the 37th Division returned to Louisiana to participate in the big, big maneuvers of the 2nd and 3rd Armies. Here, Uncle Sam put 550,000 soldiers in the field for the largest peacetime maneuvers in the history of the United States of America. The maneuvers were much the same as the June maneuvers, only on a much larger scale. The rank-and-file soldiers in general and the foot soldiers in particular found the maneuvers to be an endurance test. They were toughened and hardened to the 9th degree. The soldiers were confident; if one could endure the Louisiana maneuvers, they individually could take on Hitler and Tojo single-handed.

On October 4, the 37th Division returned to Camp Shelby to continue where they had left off. There were more extensive trainings, more forced marches, and more night problems. The one year of active duty for the National Guardsmen and draftees was extended for an additional 18 months. This was somewhat ameliorated by the War Department's release of over-aged, enlisted men and officers and those in certain other categories. Furloughs were granted in November.

The 37th Division received a contingent of draftees from Camp Wolters, TX, who hailed principally from the western states. They were slightly of a different breed, but they soon found their places within the ranks of the 37th's units.

On December 7, 1941, many troops were on liberty in the surrounding communities. The new regimental chapels had been completed, and it was dedication day. Among the troops attending the dedication services were those of the 147th Infantry. Upon returning to their quarters, the radios were turned on and the troops learned that the Japs had bombed Pearl Harbor. It is hard to express in words how this awful and dreaded news was received by the officers and soldiers of the U.S. Army. Beyond words, they knew that these little-yellow-bellies had brought their challenge to America's doorstep, and She had no other choice but to respond.

On the heels of Pearl Harbor, the United States declared war on Japan, Germany, and Italy, which was endorsed by the masses at Camp Shelby. Those classified as overage and so forth and released in October, November, and December were recalled to active duty. Discharges in general were canceled for the duration of the war, plus six months. The 37th Division was triangulized to make it more streamlined and comparable in size to the Allied divisions. The Division was alerted for overseas service; all units were brought up to full wartime strength; the vacancies in the chain of command were filled; and the newest and most modern equipment was issued to the combat units. In February 1942, the Buckeyes were transferred to the Military Reservation at Indiantown Gap, Pennsylvania, which was merely a stopover. The Division and all of its units were on their way to where the war was being fought. Its performance is now history.

On the departure of the 37th Division, the role played by the participants at Camp Shelby continued to expand and enlarge. In addition to the 37th and 38th Divisions, the 43rd, the 65th and the 69th Divisions trained at Camp Shelby for their World War II roles. Also trained was the famous Japanese-American 442nd Regimental Combat Team, which became the most highly decorated unit in the European Theater. WAC units also trained at Camp Shelby. The post contained a large convalescent hospital and a prisoner of war camp, which initially housed members of the German Africa Corps. At one time, the population exceeded 100,000 troops, making Camp Shelby the largest military training center and post in the world.

After World War II, the post was again closed. The War Assets Administration sold the federally-owned property. Even the water pipes were dug up and sold, most of them going to Oklahoma City where some are still in use.

During the Korean Conflict, Camp Shelby was developed as an emergency railhead facility. Three million dollars was spent to restore rail, water, and electric services. In the summer of 1954, non-divisional National Guard units trained at the post; and in 1956, the Continental Army Command designated it as a permanent training site directed by the 3rd Army Headquarters.

Traditionally, troops at Camp Shelby have been housed in tents; but in 1958, Congress allocated money for the first of the permanent type barracks. In 1959 the Department of the Army approved the overall Camp Shelby plan and adopted it as the model for future construction at all field-training sites.

Today, Camp Shelby is the largest state-owned-and-operated training site in the United States. There are over 132,000 acres available for training, over 750 buildings, over 50 ranges, 64 numbered training areas, an airfield, and an airborne drop zone. The camp had 92 surveyed artillery firing points and has accommodated seven artillery battalions training simultaneously. It is especially suitable for tank and mechanized infantry training. The camp has extensive maneuver areas and six tank-firing ranges. Its newest addition is the M-I tank training program being conducted by the 155th Armored Brigade, Mississippi National Guard. Its National Guard OCS Academy is currently in its 28th year of operation; and it has graduated 819 officers of whom 400 continue to serve. It had an NCO School which has trained and graduated 1,014 non-commissioned officers, among its many, many functional activities.

At the present time the post has nearly 300 barracks and 127 headquarters buildings—enough to support an entire division or its equivalent. It has dining facilities, capable of serving 14,000 troops at one meal, and medical facilities. Troop welfare and recreational facilities are also available.

Camp Shelby is an annual training site for over 30,000 National Guardsmen and reservists from a dozen states, but it is also used throughout the year—typically 280 days out of 365 and 42 weekends out of 52. In 1985, 101,748 troops trained at Shelby. The camp's wartime mission is to serve as a major, independent mobilization center under Forces Command.

Camp Shelby beckons the second line of our defense to use its facilities should a national emergency arise.

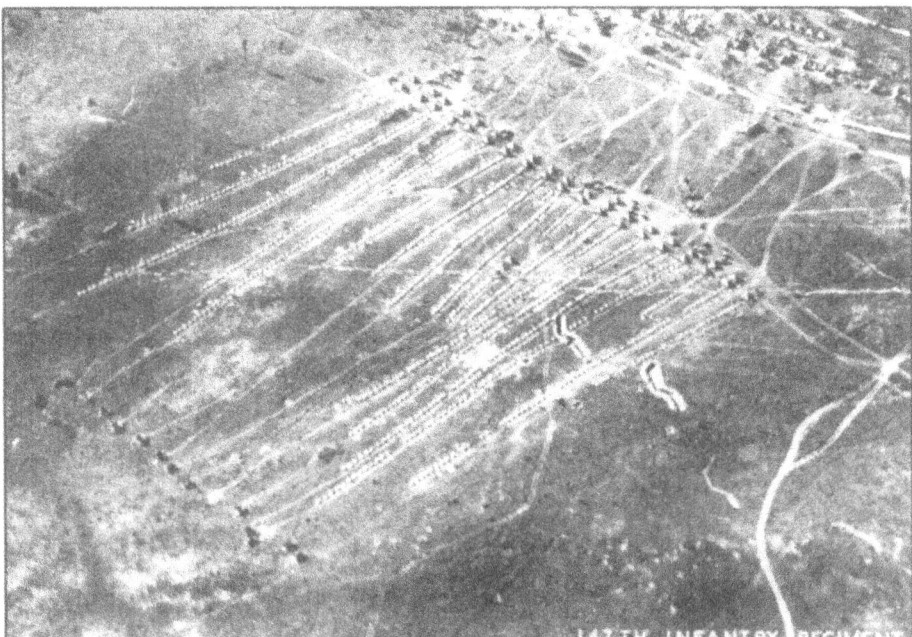

Camp Claiborne, Louisiana Outskirts, June 19, 1941. Division reserve. (Courtesy Chaney)

KP duty, May 1941. Ralph T. DiLullo on left.

Indiantown Gap, Pennsylvania

Ah! Yes: "We Remember"

by William Marshal Chaney

This year the United States of America and her World War II Allies will observe the 42nd anniversary of the victorious conclusion of World War II.

On "Pearl Harbor Day," December 7, 1941, B Company, 1st Battalion, 147th Infantry, 37th Infantry Division was at Camp Shelby, Mississippi. The Division was under command of Major General Robert S. Beightler, an Ohioan whose military career dated back to August 11, 1911. The Division had been in federal service since October 14, 1940, and practically in constant training since the Wisconsin 2nd Army Maneuvers of the preceding August. The Division, like a gamecock, was primed and ready for action, with the exception of being slightly understrength. That not withstanding, almost immediately after "Pearl Harbor," the Division was alerted for overseas duty.

In February 1942, the 37th Infantry Division was transferred to the Military Reservation at Indiantown Gap, Pennsylvania. Rumors were hot and consistent that the Division had been consigned to the ETO. However, our defenses on Guam, Wake, the Philippines and elsewhere in the Pacific fell rapidly before the Japanese onslaught. In order to protect Australia and New Zealand, and keep the sea lanes open, it was necessary to occupy the New Hebrides, New Caledonia and Tonga.

The 1st and 3rd Battalions of the 147th Infantry were pulled out of the 37th Division, along with the 134th Field Artillery, and combined into the 147th Infantry Regimental Combat Team. It, and elements of the Division's service troops, were assigned to Task Force 0051. On April 7, 1942, the 1st Battalion boarded the USS *American Legion* and the 3rd Battalion, Service Company and Regimental Headquarters Company of the 147th. Infantry-RCT boarded the USS *Hunter Liggett*. On April 9, 1942, in Brooklyn, New York, they got underway with seven other ships loaded with Task Force troops, materials and equipment, embarking for Tonga Tabu via Panama Canal. They picked up the balance of 23 other ships off Newport News, Virginia, en route.

Upon reaching the high seas each individual soldier was issued a copy of a form letter from the President of the United States. We young GIs who were venturing out on the war-torn seas for our first voyage, with thoughts of home and the loved ones we were leaving behind, found the President's letter very comforting and it instilled in we GIs a sense of purpose.

On the morning of May 10, 1942, the Task Force landed at Tonga Tabu unopposed. While there we never found time for many dull moments. The personnel of the 147th Infantry-RCT unloaded numerous ships, built and manned gun positions along the coastal areas, did some jungle training in the island's interior and practiced assault landings.

On October 20, 1942, the 1st Battalion, 147th Infantry boarded the USS *Neville* and sailed via the New Hebrides, landing at daybreak on November 4, 1942, at Aola Bay, Guadalcanal. We were an element of a Task Force consisting of a Battery from the 246th Field Artillery Battalion, the 5th Marine Defense Battalion, the 14th Naval Construction Battalion, and the 2nd Marine (Gung Ho) Raider Battalion, under command of Colonel Evans F. Carlson. Lieutenant Colonel James "Jimmy" Roosevelt (FDR's eldest son) made an appearance at the landing site. During the landing, American fighter planes and Jap Zeros were dogfighting overhead; otherwise, the landing was unopposed.

The combat units moved inland and established a perimeter defense, with the reserve units participating in securing rations and supplies as they were delivered from the ships to the beach. The temperature was always hot and the humidity high, and it rained often, even occasionally when the sun was shining. The mud and swamps were everywhere, as were the insects and anopheles mosquitoes. We GIs were assured if the nips didn't get us, the mosquitoes would. Our rations were of poor quality and our diet reminded me of a neighbor back in southeastern Kentucky wintering his horses on corn-fodder. Within a week after the landing, an army of insects had invaded our dried beans, soup and cereal. Initially we tried to sort the bugs out as we ate, but due to their colors they blended in with our food. In disgust we gave up, consoling ourselves with the thought that nature had provided us with meat, to spice our dried milk, dehydrated eggs, and other goodies, such as GI chocolate bars (which were as scarce as hen's teeth).

Patrols operated daily in front of the perimeter and the 2nd Marine Raider Battalion penetrated deep into the interior northwestward of Aola Bay, making sporadic contact with the enemy. Shortly after the landing, a group of natives informed our headquarters that several nips were biv-

Camp Shelby, Miss., October 14, 1990. The 37th "Buckeye" Division was honored for its service and contributions with this monument.

ouacking in a village some 10 miles or so northwest of our perimeter and inland some distance from the coast. A patrol from B Company, 147th Infantry and a detachment of Marines made a daylight attack on the village, killing all the Japs but one. The native guides lashed his (the Jap's) hands and legs together, strung him on a pole and carried him into the 147th Infantry, 1st Battalion Headquarters. He was interrogated by a Japanese speaking American soldier and then sent to the island stockade.

Rear Admiral Richmond Kelly Turner had directed the operation at Aola Bay with the intention of building a secondary airfield at the site. However, the Seabees found the ground to be unsuitable. As a result, on Thanksgiving night of 1942, the 1st Battalion, 147th Infantry was moved up the coast by Higgins boats northwestward to Koli Point. There it was joined by the 3rd Battalion, Service Company and Regimental Headquarters Company on November 29, 1942.

The two battalions moved inland to near the foot of Gold Ridge and established an outpost line of resistance where they operated daily patrols while the Seabees and the Army Corps of Engineers were constructing a heavy bomber base to be known as Carney Field.

As the Japs threw in reinforcements so did the U.S. Armed Forces. In addition to the personnel of the 147th Infantry, the U.S. Army's Americal Division and the 25th Infantry Division joined the battle for Guadalcanal between October through December 1942. Several bomber and fighter squadrons, in addition to coast artillery and antiaircraft units and the 2nd Marine Division arrived in December 1942. This was to bring relief and support to the U.S. 1st Marine Division-Reinforced, which made the initial landing at Guadalcanal on August 7, 1942.

On December 9, 1942, Major General A.A. Vandegrift and his 1st Marine Division were relieved and Major General Alexander M. Patch, United States Army, assumed command of all combat operations on Guadalcanal. In early January 1943, General Patch called on the nips to surrender by having thousands upon thousands of pamphlets dropped by planes over the Japanese held section of the island, which the Japs ignored. The general then launched an all-out campaign to secure the island, contending there wasn't room for both the Americans and the Japs, too.

The 1st and 3rd Battalions of the 147th Infantry, less I Company, which had been detached to Beaufort Bay (to block the possible Japanese use of the Beaufort Bay-Kokumbona Trail), were assigned as line units in the newly organized Composite Army-Marine Division.

On January 19, 1943, the 1st and 3rd Battalions of the 147th Infantry moved into the frontlines, flanked by the 6th Marines on their right and the 182nd Infantry on their left. The Battalions were in almost constant contact with the enemy. On the morning of January 20, 1943, B Company's 1st Platoon was on the right flank of the regimental sector. As the platoon went through the valley, between Hills 96 and 98, and as it neared the river bank in the valley floor, a group of dazed and confused Japs, but full of fight, were encountered. The 1st Platoon responded quickly. When the firefight was over, 17 nips had been made good ones and laid on the valley floor. During this initial operation the 147th Infantry units advanced 8,350 yards, sustaining light casualties and inflicted heavy losses on the enemy in both personnel and materials.

After arriving at Kokumbona on or near January 24, 1943, and remaining in reserve briefly, the 147th Infantry was chosen by the 14th Corps Commander to continue the attack and pursuit of the enemy.

On January 30, 1943, as the regiment advanced through a coconut grove, running parallel with the coast and on approaching the east banks of the Bonegi River, all hell broke lose. The fight developed into a full-scale battle. Artillery fire was stepped up and the Navy and Air Arms were called upon for support. Three destroyers were sent up from Henderson to shell the Japs on the west bank of the river and they were strafed by several planes. Halftracks were brought up to reinforce the 1st Battalion sector; it was a hell-of-a-fight.

B Company earned more Purple Hearts on January 30, 1943, than at any time during their long stay on Guadalcanal. Two B Company Sergeants, Robert J. Schwing of Cleves, Ohio, and H.L. Wright of Hooven, Ohio, and the 1st Battalion Commander, Lieutenant Colonel Robert C. Hanes of Springfield, Ohio, were awarded the Silver Star Medal for gallantry in action as well as PFC, Thomas Hughes, and Sgt. Buesher, both members of Co, B, 147th Infantry. They were several other GIs of the 147th Infantry awarded Silver Star medals.

Despite all the efforts, however, units of the 147th Infantry did not cross the Bonegi River until February 5, 1943. In the meantime, Japanese planes sunk the destroyer, the USS *DeHaven* between Savo Island and Guadalcanal as she supported the advance of the 147th Infantry. It was later learned that the nips had amassed 10,000 to 12,000 troops in the vicinity of the west bank of the Bonegi River, extending to the Cape Esperance area, for evacuation, which they slipped off the island under cover of darkness during the early nights of February 1943.

On February 7, 1943, the 2nd Battalion, which had been attached to the 37th Infantry Division in Fiji, was reunited with its parent regiment. At 1600 hours (4:00 p.m.) on February 9, 1943, Guadalcanal was officially secured. However, the 147th Infantry remained on Guadalcanal until May 12, 1943. It continued mopping up, patrolling and training exercises. All personnel of the regiment had contacted malaria and practically all had been hospitalized many times. In addition to the regiment's combat encounters, it had survived 133 Jap air raids. To a man, they were veterans in their own right.

After Guadalcanal the 147th Infantry-RCT USA was transferred to British Samoa and then to New Caledonia, Emirau, Iwo Jima, Tinian, and Okinawa and was deactivated on Christmas Day 1945, at Fort Lewis, Washington.

P.S.: According to Robert Leckie's book, *Strong Men Armed*, the last nip surrendered on Guadalcanal on October 27, 1947.

P.S.S.: The 147th Infantry USA didn't merely mark time on the sands of Iwo Jima. During its piece of the action, it captured over 800 nips and killed 1600 and some odd. Get the facts! Read *The Two Ocean War* by Samuel Elliot Morison, published by Atlantic, Little and Brown, and/or *Iwo* by Richard Wheeler, published by Lippincott & Crowell.

Maj. Gen. and Mrs. Robert Beightler, Labor Day weekend 1977, 37th Infantry Division Reunion. (Courtesy Chaney)

Memories of the 37th

W. Marshal Chaney, veteran of Co. B, 147th Inf. and Capt. Ed Miller, both Kentucky natives, visit during 50th Anniversary Commemorative Ceremony, September 6, 1990.

March 1945, Co. F, 147th Inf. Jap cave on Iwo Jima. (Courtesy McGuire)

Administration Building, Manila, 1945. (Courtesy Atkins)

Bougainville

*Submitted by William Marshal Chaney,
Chairman 37th Inf. Div. History Book Committee*

Bougainville was the largest of the Solomon Islands, and even more primitive than Guadalcanal. The jungle clad terrain was a challenge within itself, and there were the tropical diseases to contend with. There were many combat veterans among the occupying Japs, and they were dug-in, in many of the strategical positions. America's armed forces and her Allies had their work cut out for them.

Hats off to the U.S. Navy; her sea going sailors that man the ships, the seabees who were second to none, when it came to building airports (fields), roads, and harbor facilities, the special seabees (stevedores) and air arms, and the U.S. Marines' Air Arms. And there was the U.S. Army's Air Force, the masters of Air Warfare.

And a big thank you to the Corps Artillery. The big guns and the ack-ack with their searchlite batteries. They were part of the team that tore up the Japs playhouses, and sent them home to their Sun - God or that place below to shovel coal.

Thanks to God, the 37th Infantry didn't have to carry the fight to the enemy all alone. There was the U.S. 3rd Marine Division reinforced; the USA's Americal Division; veterans of the Guadalcanal Campaign; the USA's 43rd Infantry Division, who like the 37th Division were veterans of the New Georgia Campaign; and there was the USA's 93rd Infantry Colored (Negro) Division, with a sprinkling of white commissioned officers.

There was also an Australian contingency, troops that perform superbly on any field; there were also a contingency of Fijian Scouts intermingled with Tongans, and perhaps a number of other islanders.

We veterans of the 37th Infantry Division humbly thank God, that the "Buckeyes" didn't have to go it alone at Bougainville. We appreciate the achievements of all the services that were involved in the Bougainville Campaign, who were members of the Allied Services.

Bougainville Island, 1943. Volcano atop 10,000 foot high Mount Bagana (Courtesy Chaney)

Bougainville, 1943. U.S. Navy smoke shells exploding during the initial naval bombardment of Empress Augusta Bay. (Courtesy Chaney)

Wilfred D. Hendershot after getting a haircut at Bentley's Bougainville Barber Shop. (Courtesy Hendershot)

A mass grave of 250 Japs who freely gave their all for the Emperor and Tojo. The Japs were known to take cover among their dead and attack their enemies as they passed by. (Courtesy Chaney)

Emirau Island of St. Matthias Group

by LTC Gordon W. Bailey, USAR RET, 147th Inf. AUS, WWII

Emirau Island was relatively small, but the largest island in the St. Matthias Group, which was located in the Bismarck Archipalago, in a fringe area of water dominated by Japanese forces. Kavieng, New Ireland was only 65 or 70 miles away, where it was estimated that the Nips had 90,000 troops based. The big Jap base at Rabaul was within striking range.

The Allies were determined to neutralize the Jap base at Rabaul and to by-pass Kavieng, New Ireland. Admiral William F. "Bull" Halsey, Commander of the South Pacific Allied Forces targeted Emirau Island as his final operation before stepping down as Commander of South Pacific Allied Forces.

Initially the 147th Infantry, reinforced, was alerted on March 17, 1944, for the invasion and occupation of Emirau. However, the 4th Marines, which had recently been reconstituted by the 1st, 2nd and 3rd USMC Raider Battalions, reinforced, who were located closer to Emirau than the USA's 147th Infantry, were chosen as the initial invasion force. And on March 20, 1944, the 4th U.S. Marines landed without opposition. They found no Japs, and the only occupants of the island were a small band of lepers in a village on the west end of the 10 mile long island. Although the 147th Infantry didn't participate in the initial invasion, it was chosen to relieve the 4th Marines.

The USA's 147th Infantry at full strength and fully equipped, embarked at Noumea, New Caledonia on April 2, 1944, aboard the transports USS *Dupage, Elmore, Wayne* and *Crescent City*, and the cargo ship *Aquarius*. Much special equipment was among the gear, and attachments for the mission included a postal unit, a signal service detachment, a bomb-disposal squad and CIC, Public Relations and Nisei personnel. The convoy sailed April 4. After making an overnight stop at Guadalcanal, it resumed its northwest voyage, passing west of Bougainville, bearing northeast between Green and Buka Islands and then to the northeast, but keeping out of visibility from New Ireland, and arrived off Emirau at dawn on April 11.

The GIs unloaded the ships holes quickly at three beaches along the north coast, the 147th affected relief at all tactical positions by early afternoon, enabling the Marines to board the same transports and sailed before nightfall, 24 hours ahead of schedule. Emirau had heavy jungles, weeping weather, hub-deep mud and the roads were almost impassable trails, along with the normal confusion ever present with the establishment of a new base; to test the mettles, ingenuity, and the morale of the regiment. In less than a month it was apparent that these tests and others were cleared with ease.

The construction troops went to work immediately, and in short order, they had operational runways constructed, as was the norm for Seabees. They soon had developed the most advanced B-29 Airbase in the Asiatic-Pacific and put us Americans and our Allies just a little closer to Tokyo. Major Joe Foss, one of America's early Aces and a recipient of the Medal of Honor, came in with a squadron of Corsairs to provide fighter protection, and ack-ack units were stationed everywhere around the island, but more heavily near the airfield runways.

Like an opossum, the Japanese who occupied nearby islands in strength and in easy striking distance, were very coy, and made no effort to attack us Americans on Emirau, neither by air nor water. They acted as if they thought by ignoring us, we would go away.

MG James T. Moore, USMC, was island commander when the 147th Infantry reinforced arrived. Comgensopac designated Colonel W.B. Tuttle, CO 147th Infantry, as Commander of all Army troops, including the 14th AAA Group, a service command, and smaller attached units. General Moore was transferred on May 25 and five Seabees' battalions, having completed two landing strips, were also transferred and shipped out of Emirau to assume other assignments. On June 6, BG Leonard R. Boyd, assistant CO, 93rd (Negro) Infantry Division arrived at Emirau and assumed command of the island.

The 147th Infantry remained under the command of Comgensopac, however. The 147th as the principal garrison force on Emirau was relived by the 365th (Colored) Infantry, and sailed to New Caledonia July 9, 1944. Debarking at Noumea, New Caledonia on July 16, 1944, where it resumed training and preparations for future assignments.

Emirau, 1944. Romisher and Vaccariello at still. (Courtesy Seibert)

Emirau, 1944. Seabees building sailboats out of airplane auxiliary tanks. (Courtesy Chaney)

Sawmill, Emirau, 147th Inf. Service Co. (Courtesy Estes)

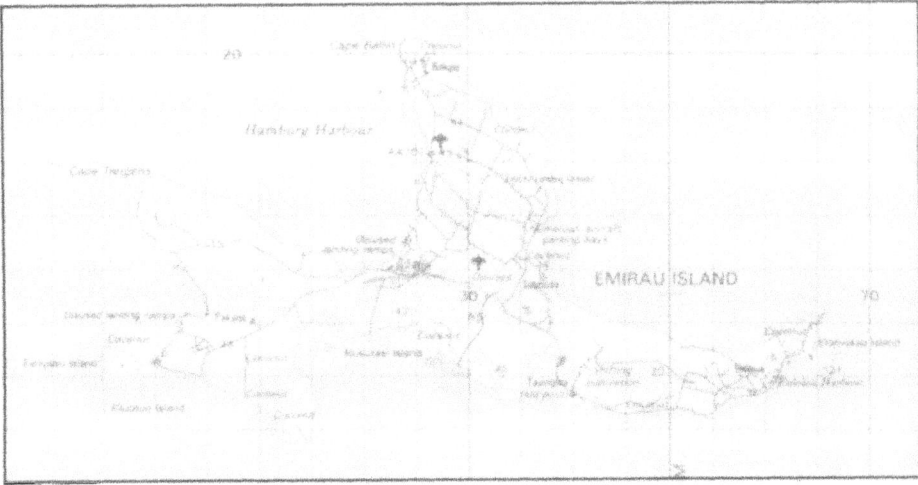

Map of Emirau Island. (Courtesy Chaney)

Evolution of the 147th Inf. Reg.

By Maj. L.K. Shropshire (excerpts)

The 147th had been inducted under the command of Col. John A. Blount of Hillsboro, a veteran of the National Guard organization in the Buckeye state. In keeping with the U.S. policy of relieving all officers above specified ages in the various grades, Col. Blount left the regiment on the last day of the year. Following this the regiment was commanded for varying periods by senior officers assigned and present including Lt. Cols. Edwin D. Woellner, James Glore and A.G Lockhart...

Streamlining of the old Infantry square divisions was being accomplished throughout the army, and in March the 147th was detached from Maj. Gen. Robert S. Beightler's 37th Division and designated, less the 2nd Bat., as the Infantry element of a task force formed for duty in the South Pacific. The 2nd Bat. was attached to the 148th Inf. and the remaining unit of the 147th were filled with transfers in order to be at full strength upon departure from the states ...

The first actual change in the 147th organization while overseas had occurred in October 1943, when the regiment was reorganized under a T/O dated July 16. 1943, less Cannon Company . . . Another change in the organic structure of the 147th occurred in December when, under a War Department directive changing the organization and distribution of all Army Bands, the regimental band was relieved from attachment to the 147th and redesignated the 202nd Army Band. It was promptly attached to its parent organization. A third change took place in mid-March when the 147th Inf. Cannon Company, which had just completed its training in the states, arrived at New Caledonia and joined the regiment.

Ayers' Log puts One Four Seven Doggies on Okinawa

Following the Iwo Jima Campaign, and a short tour of duty for the 1st Battalion, 147th Infantry Regiment, USA, on the Island of Tinian, the regiment embarked by battalion for Okinawa.

LTC Marvin V. Ayers, CO, 2nd Battalion, 147th Infantry, was on Okinawa only for a few weeks before being rotated to the States, after 40 odd months of service in the Asiatic-Pacific Theater. Colonel Ayers, through his graciousness, has made available the daily notes from his log of September 8-October 5, 1945.

Upon reviewing the Colonel's notes, one can readily understand how life was for the troops onboard the USS *Alcoa Polaris*, and the situation that confronted them, following their embarkation at Okinawa.

Alcoa Polaris

Saturday, September 8 - Commenced boarding at 1700, finished at 1800. Worst accommodations I've ever had. Hot, #5 hold.

Sunday September 9 - Nothing much. Read *Enter The Saint*, bored. Fair night's sleep, although sea was calm.

Monday, September 10 - Nothing much. Few drills. Wrote Chris. Sea a little rougher.

Tuesday, September 11 - Finished *Night Life of the Gods*. Wrote Chris and Mom. Played Cribbage most of afternoon and night. Not scheduled to arrive until tomorrow now.

Wednesday, September 12 - Up 0530. Still dark but could see lights on Okinawa - past Kerami Retta-Naha and anchored in Hagusha Bay between Kadena and Yontana airfields at 1100. No signs of our advance detachment - no word on unloading. Bay is full of ships, all kinds, except warships. Advance detachment out at 1600. We are to unload troops tomorrow but not cargo. Silly as heck. Wrote Chris, Mom, and Kay.

Thursday, September 13 - Up early expecting to debark when Captain Collin came after Colonel Davies to take him to General Lawson, Island Coast Guard. I had orders to stand by. Two LCMs arrived to take us, but we didn't load. About 1400 received word to debark and did so (Haguchi River) bivouacked on beach for night, eating K rations.

Okinawa

Thursday, September 13 - Onboard *Alcoa Polaris*. Up early expecting to debark, but received orders to stand-by until further notice. About 1400 received notice to debark (accomplished) Haguchi River. Bivouacked on beach for night, ate K rations.

Friday, September 14 - By end of day had all troops moved to old 1st Battalion, 105th Infantry area, two miles north of Onna. On ridges, plenty of mosquitoes, managed to secure former 105th Regimental CP area for Battalion CP, former colonel's house with shower, wash basin, urinal. No transportation all day, so no dope on what is going on. All Battalion Headquarter officers slept in house on floor of porch which faces toward Ie Shima where Ernie Pyle was killed. All roads are coral and not bad. Island reminds me of New Caledonia.

Saturday, September 15 - Down to Regiment to check on situation. Colonel dispatched me 30 miles to Machinato for situation. Our ship is being unloaded; saw Lieutenant General Buckner's grave. 1st Battalion arrived last night and debarked; 3rd Battalion is north about 15 miles at Nago. Wrote Chris.

Sunday, September 16 - Meeting with Colonel Davies. To Island Commander G-1, CO, 25th Replacement Depot (Colonel Wood), CO, 74th Replacement Battalion (Major Hanley). My battalion (less two rifle companies) to take over 74th Replacement Battalion and 2,000 readjustment personnel within two days. Checked on procurement of extra supplies, etc. Typhoon hit island, halting ship unloading. We do have three kitchens off, rain, and 50 mile winds.

Monday, September 17 - Typhoon still raging. Planned to take over 74th Replacement Battalion Tuesday. Wrote Chris and Mom. Winds continued all night.

Tuesday, September 18 - Moved Battalion (less E and G Companies) to 74th Replacement Battalion are preparatory to taking over their duties. Set up temporarily until they move out.

Wednesday, September 19 - Met Lieutenant Colonel Shields, CO of ASCOM Personnel Center, whom I'm responsible to. The 74th was supposed to leave today, but postponed until tomorrow. Went to Machinato. Ship still is not being unloaded. Letter from Latwer, wrote Chris.

Thursday, September 20 - 74th Replacement Battalion departed, Cargo started coming in off our ship. Took look at prospective camp areas for E and G Companies (to guard ammunition dump). Word received that 1494 casuals leaving tomorrow—contacted processing team. Lots of mail at 2100: Chris through September 5, Mom (including pictures of Norb, Chuck and Ann, Herrmanns, *Time*, *Newsweek*, Bank September 4 with statement, P&G with invitation to dinner, Glennis August 25, Jr. Price August 28, Aunt Irene, Skippy. Have been playing Gin Rummy with Stewart. Owe him $8.00.

Friday, September 21 - Shipped out 1,500 high point men. Received about one hundred 38-year old men. Wrote Chris and Mom.

Saturday, September 22 - Moved E and G to Ordinance area to take over guard-21 posts, three and a half miles from here. Passed General Stillwell in a jeep. Still haven't got all the cargo off the ship. Got in 500 38-year old and high point men—lost 38. Tried to write some letters, but gave up when bugs got the best of me. So retired.

Sunday, September 23 - Colonel Davies visited. He said I should let Major Senter take over as I should be leaving soon. Still unloading the ship. Wrote letters. Went to Machinato to pick up my 1/4 ton trailer with footlockers and bed roll. Started to rain. Tent leaks. What a mess! Uncomfortable night's sleep.

Monday, September 24 - Shipped out 300 38-year old men. They are still coming in fast though. We are about filled up. Checked on E and G Companies this morning. Mail service is good: Chris 9/11; Mom, Kay 9/12; Ralph, Lucy. Still raining, damp bed again.

Tuesday, September 25 - Word from Regiment to submit addresses of 85 point company grade officers and 100 point field grade officers. I've only got about 135 so worked on this roster immediately and delivered to regiment personally. Not much else—still raining. Wrote Kay, Skippy and Glennis. Bugs so bad, went to bed.

Wednesday, September 26 - Finished letter to Glennis and wrote Chris, Mom, Jr. Price. Still raining. Got the $125 check cashed—all in yen. Tried to play Gin Rummy but too many bugs and so went to bed early again.

Thursday, September 27 - Fairly quiet. Colonel Davies here. Harper said orders for eight of us with over 100 points as of 5/12 will be out by Saturday. So packed footlockers and Val Pack.

Friday, September 28 - To Regiment - Efficiency Reports, etc. Came back down eastern side of Island. About 1600 saw copies of orders assigning us to ASCOM Personnel Center (eight of us: Lieutenant Colonel Lovko; Majors Morrison, Williams; Captains Braden, Harper, Steele and Lieutenant Moody, and, of course, the most important one, Lieutenant Colonel Ayers.

Saturday, September 29 - Checked packing. Saw Captain Roberts and converted yen to dollars. Had luggage checked. Typhoon warning of 150 mile winds received. Wrote Chris and Mom short letters enclosing pictures. Mail from Mom, Norb, Woody. Farewell party at Regiment, but didn't drink too much. Back to area by 2000.

Sunday, September 30 - Reported to Personnel Center with records. To report back tomorrow for processing. Other seven officers moved in here at 2nd Battalion. Had baggage inspected. Mail call. Typhoon still hasn't hit us too hard although quite windy.

Monday, October 1 - Reported to Personnel Center for processing. Wrote Chris a 10 page letter. Took a ride in southern part of island: Kakasu Ridge, Hacksaw Ridge, Shirri-Naha-Yonabaru-Buckner Bay, etc. Can sure appreciate the toughness of the fighting that took place here. Some ships coming in looked like baby carriers. Played poker using yen only (such paper) lost $20. Can see harbor of ships from this hilltop where tent is located.

Tuesday, October 2 - Played Cribbage with Braden. Heard we were to leave Friday or Saturday on the *Sea Bass*. Wrote Colleen, Kay, Norb, Schuler, Mom, and Chris. Later in day heard that ship had been taken by Navy and we wouldn't leave for at least 10 days; phooey. This waiting is for the birds.

Wednesday, October 3 - Verified report of delay to Inspector General, but no help there. Have a terrific head cold now. Letter from Mrs. Bollinger enclosing pictures of her girls 9/17. Rained all day, everything is soaked. Major Senter returned to hospital. Played Gin Rummy with Lovko and broke even. Wrote Chris, Ralph, Irene. Mail call at 2200; orderly couldn't make it back from regiment because of road conditions. Chris 9/24. What a miserable day it has been. Rations are low on this island due to the inclement weather preventing unloading and the fact that the Japanese occupation troops took so much with them. Supposed to have "C" and "K" rations.

Thursday, October 4 - Still feeling lousy with this cold, saw Doc and got some pills. No rain although wind still blowing. Cooked own meals. Retired early.

Friday, October 5 - Heard we might leave Monday, but all medical officers have priority; may turn over hold to officers. Went out to see Major Senter at 233rd General Hospital. Played Gin Rummy all day. Wrote Chris and Mom.

LTC Marvin Van Horn Ayers, in response to the summon of the Grand Commander of the universe, mustered for the final roll call, in the land beyond the sunset, June 1, 1994. He was revered by all who knew him, as the officer and Christian gentleman that he was.

G.I. Jive

by Frank F. Mathias

The Army has a saying about travel: "No matter where you've been, where you're going is worse." I learned that the hard way. Things went downhill rapidly after I, an 18 year old draftee, left Fort Thomas, Kentucky in mid-1943. Infantry basic at Fort Benning, Georgia ran me ragged, yet things looked up when I won a spot in the post band. Then the band disbanded! I wound up taking advanced infantry training at Camp Wheeler, Georgia. All here were destined to be replacements for shattered line companies overseas. Everyone in my group except my buddy, Walter Clark, and myself, were shipped to Europe. We were sent to "the great unknown," a generally dreaded place without wine, women, or song—the South Pacific.

I saw New Guinea off the port side of the *Monterrey*. Hulking dark mountains plunged from the clouds to black beaches and surf, a gloomy welcome to this vast, disease ridden, embattled island. We landed at Oro Bay. Trucks hauled us inland to the 5th Replacement Depot, a sprawling tent city. Tough jungle training started immediately. Near the end of this exhaustive training period, we were ordered to line up for inspection. I stood at the left end of the long line with Walter Clark and Marcel Veilleus, a new buddy we picked up aboard the *Monterrey*. An officer strode up to the middle of the line. He divided it. The men on the right were sent as replacements to the 43rd Division; those on the left were assigned to the 37th, the Buck-eye Division.

The *Oconto* dropped anchor at Empress Augusta Bay, with Bougainville's 10,000 foot volcano, Mount Bagana, looming in the background. Someone shouted and pointed to the ridges near the volcano. An artillery barrage was falling with flashes of fire, the lazy white fingers from exploding white phosphorous shells curling through the foliage and falling debris. War's horrible reality hit my mind for the first time. My mind locked tightly on one thought: "My God, this is the real thing, this isn't practice, this is the real thing."

About 20 of us piled into a shipside Higgins boat and headed for shore. The sailor had forgotten to close the drainage bung, so we sunk onto a shallow part of the offshore coral reef. We were rescued by other craft, but the trucks sent to pick us up found a gang of dripping and depressed replacements. Our truck passed hundreds of tents and Quonset huts connected by a filigree of coral roads. My optimism returned. Clark and I and several others were unloaded at G Company, 145th Infantry Regiment. Marcel went on to the 148th AT Company and later was to die of wounds, February 12, 1945, on Luzon.

This was it! A veteran line infantry company. Instead of the grim, hard-bitten, rifle-toting old vets of my imagination, there were friendly faces everywhere. They trotted to meet us. None had on regulation issue; some wore nothing. A welter of Marine shirts, soiled Navy caps, Aussie short pants and odd bits of fatigues swirled like a drab pinwheel. They reminded me of a friendly bunch of pirates.

"You're in Ohio now," someone cried.

"The hell I am, I wish I were."

"Well, you are, all right. This is the 37th, an Ohio National Guard outfit."

Raisin jack and stocky green bottles of Aussie beer appeared. We felt like knew men as we went to supper; it was good to belong to something again. After supper, the regimental commander, Colonel Cecil Whitcomb, untidy and tough looking, climbed on a chair to welcome the replacements.

"You're in the best damned battalion, in the best damned regiment, in the best damned division in the South Pacific, and you damn well better not forget it." We replacements were in an expansive mood after this fine welcome to our new home.

A few nights later a patrol out past the Bougainville perimeter forced me to acknowledge my true position as a replacement "cannon fodder." As we moved out, I repeatedly worked the action of my M-1 Garand and examined the bullets. We followed a trail into the murk. I strained to

Frank J. Mathias.

probe the flickering, misty twilight. We skirted the shore of a large lake. Stars were reflected in the water. Something broke the surface, scattering these points of light. I snapped up my rifle. The squad leader laughed, telling us that big crocodiles lived in the lake. The stars disappeared and a heavy rain pattered on our caps. The blackness was almost total. We paused in a hut. An almost unreasoning fear constricted my throat. We doubled back over the trail. In my dry tent I prayed for deliverance and dropped off to a few hours of fitful sleep.

I shuffled off to breakfast, finding that my worries were shared fully by Clark and the other replacements. I sulked in my tent after breakfast. The door flap opened, and a top kick peeked in. I was sure I was going to get another patrol.

"Is a fellow named Mathias here?"

"Here I am."

"Good. I've been looking for you. Your military occupation serial shows that you played sax and clarinet in a Fort Benning Band. You've been transferred to the division band." I put in a word for Clark, but no brass men were needed.

My joy knew no bounds. What luck! I decided my prayers after the patrol had done it. In any event, I bunked with Glenn Crosby, a stubby, powerful Charles Atlas devotee from Toledo, and two Mexican reed men from California, Chick Cervantes and Rudy Panol. All three had been in combat. They dubbed me "Paco."

The three 28 piece regimental bands had recently been weeded down to a 56 piece division band assigned to division headquarters. The full band played for parades, ball games, concerts and the like, while the show and dance band often played at "Lowe's Bougainville," a large open air theater that hosted touring USO shows. This excellent band has something of Count Basie's power tempered with Glenn Miller's taste and precision.

Among the division headquarters characters I met was "Chalkeye," a talkative GI with a white speck near the pupil of one eye. He told me, as he told everyone, I later learned, of his encounter with Eleanor Roosevelt: "I was down on Espiritu Santo and decided to take a swim off the one lane Baily Bridge. Now Mrs. Roosevelt, you know how she is always traveling everywhere, stopped off to see Santo. While she's coming down my road in a jeep, I'm stripped naked, getting ready to dive off the bridge. Her jeep driver stopped to wait his turn on the bridge. I'm just standing there, not expecting anything exciting. Then I saw her and she saw me, just as her jeep pulls up. She waved and shouted 'Yoo hoo' as I leaped for the water."

I laughed. Chalkeye shushed me.

"That's not all of it, boy. Eleanor has sent me complimentary letters ever since."

One hot December afternoon an officer told the assembled bandsmen that the 37th was to spearhead a drive on Manila after the 6th Army landing planned for January 9 on Luzon's Lingayan Gulf. "General Yamashita," he said, "can count on some 275,000 soldiers to defend Luzon, so this will be a hard campaign."

I heard coughs and sighs.

"The band will land with the assault wave."

His words parched my soul. My thought turned to G Company. I fought off a growing suspicion that the Lord may have been playing games with me. The lousy band would hit the beaches first while G Company and the 145th would float away invasion day in a reserve role aboard their ships.

The band was reformed into a heavy weapons platoon and assigned the defense of division headquarters. Rudy Panol and I were teamed behind a .30 caliber light machine gun. We were loaded aboard the *Simon Bolivar* for the trip to Luzon. A few hours before we sailed, an officer shot himself. The corpse flipped over the side of the ship and slapped into the sea. It bobbed until some sailors fished it out. I tried not to think about it.

A double line of ships stretching for 40 miles carried the 6th Army and supporting units to the Lingayan Gulf. Kamikaze attacks sunk 24 of the 1,000 ships in the invasion fleet, two of which barely missed the *Bolivar*. I joined my fellow bandsmen as we descended rope netting into our landing craft early in the morning of January 9, 1945. Our boat bucked forward as the thunderous fleet barrage continued. We passed the stern of the battleship *West Virginia*. She squatted on her haunches and bellowed; broadsides flamed from her 16-inch guns. The assault wave landed at about 9:35 a.m. and we waded waist-deep and dripping out onto the wide, beautiful beaches of Luzon. The Japanese had decided to let us land, then fight later for control of certain Luzon regions.

The 37th traversed 70 uncontested miles of Luzon's central plain before running into heavy resistance at Clark Field. Following this, we drove straight into Manila, some of us pausing to lap up gallons of green beer "liberated" at Balintawak Brewery. Such signs of civilization were everywhere, welcome beyond measure to older Buckeyes who have been in isolated island jungles since going overseas in early 1942. Once in Manila, enemy resistance became rock hard. Division Headquarters was set up in the Ang Tibay shoe factory, along northern Rizal Avenue. I watched downtown Manila burn from the roof of this factory. Great sheets of flame soared skyward into the night.

The Japanese made their last stand inside Intramuros, the impenetrable walled inner city built by Spain in the 16th century. My buddy and I were assigned duty with some 30 other machine gun crews to support the infantry attack on this bastion. We were to fire from sandbagged window positions in commercial buildings directly across the Pasig River from Intramuros. We waited all night for the 8:30 a.m. attack made in assault boats by the 3rd Battalion, 129th Infantry. We jumped as the air shuddered with a sharp swishing sound heralding the instantaneous arrival of a thunderous artillery barrage. We began firing at anything suspicious—wall slits, movement, doubtful rubble. Smoke shells covered the approaching landing craft. The troops rushed out on the opposite bank, and they, with other units of the 37th, would take Intramuros and end the Battle of Manila.

After the battle, our band picked up its instruments and began playing for regimental dances, concerts of all kinds, and most importantly for the recently liberated POWs at Santo Tomas and Bilibid. Music filled the air as life slowly oozed back into the veins of this horrible mangled city.

One day our leader, CWO Charles B. Hower, presented the bandsmen with a rather unique problem. General MacArthur had recently received a fifth star, a new rank, and we were to play the *General's March* to announce his arrival at festivities the next

129th Infantry's famous "Mosquito Bar" where Division Combo Band is playing. Frank Mathias, sax; Walter Groves, trombone; Bruce Thomson, trumpet; Ralph Freeman, guitar; Bill Rogers, clarinet; George Campbell, drums; Gil Silbius, bass fiddle. (Courtesy Mathias)

day, welcoming the first train over rebuilt tracks from Lingayan. The rules strictly held four trumpet flourishes as the absolute limit to denote the stars on the shoulders of any general. Should we blow five flourishes? Our "philosophers" argued that MacArthur could change the rules anytime, but not his ego. That did it. We blew five, and I peeked up from my clarinet in time to see his head lift a bit as the fifth flourish announced his nearly unique status. He spoke briefly as the cameras whirred, then strode quickly to his staff car.

Following the capture of mountainous Baguio, the division launched a veritable blitzkrieg up the lengthy Cagayan Valley of Northern Luzon. On the way we discovered a charnel house, a Japanese hospital at Bayombong where over 200 sick and wounded had committed suicide rather than surrender to Yankee soldiers. After burying the dead with a bulldozer, we moved on north of Tumauini, setting up the division command post between the hills and the Cagayan River. I dug a shallow hole, set up my machine gun covering a nearby airstrip, and went to bed under a bright midnight moon.

A shattering roar pitched me from my cot. Even as I tumbled I scurried for my foxhole. Incoming artillery smothered hysterical shouting. Suddenly the entire area lit up; they had hit the airstrip gasoline dump creating a perfect target. They poured it on, dropping in hundreds of shells over the next three hours. I hung on, numb but praying they would not use "timers" that would burst above us, spraying shrapnel. The sounds above me became puzzling. Shells seemed to be going both ways. We cheered when we realized our 140th Field Artillery had moved up to mount counter-battery fire. But the 140th was unable to pinpoint the well-hidden enemy, so the Japanese gunners turned back to us, dropping in several hundred more shells before an observation plane laid our artillery on them by dawn's early light. The division had by-passed three batteries of 105mm guns (12 in all). There were scores of casualties including three men I had been with throughout the campaign. It was the worst day of the war for me.

A month later I came down with malaria, and wound up in the 43rd Field Hospital in Tuguegarao. I also had jaundice, and this, along with the atabrine for malaria, turned my skin and eyes yellow and my urine the color of Coca Cola. Blue lines, like highways on a map, marked my veins. I became a sideshow in the shower stalls. The war ended while I was in the hospital, and two weeks later I was able to rejoin the band.

The division moved some 200 miles south to Cabanatuan, a town that had once held prisoners from the Bataan Death March. We were preparing for shipment home at some later date. Our combo began playing in the ramshackle clubs and bars in Cabanatuan. One night, I called up the *Clarinet Polka*, a rollicking number I had memorized back in the Benning Band. Many GIs cheered and danced, but a number stood in front of the bandstand with tears flowing down their cheeks. Astonished, we gave them what they wanted—more polkas: *Beer Barrel, Liechtensteiner, Friendly Tavern, Chihuahua*. Pandemonium swept the crowd when Chubby Malewski grabbed the mike and sang, "I don't want her, you can have her, she's too fat for me." We finally understood that our music was blowing the dust of war from their souls; they had survived to make it back to their homefolks and girl friends in Cleveland, Dayton and elsewhere. They cried for joy.

On the anniversary of the Lingayen Gulf landings, I visited the military cemetery in Manila's Grace Park. White crosses spread like a cloud over the charred ground. The 37th had suffered over 11,000 casualties, and hundreds of those were buried here. I went to Marcel Veilleus' grave, but was unable to find the graves of my three friends killed at Tumauini. I thanked God for his guidance, crossed myself, and was soon aboard ship heading for home. And for the first time in two and a half years, I was able to turn around that old Army saying, and truthfully declare that "no matter where I had been, where I was going was bound to be better."

The "Old Man"

By Fred J. Reichelderfer

Every man loved and swore by our Company Commander Emile J. Correages. He loved us all and tried to keep us intact. We had him as Co. Commander for most of the war. This tale is about him.

After the Battle of Manila, our 3rd Bat., 145th Regt. was loaded up quickly and moved Northeast of Clark AFB some thirty miles from Manila where, in an area of low hills, a lake and a dam system provided Manila with most of their water supply.

Later, according to Division records, some 4500 Japanese soldiers from the remainder of their forces in the Philippines had gathered, holding out and desperate to the end. The Japanese had cut off their water supply. Most Companies were way under strength. My squad only had five men left in it.

The place was one of those hills in the late summer of 1945. we were stuck on one of those hills called "X" on the map for three terrible nights. Down to one half Company strength, lots of casualties, some holes with only one man in each and morale as low as I had ever seen it.

The next morning our Platoon leader, another squad leader and I had gone back to the sea side of the hill to see what "the old man" had been doing to get us out of this mess.

To make a long story short, I'll give you his quick answer, which put sand in our craw and stiffened our spine.

First, he said that he hated a delegation. Second, he had talked to the Colonel and no one was coming to help for three days. If things got worse, he intended to bring the holes back up the hill, another 75 yards, dig them in tighter and give "'em" more open space to come at us.

Then the earth shaker! He looked our Platoon leader in the eye and said real slow like, "And if it comes down to only two holes are left in the field, you (Rodman) and I are going to man them!" We knew his "two holes" were only a figure of speech, but the word was plain. We stayed and slugged it out. Forty years later on a return trip in a small plane ride over the area, I realized how these hills commanded access to the dam. It was very imperative to hold them.

We got up, not a word was said. Rumors circulated the hill. I got wounded the next night, but Co. L held the hill for 15 more days. 3rd bat. had a total of 166 men left when relief came.

"The old man" died a couple of years ago in Houston, TX, but for many of us, he'll live forever.

April 1945, Manila. 4,000 feet in the hill, firing over the main road. (Courtesy Gajewski)

Guadalcanal

Clockwise from top left: Service Co, 147th Inf., Christmas, 1942, Koli Point. Back, Recher, Romisher, Goldsberry, Vaccariello. Front, Seibert, Linneman, Volk, White, Kock.. Sign erected by 164th Inf. Brig. on road in Lunga Point perimeter. Jap ship off Bunina Point. USS Neville APA 9, transport which brought 147th reinforcements from which landed the 1st BN, 147th Infantry RCT. at Aola Bay, Nov. 4, 1942. Captured Jap field artillery piece. (Wooden wheels, WWI vintage) Melanesian women of Guadalcanal. Sgt. Stanley F. Beck and Cpl Dillard S. Burroughs furl their squad tent in Guadalcanal jungle. (All courtesy Chaney)

147th Infantry Dogfaces on the "Canal"

by William Marshal Chaney

The 147th Infantry (less the 2nd Battalion) with the 134th Field Artillery Battalion attached, and redesignated the 147th RCT (Regimental Combat Team), landed on May 10, 1942, as a component of Task Force 0051 at Nuku'alofa, Tongatabu. The Task Force relieved the occupying New Zealand troops, forthwith.

The Task Force was under the command of BG Benjamin C. Lockwood, who was known among his peers as "Old Frosty." General Lockwood was a career soldier, and his Task Force systematically, in relays, unloaded ships and secured the strategically points of the Tongan Islands. To maintain discipline and further condition the troops and to prepare them for future operations, the General immediately scheduled an advanced tactical training program and ordered its implementation without delay.

The 147th RCT was also commanded by a regular Army officer, Colonel W.B. Tuttle, a native of the "Lone Star State of Texas." His military biography read like that of a Kentucky thoroughbred's pedigree. His entry into the U.S. Army pre-dated the DOB (date of birth) of many of the officers in his command. Whatever the assignment was, the Colonel merely considered it SOP (Standard Operating Procedure). Those who knew the Colonel best, knew him as "Smash and Drive." His advice to the officers and GIs of his command was, "If you have a problem, work it out."

No sooner had the GIs and some of the junior officers started making headway with the Polynesian Tongan maidens, when orders were received for the 1st Battalion, reinforced of the 147th RCT, to board the USS *Neville* on October 20, 1942. It sailed via the New Hebrides, and landed at daybreak on November 4, 1942, at Aola Bay, Guadalcanal. The dogfaces of the 147th's 1st Battalion were again an element of another Task Force consisting of Battery K, 246th Field Artillery Battalion, Americal Division; the 5th Marine Defense Battalion; the 14th Seabees (Naval Construction Battalion); and the 2nd Marine (Gung Ho) Raider Battalion under command of Colonel Evans F. Carlson. Lieutenant Colonel Jimmy Roosevelt (FDR's eldest son) made an appearance at the landing site. Lieutenant Colonel Robert C. Hanes, CO, 1st Battalion, 147th Infantry, exchanged greetings with the other unit commanders and went about the task at hand. During the landing, American fighter planes and Jap Zeroes were dogfighting overhead; otherwise, the landing was unopposed.

The combat units moved inland and established a perimeter defense, with the reserve units participating in securing rations and supplies, as they were delivered from the ships to the beach. The temperature was always hot and the humidity high. It rained often, even occasionally when the sun was shining. The mud and swamps were everywhere, as were the insects and anopheles mosquitoes. We GIs were assured if the Nips didn't get us, the mosquitoes would. Our rations were of poor quality. Our diet reminded me of a neighbor back in southeastern Kentucky wintering his horses on corn fodder. Within a week after the landing, an army of insects had invaded our dried beans, soup, and cereal. Initially we tried to sort the bugs out as we ate, but due to their colors, they blended in with our food. We gave up in disgust consoling ourselves with the thought that nature had provided us with meat to spice our dried milk, dehydrated eggs and other goodies such as GI chocolate bars (D Rations, which were as scarce as hens' teeth).

Capt. John W. Rosskopf, Co. B, 147th Inf.

Maj. John M. McGuffin, CO, 3rd Bat, 147th Inf.

LST that brought in units of the USA's 25th Division at Kakum Beach, Guadcanal, January 1943. (Courtesy Chaney)

Lt. Col. Robert C. Hanes, CO, 1st Bat., 147th Inf.

Col. William B. Tuttle, Commander, 147th Inf.

Lt. Col. DeForest R. Roush, Commander, 2nd Bat., 147th.

Top, Falls, Watkins, Smith, Day. Middle, Pennoyer, Boise, Teeters, Lyons. Bottom, Henne, Schultze. (Courtesy Henne)

Patrols operated daily in front of the perimeter, and the 2nd Marine Raider Battalion penetrated deep into the interior northwestward of Aola Bay, making sporadic contact with the enemy. Shortly after the landing, a group of natives informed our 147th Battalion Headquarters that several Nips were bivouacking in a village some 10 miles northwest of our perimeter, and inland some distance from the coast. A patrol from the 147th Infantry and a detachment of Marines made a daylight attack on the village, killing all the Japs but one. The natives lashed the Jap's hands and legs together, strung him on a pole and carried him into the 147th Infantry's Battalion Headquarters. The prisoner was then interrogated by a Japanese speaking American soldier and sent to the island stockade.

Rear Admiral Richmond Kelly Turner had directed the operation at Aola Bay with the intention of building a secondary airfield at the site. However, the Seabees found the ground unsuitable. As a result, on Thanksgiving night of 1942, Lieutenant Colonel Hanes and his 1st Battalion, 147th Infantry were moved up the coast by Higgins boats, northwestward to Koli Point. There it was joined by Major John M. McGuffin's 3rd Battalion, Service Company, Anti-tank Company, Regimental Headquarters Company, the Regimental Medical Detachment (less those troops that had reinforced the 1st Battalion) and Regimental CO Colonel W.B. Tuttle, which landed off the USS *President Hayes*, November 29, 1942.

The 147th Infantry, less its 2nd Battalion, moved inland (south) to a point near the foot of Gold Ridge and established an outpost line of resistance. While the 9th Marine Defense Battalion manned the Koli Point Coastal defenses, the 14th and 18th Naval Construction Battalions constructed a heavy bomber base, which was later named Carney Field in honor of the island's ranking CB, a USN Captain, who was killed on December 17, 1942 in an airplane crash.

As the Japs threw in reinforcements, so did the U.S. In addition to Colonel Tuttle's 147th Infantry, the USA's Americal Division was committed, piecemeal from October through December 1942. Major General J. Lawton Collins' 25th Infantry Division joined the fray between December 17, 1942 and January 4, 1943. Brigadier General Alphonse DeCarre's 2nd Marine Division was committed, piecemeal between August 7, 1942 and January 4, 1943. In the meantime, several bomber and fighter squadrons of the 13th USAAF, coast artillery and antiaircraft units arrived, which gave relief and support to the 1st Marine Division-reinforced, that made the initial landing at Guadalcanal and Tulagi on August 7, 1942 and lessened the load of the 1st Marine Airwing.

On December 9, 1942, Major General A.A. Vandegrift and his 1st Marine Division were relieved, and Major General Alexander M. Patch, USA, assumed command of all combat operations on Guadalcanal and the surrounding islands. General Patch formed and assumed command of the XIV Corps. In early January 1943, General Patch called on the Nips to surrender by having thousands of pamphlets dropped by planes over the Japanese-held section of the "canal;" which the Nips ignored. The General then launched an all-out campaign to secure the island, contending there wasn't room for both Americans and the Japs too.

Meanwhile, the USN with token Allied assistance had fought eight major engagements securing the waters of Guadalcanal, with heavy losses. The 3rd Battle of Savo convinced the Japs that reclaiming Guadalcanal wouldn't be worth the cost the ordeal would entail.

Company I, 147th Infantry, reinforced by squads and sections from M and Anti-tank Companies, was dispatched to Beaufort Bay on January 8, 1943, under command of Captain Charles E. Beach, to block the possible Japanese use of the Beaufort Bay - Kokumbona Trail. Shortly thereafter, the re-

Captured Jap submarine off the coast of Guadalcanal. (Courtesy Chaney)

37th Infantry Division—37

maining units (less Company A, which was on Florida Island) were assigned to the CAM (Composite Army Marine Division) under command of Brigadier General Alphonse DeCarre.

On January 19, 1943, the 147 Doggies (less the 2nd Battalion), moved into the front-line on the western sector. Flanked by the 6th Marines on their right and the 182nd Infantry on their left, the 147th was in almost constant contact with the enemy. On the morning of January 20, 1943, Company B's 1st Platoon was on the right flank of the regimental sector. As the platoon advanced across the valley, between Hills 96 and 98, and as it neared the east bank of the Kokumbona River in the valley floor, a group of dazed Japs, but full of fight, were encountered. The 1st Platoon responded quickly. When the fire fight was over, 17 Nips laid on the valley floor. During this initial combat operation, Colonel Tuttle's 147th Infantry advanced 8,350 yards, sustaining light casualties and inflicted heavy losses on the enemy in both personnel and materials.

On arriving at Kokumbona on January 24, 1943 and remaining in reserve briefly, the 147th Infantry was chosen by the XIV Corps' Commander to continue the attack and pursuit of the enemy. Company A was returned from Florida Island, and those elements of Antitank Company at Kukum Beach were brought forward.

On January 30, 1943 as the 147th advanced through a coconut grove, running parallel with the coast, and on approaching the east banks of the Bonegi River, all hell broke loose. The fighting developed into a full-scale battle. Artillery fire was stepped up. The Navy and Air Arms were called upon for support. Three destroyers were sent up from Kukum Beach to shell the Japs on the west bank of the Bonegi, and they were strafed by several P-38s from Henderson Field. Half-tracks were committed in the 1st Battalion sector. It was a hell of a fight!

The 147th Infantry earned more Purple Hearts on January 30, 1943 than at any other time during their long stay on the "canal." After the sound of battle had died, many of the GIs were decorated for distinguished service. Three Company B Sergeants: Thomas R. Hughes, Robert J. Schwing and H.L. Wright, and Lieutenant Colonel Robert C. Hanes were among those that were awarded Silver Star Medals during the Bonegi engagement. Sergeant Bernard Buescher was awarded the Silver Star Medal for gallantry on Hill 124, February 1, 1943. This writer tips his hat to all those of the 147th Infantry who distinguished themselves under fire.

Despite repeated efforts, the 147th Infantry didn't cross the Bonegi River in strength until February 5, 1943. In the meantime, Jap planes sank the destroyer, USS *DeHaven*, between the mouth of the Bonegi River on Guadalcanal and Savo Island. It was later learned the Nips had amassed 11,000 to 13,000 in the area west of the Bonegi River, extending to Cape Esperance for evacuation in which they slipped off the island under the cover of darkness during the early nights of February 1943.

February 7, 1943, Lieutenant Colonel DeForest R. Roush and his 2nd Battalion, 147th Infantry arrived at Kukum Beach, Guadalcanal onboard the USS *George Clymer*, after embarking from Fiji where the battalion had been attached to the 37th Infantry Division. The GIs of the 147th were pleased to welcome their 2nd Battalion to Guadalcanal and invited them to take their rightful station in their parent regiment.

When the westbound 161st Infantry of the 25th Infantry Division and the 132nd Infantry of the Americal Division, which had landed at Verahue Village February 1, 1943, met in the village of Tenaro at 1600 hours (4:00 p.m.) head-on on February 9, 1943; Guadalcanal was officially secured. However, the 147th Infantry remained on Guadalcanal until May 12, 1943. It continued mopping up, patrolling, and training exercises. All personnel of the regiment had contacted malaria and practically all had been hospitalized many times. In addition to the regiment's ground combat encounters, it had survived 133 Jap air raids. To a man, they were veterans in their own right.

Following Guadalcanal, the 147th Infantry was transferred to British Somoa, New Caledonia, Emirau Island in the St. Mathias Group, Iwo Jima, Tinian, Okinawa and was deactivated on Christmas Day, 1945 at Fort Lewis, Washington.

Guadalcanal (Courtesy Estes)

GIs looking for survivors among the Jap bodies. (Courtesy Chaney)

The price of victory. Temporary military and naval cemetery for America's fallen heroes at Guadalcanal. (Courtesy Chaney)

Dear Mary (Ambush Patrol)

April 7, 1945—Iwo Jima

Dear Mary,

Can't sleep today, so I think I'll write to you. I had all the intentions to do so anyway. I was out all last night as am ambush patrol and I kept thinking of you and made up my mind to write to you. I wish someone would invent a device to record all your thoughts for future reference. I think of a lot of things to say and generally forget them

Yesterday I made a reconnaissance and came across a spot where I noticed a lot of Jap activity and I decided I would operate in the area that night. I cam back to the command post and decided to take two machine guns with me.

We waited until an hour before dark and left the company area. On the way out we captured a Jap. I wanted to shoot him, but I realized he was more valuable alive than dead. I sent two men back with him to the battalion CP.

Well we finally set up and began that long, long wait for the enemy. About 0100 hours, we saw five of them coming up the road. I told my machine gunner before he opened fire to wait until they closed to ten feet; just in case more of them behind them. (sic) There were four of us in our position. I made sure every man knew what he was to do. One man had an M-1 rifle; another a carbine and I had a sub-machine gun.

When I gave the order to fire, the machine gun did not fire. Neither did the M-1 rifle or sub-machine gun. I picked up a grenade and threw it. Then the machine gun opened fire. We killed three and wounded one. What a feeling when everything fouled up. It is a good thing there weren't more behind them.

Another night it was black as the devil and we went out to set up an ambush. I decided not to move around, but to stay in one spot. I could cover four roads and a few trails. Evidently the Japs saw us get into position. At 2200 hours a couple of shots went over my head. I became angry because I thought my own men had opened fire. That is, until the next couple of shots wend over my head and then I recognized the shots were .25 caliber Japanese rounds.

The next thing I heard was a grenade hit next to my position. I ducked and then it went off. That grenade attack lasted half an hour. We tossed a few grenades and sent up some flares. We killed three of them

The second attack was a little rougher, as were the next two. I kept saying to myself, "Lord, you made the night too long."

I received your four letters. I appreciate them.

All my love,
Jim

Ed. Note: This letter was written by Lt. James J. Ahern, Co. F. 147th Inf. Reg. to Miss Mary Eells. She would marry him in 1946.

Jim Madden, Joe Casteneda, Jim Payntor, Bill Pawlowski, Vince Locurcio.

Japanese Lance Corporal

Early in the Iwo Jima Battle we took prisoner a Japanese non-comm. He was favorable impressed with the treatment of POWs by our units and volunteered to assist us in the taking of prisoners.

He reported to me early one morning resplendent in a spotless uniform. He was very official and military in his greeting to me which included a precise salute since I outranked him.

The corporal was very intelligent and efficient in helping us. He spoke English perfectly. I remarked to him that he spoke our language better than I (sic) or my men. He answered, "I should speak it well. I graduated from the University of Southern California."

Frequently he entered underground positions containing Japanese defenders and on several occasions when he outranked the occupants he ordered them to come out and surrender.

One morning he went down into a very large complex and shortly after we heard muffled gunfire. He came scrambling breathlessly out. When he regained his breath I asked him what happened. With some hesitation he said, "I made a big mistake. I couldn't get a good look at the man I was talking to and I ordered a Captain to leave the position."

Routes to Mundo

By Col. Charles J. Henne, USA Ret.

It is unlikely that Munda and other Japanese garrisons were supplied by sea prior to the American invasion of Rendova Island. Losing the sea route forced them to use one of four other routes. By the time of the 3rd Battalion, 148th Inf. Reg. July landing, the Mundo-Bairoko Trail was but one of four routes to Munda.

• The Mundo-Bairoko trail started at Bairoko Harbor and ended at Munda. It ran through heavy rain forest most of the way. Upon reaching Mount Tirokiamba it forked with one branch continuing to Munda and the other to Zieta.

• Only one other route used Bairoko as a staging point. Its first leg was by water to the shoal end of Bairoko Inlet. from there it continued as a foot trail to Zieta.

• The third land route began on the northwestern tip of Arundel Island and ran its length to a crossing point at the southeastern end of Diamond Narrows. The Japs may not have used this route to send men and supplies to Munda, but it was used as an escape route by the survivors of the Munda battle.

• The fourth route was a water route trafficable by barges and other low draft boats. It ran from Vila across Kula Gulf to Hathorn Sound. It transited Hathorn Sound and the Diamond Narrows to a barge station near Zieta.

The water route was a long, narrow waterway. It lay between the main island and Arundel Island. Hathorn Sound and the Diamond Narrows canalized movement but the shore lines were extensively indented providing innumerable hiding places for barges. During the campaign Solomon Air Command fighters made it a daytime deathway. Although protective, the nighttime dark made navigation difficult, and Japanese coxswains had to be on the lookout for lurking American PT boats.

From the beginning, I believed what I had been told. Our mission briefing informed us that the Munda-Bairoko Trail was the main Japanese supply route linking Kolombangara depots to Munda. Therefore, cutting the trail would prevent resupply and reinforcement of Munda. The implication was that as soon as we blocked the trail we would have a fight on our hands. Maps showed that the Munda-Bairoko Trail was the most direct land route connecting Bairoko and Munda, and that it was a relatively covered route that ran through rain forest most of the way. I did not know that there were three other routes that be as important, in fact, more important to the Japanese. When I inspected the trail on the 8th, the lack of signs of use raised questions, but the operational telephone lines supported what we had been told. These questions lingered until a Jap carrying party was ambushed and from that time I believed we had a fight brewing.

The Japanese Southeastern Detachment was a walking command. It either moved men and supplies by water or the troops carried their needs on their backs. When denied the sea route and daytime use of Hathorn Sound, logistics became the Japanese nemesis. Of greater importance, their inability to protect transport and cargo ships forced them to make night runs with destroyers and submarines—neither designed for transporting men and supplies. Gen. Sasaki's enormous logistical problems proved insurmountable, and when the noose tightened his men starved and died of treatable wounds and diseases.

The Japs never used native porters to backpack supplies to their fighting elements, although it was common for the Allies to do so. If the Japs had such intentions, the native must have eluded them. Of course, the Allies paid, fed and protected their porters, treatment that may never have occurred to the Japs. On New Georgia, different from Bougainville, they would have had to catch the natives first, for the New Georgians were Jap haters.

MOBILIZATION - 1940
CAMP SHELBY

by Orland T. Outland

In the late summer of 1940 it was quite clear the National Guard was going to be mobilized, activated into federal service. War was raging in Europe, Japan was on an expansionist path, and the principal strongholds of isolationism in the United States had been breached.

Since 1936, when I read a fictionalized account of Japan's attack on, and invasion of, the United States I was convinced it was only a matter of time before the United States and Japan would be at war with each other.

In September 1940, I enlisted in the Ohio National Guard; I had tried to enlist in the U.S. Army, but my nearsightedness and low weight disqualified me, and I couldn't qualify for the Civilian Conservation Corps (CCC). Bonuses were still being paid to Guard members for bringing in new recruits. A friend of mine sponsored me, but I still didn't weigh enough. The doctor overseeing the physical examinations had a penchant for the "sauce." As I recall it, he was not a member of the Guard, but functioned on some sort of contract arrangement for certain services, examining potential recruits being one of them. My friend and I were determined to get me enlisted. At that time I was 17 years old and homeless. I just knew war was coming and I wanted to be a jump ahead of the others who would come later; besides, I needed a job. My friend wanted to help me, and bonuses were getting harder to come by. So we mounted a campaign. I set about memorizing enough of the eye chart to meet the minimum qualifications and I went on an enforced diet including bananas, water, and salt in order to put on weight. Also, I had to come up with enough money for a pint of whiskey to keep the doctor occupied while his assistant read the scale and reported on my reading of the chart. During the week just before my exam it seemed I always had a banana in my hand and as though I was constantly washing down handfuls of salt. On the night of the examination, I was so bloated if I had been a girl I would have been presumed pregnant. The doctor got his pint well in advance of the examination so we were able to pretty well control the routine and everything worked according to plan, and I was declared fit for service.

Now my only problem was in convincing the company commander that yes, I knew the Guard was going to be mobilized, and yes, I realized that there was every likelihood of going to war. I don't think the old gentleman liked signing me up, but he couldn't find any good reason to refuse me and on September 15, 1940, I became a member of Company K, 145th Infantry Regiment, 73rd Brigade, 37th Infantry Division. Unfortunately for those of us under his command, he was not included in the mobilization as he was afflicted with tuberculosis and failed his physical. He was a gentleman and a good leader, respected as well as liked by all his men. We were to miss his leadership more than once.

On September 26, 1940, the division was alerted to its pending mobilization; on October 4, an order was issued directing units of the division to assemble at their respective armories on October 15 and begin the process of induction into federal service. From the 26th of September until the 18th of October, when we left for Camp Shelby, we were busy in the armory practicing close order drill and packing and crating equipment for the trip.

We left for camp as federal troops, departing at night so as to arrive in the daylight hours. The evening of our departure, friends and relatives in the spectator seats of the basketball court of the armory watched us form into units and prepare to depart. Then there was a brief mingling with friends and loved ones, some crying, kissing, and shaking of hands as a very somber mood settled over the arena; the future held so many unknowns for everyone, with the portents of death seeming to lurk in the darkness outside.

Finally, through the darkness, we marched the short distance to the train with many well-wishers trailing along. There was a subdued tenseness at the depot; the reality of the world situation was hovering in the air, unarticulated and undefined and with an uncertainty as to what lies in the future for everyone. Tearful farewells were groped and wept next to more formal ones. We boarded Pullman cars and what windows could be opened were, and the waving farewells continued as the train pulled away into an unknown and uncertain future. For many it was the beginning of a voyage where they couldn't, or wouldn't, go home again, some in the light of Thomas Wolfe and some in the light of fate.

Out of sight of the station, depression still lingered in the coaches. Then, to break the tension, someone started to sing and bit by bit most all joined in. The songs ranged from *The Old Oaken Bucket* to *Ace in the Hole*. Someone produced a bottle of whiskey and the tension was really broken. It wasn't long until somberness gave way to gaiety as one bottle after another surfaced, and one really expressive soul was prancing up and down the aisle, naked, with a pint of whiskey in one hand and waving a wand you couldn't possibly buy in any store in the other.

We finally pulled into some nondescript siding in McLaurin, Mississippi, and stumbled out of the train in what loosely might be described as a formation. We were stiff and sore, and our packs hadn't fared too well, either. We were carrying "full" packs, which meant we were carrying all our personal gear, including blankets, a horse-shoed overcoat, and an extra pair of shoes, most of which was really not too well or tidily assembled.

An attempt was made to have us march all in step, as good little soldiers making a great impression on ourselves, as well as others witnessing this grand spectacle. But that didn't last even 100 yards before we converted to "route step," each setting his own pace.

What a motley looking group! Here we were struggling down a dirt road in campaign hats, breeches and wrap leggings that were drooping down around our ankles, trying to balance packs that kept shifting, with shoes on the packs that had come loose and were bumping you in the side or the arm, and an overcoat that didn't know enough to stay in place either; there was always someone reaching out to help push another's gear back into place for as long as it was willing to stay there - which wasn't long at all.

Finally, we came to a row of wooden buildings, which were company mess halls, and staggered down behind them into what were to become our "company streets." We stacked rifles (which we were constrained to call "pieces," suffering punishment if we did otherwise) in grass and weed so high you couldn't see the trigger guards. Pyramidal tents lay in an irregular row of dark green globs, yet to be unpacked and erected.

Slowly, the tents were put up, canvas cots appeared and were put in the tents, and we were assigned to our new homes. The cots had been stored so long the canvas had shrunk and trying to stretch the canvas so the wooden end crosspieces would fit created a sideshow of frustrated, angry antics, with some cots not getting completely assembled until a night or two of sleeping on them had stretched the canvas to manageable lengths.

Our company street was next to the battalion "officers row," which figured in a later escapade that approached "crisis" proportions in some peoples' minds.

If I remember correctly, our company

contingent consisted of 59 men; 56 enlisted men and three officers, and that, too, was to bear heavily on the making of that unfortunate "crisis."

At the head of the company street stood the company mess hall, then our row of tents extended away from it, with the orderly room tent closest to the mess hall and a Lister bag of drinking water between them.

At the end of the street a wooden stand had been erected to hold wash basins where we washed and shaved; we had to go to a "water point" in order to get the water we used. Usually, someone was detailed to that task the last thing at night so the water would be available at reveille, although quite often a thin crust of ice formed on the water in basins overnight and that made washing and shaving a brisk experience. I was bothered less than others as I had to shave only about once a week, although the 1st Sergeant soon made me shave twice weekly just to add more masculinity to the troop.

There was a communal shower shed that accommodated each battalion, and each company had an outdoor two or three holer, which made for an interesting arrangement when there was a plague of the "mess-kit blues."

The mess hall stove sat flat on the ground and was fueled by wood. Food was prepared in deep pans about two to three feet square and hard as hell to clean and keep hygienic, resulting in more than one case of those "blues." Practically everything was of World War I vintage, including the rations. We ate from our mess kits either standing or sitting on the ground, although the officers had a form of table. Three large garbage cans of the 35 gallon variety, outdoors, over open flames, held the wash and rinse water for our mess kits.

At first, we had to suffice with the toiletries we had brought with us, although soap and razor blades were issued items, but then two sources of supply appeared.

A circus-like tent was erected as a Post Exchange. Some low-wattage electric lines and bulbs were strung inside from pole to pole, but the best illumination came from Coleman gasoline lanterns as the electric power was not too reliable. There was a supply of candy, toiletry items, soft drinks, and beer; the beer was very popular, but someone squealed on me about my age and my supply was cut off. Beer was in short supply so it figured the fewer drinking it made it better for those of heavy thirst for the stuff. There was no flooring and the ground was uneven in spots, with a little trough here and there and a tuft of grass rising to invite a stumble, and dust combined with smoke to develop a light haze, further reducing the already dim light. But it was the place for relaxed social contact away from the inhibiting company street.

Our other source of supply came as sort of a mobile sutler, appearing in a rumpled suit and a well-worn car on the road at the end of the company street. He had a slender stock of candy bars and some cigarettes. He was from Cleveland and it was obvious he would never be a soldier; he had driven to Mississippi to see if he could be of help to us in our wilderness and to be our envoy into the town few of us would see for quite some time. Of course, he wanted to make some money, but I have never met or traded with a more fair and considerate person. He was our link to Hattiesburg for legitimate purposes, that is, he did no bootlegging. He took our film into town to be processed and as the post exchange system developed, partially eliminating that need, he ran a laundry and dry cleaning service, picking up clothing from your bed and returning the finished product to the same location, unerringly, meticulously, and honestly. He followed us into maneuver areas and brought us cold drinks and other goodies. From the "old area" to the "new area" until our departure from Camp Shelby, he was an institution, unfailing in his efforts regardless of weather. I think in the early days he served best in an unintended capacity: we were isolated and struggling in a new, harsh environment and here was someone who cared about us.

And say, who can ever forget that impromptu reveille call from the Hattiesburg radio station playing daily at dawn *You Are My Sunshine?*

We were a sorry sight in the early days. The regimental band would accompany us to our training area, playing march music to bolster our spirits and to sharpen our cadence. We couldn't keep step, and in derision, as we left the road to enter the training field, the band would blow discordant notes as a form of critique to our marching. The first day we marched in an orderly fashion, the band sent up a cheer; it was a bench mark of sorts. The regimental theme song was *Skoda Lasky,* more popularly known as *The Beer Barrel Polka.* It always gave morale a lift whenever we came out of the training area and the band would greet us at a marching point, playing that song. Later, in the Fiji Islands, we would be assigned a new regimental commander who, as a West Pointer, found the song unfitting for an Army unit and banned its playing. He composed a new song for us; although he was disliked and unrespected for many other flamboyant and cowardly acts, the origins for his loss of support and respect lay in those two acts. (On Guadalcanal, during air raids, even though he had no role in the air action other than to "hunker in the bunker," he wanted to listen to the fighter pilots' radio traffic, so while he would stay down in an air raid shelter, he had a radio operator sit in his command car, exposed to the bombing attacks, monitoring fighter transmissions so the colonel could listen to them on a speaker extension in the bunker.)

But training was sporadic. Stove pipe represented cannon and large, crude crates or trucks were marked "TANK" to represent tanks, because we didn't have any. We were exposed to "extended order," learning to "hit the dirt" and to move "as skirmishers;" we were being acquainted with basic infantry tactical moves, and it was all very basic. We were lectured on hygiene by regimental doctors, being warned against sitting on cold rocks to avoid developing hemorrhoids, all the while sitting on the cold ground; the chaplain waxed about being good boys and refraining from frequenting the sin spots that were beginning to flourish in the area. But we didn't get that training every day.

Owing to the small number of men in the regiment, one was placed on a regimental duty roster every third day; it rotated from regimental guard duty to regimental garbage detail to regimental work detail. Then, in addition, there were company detail and "kitchen police" chores to be performed. Even though non-commissioned officers were not supposed to do manual labor, corporals were included in the regimental rosters. So it was hard to develop a sense of order; you didn't know from one day to the next what your routine might be. There was a feeling of being pulled in all directions

USS Hunter Liggett carried the 1st Bat., less Co. B, 147th Inf-RCT and other troops of Task Force 0051-13 to Nuku'alofa, Tongatabu via Panama, April -May 1942. (Courtesy Chaney)

at once. And this underlying feeling fed resentment at being called to duty out of turn.

It was traditional that payday had its own schedule. Drills and details were confined to the company street while the pay officer went for the pay. Once the pay officer was set up to pay and Pay Call was sounded, work and drill for the rest of the day was over, unless you had been posted to guard or work detail on a roster.

One particular payday, we found ourselves off the regimental roster and, except for the very few who didn't drink, availing ourselves of the services of the company bootlegger. It had been a hard month - a healthy, comradely month, but a damned hard one, nonetheless. Actually, it was more than a month, more like a month and a half, but it was the first full payday that gave that period the character of a month, a hallmark month for it marked the end and the beginning of two lives, two eras, two worlds. It was the end of peace and the beginning of the preparation for war. We were really enjoying our day off when word came that G Company, which had posted to the regimental guard detail, had been quarantined with a suspicion of chicken pox. Every other company in the regiment, except ours, had granted passes to so many men that a full guard detail could not be formed other than by our company. By this time most of us were fairly neatly snockered, but the head count was there and we were selected.

Ho, ho, ho; now the fun begun. It was mid-to-late afternoon by the time we got the word. The regimental duty officer was informed as to our condition, but a sufficient muster could be made only by our company so the word was: "put them on guard and keep your fingers crossed." After all, what could possibly happen in some desolate fields in Mississippi when there wasn't even a war on yet.

Guard mount was a spectacle unto itself. The lieutenant who was assigned officer of the guard was really a decent sort and a good officer, but he was fired with the enthusiasm of his office. He loved a formal guard mount with all the movements of the ranks and the flourishing of the saber; he was, in a sense, an anachronism - he belonged to the hussars or the lancers. He enjoyed fencing and frequently tried to recruit foiling partners, although he was impatient with the uninitiated. There just wasn't enough flair for him in the infantry; it was too mundane, although time and duty gradually wore away the gloss and left the true man standing firm and reliable. But here was his opportunity to conduct, as the sole officer in charge, a formal guard mount. He tried; oh, how he tried. But a more uncoordinated group would be hard to imagine. When we were ordered to dress the ranks, that is, form even ranks, blurred vision and unsteady footing gave a wave-like effect to the formation. When we were ordered to open ranks so an inspection could be conducted, some of us moved the required number of steps, some fewer, and some not at all; we bumped into each other and one or two fell down. The lieutenant persisted and "took it from the top" again and again, but it only got worse. Finally, in frustration and anger, he marched away at a brisk pace looking fixedly to the front and growling to the sergeant of the guard: "Post 'em!" And so we were.

It was the "super" who started it all; that damned supernumerary who had nothing to do but sit, wait for someone's infirmity, and drink cheap, bootleg booze. The supernumerary was that extra man who was available to replace any guard who became sick or otherwise was unable to stand a tour of duty. The "super" stayed in the guardhouse, which was really a tent with nothing in it but a field table and chair and one cot, through all the various reliefs, or shifts, doing practically nothing except perhaps running a few errands. He raised the point that as we were drunk when we were put on guard duty, no action could be taken against us for being drunk or, more to the point, staying drunk by continuing to drink. If you were put on duty sober and then got drunk, that was a different story: they could send you to Leavenworth, or even shoot you for that. But being placed on duty drunk absolved us of all misdeeds; we could do practically anything and we could not be held responsible. The fault would lie with whoever put us on duty in a drunken condition. It was, after all, the responsibility of all officers to assure their men were "fit for duty." And that was his recurring theme through every change of shift.

From some unknown source, a couple of pints of cheap whiskey appeared and we passed them around as we debated the fine points of the super's logic. Was he sure about this? Would we be court-martialed and shot? In good guardhouse lawyer fashion he talked about the need to be "fit for duty" and that it was the officers who made the determination and who were held to answer if a sick, lame, or drunk man was assigned to a duty he could not perform. Well, now, here was a shift in the discussion. What right had the regimental, or for that matter, the battalion headquarters to put us on guard duty when we were so drunk. Furthermore, what right had the regiment to put us on guard, drunk or sober, when it wasn't our turn for at least another four days? Why didn't they make up a guard detail from different companies ahead of us on the roster? Weren't they really treating us like dogs what with all the work and guard details. How were we ever to get the training we came to camp for? And were we going to take this lying down or would we be men and express our objections? Well, here was another point; if we were going to do anything, what would it be and when would we do it? That really took us into some heavy discussions. But after several caucuses involving the various guard reliefs going on and coming off duty, it became apparent our only hope for self-protection was to take action while still on guard, and while still drunk and, supposedly, immune from disciplinary action.

Well, we couldn't shoot the officers; that was out of the question. We couldn't just walk off and desert our guard posts; not only was there uncertainty about our immunity if we did that, but it just did not seem a soldierly thing to do. We were resolved to do something - what would it be? Someone complained bitterly we were having to lose our sleep, pulling guard duty, while all the officers were snug in their sacks. That was it! We would go throw the regimental commander and his staff out of bed. But no one was certain where to find regimental officers' row. We did know where the battalion officers' row was; it was right adjacent to our company street! We would throw the battalion officers out of bed. That would be easy; there were only four tents. There was no problem in distributing our forces. Some were assigned to overturn the cots while others were to grab tent center poles, march out the doors, collapsing the tents. Once the decision had been made, our resolve strengthened and the whiskey flowed more freely to reinforce that resolve. We reveled in what we were going to do and who was going to do what to which officer.

There were three guard reliefs: one on post and two resting in the guardhouse. Once the 2:00 a.m. relief was posted, the other two reliefs would pull an Indian raid on officers' row; the posted relief would remain properly "on post." At the appointed time, we moved as silently as we could out of the guard tent and made our way towards officers row. We hadn't gone more than 20 yards when one of the crew, who had been dozing, realized the rest of us had gone on without him. He struggled to his feet, fixed his bayonet to his rifle and charged out to catch up with us, shouting: "Save the damned colonel for me!" Fortunately, perhaps, he woke no one and we made it unannounced to our objective, where in a matter of seconds, bedlam ensued.

Some officers were thrown from their cots, at least one tent, perhaps two, were collapsed, and cursing and struggling rent the night air. But then a visage, an apparition appeared, bellowing in rage, bringing the frenetic action almost to a halt. It wasn't the voice or the words that dampened our action and left us with mouths agape; it was the attire. The roars came from our battalion commander who was dressed in a nightgown extending down to his ankles and a conical nightcap, topped with a fluffy tassel that flopped down alongside his head. It was a sight we least expected to see and it helped put an end to the bedlam. What happened then is vague, but we were returned to the guardhouse to complete our tour and await our fate.

That decision was neither quick nor easy in its forthcoming. We had sources in the regimental headquarters who kept us informed. At first, the cry was for courtmartialing every man-jack involved. Possible charges were banded about, among them was heard the term "mutiny." Mutiny? Good Lord, mutiny had not even entered our minds; if anything it was a childish cry for attention and some decent consideration.

Mutiny? Well, yes, technically, we guessed a case could be made, trying hard enough. But wiser heads prevailed. It was pointed out that, indeed, the guards were drunk when posted and the officers in charge knew it at the time; what would be made of that in a courtmartial? And how could you possibly keep that information from reaching the War Department? What would be the reaction there? Who else, especially in the officer ranks, would be courtmartialed? And how far up the chain of command would that line of action go? Also, weren't we supposed to be a cadre for expansion, for increasing the Army? How could there be an accounting for a missing company, one regiment short a rifle company? What would this do to the Table of Organization and Equipment? The debate went on for three days, and we poor miscreants were in a constant state of high anxiety and stress.

As is so often the case when a certain level of rank is at risk and notoriety can be embarrassing, at the least, the ultimate choice is to put a lid on the incident, to cover it up, and keep it as quiet as possible. That was the verdict in our case. To keep the record clear, there was to be no courtmartial; a courtmartial would have to be reviewed and there would be a permanent record. That would be intolerable. Equally intolerable to good order would be that we go unpunished. Ah, a fine dilemma: make an example of the culprits before the rest of the regiment, but don't let anybody know why, especially anybody outside the regiment.

It was finally resolved that the entire company would receive "company punishment," which, by law, could not exceed a week, but there would be no record entered in the company punishment book to be found at a later date by an inspector-general inspection. Company punishment is conducted at the company level, involving work detail within the confines of the company sphere of operations and with the record going only into a company record and not into the service record of an individual. It relates somewhat to the Navy's Captain's Mast.

We had an interesting week. We aligned every tent in our company street and on battalion officers' row by tent stake, post, and rope with a string and if, along the way, one post or rope was out of alignment, our sergeants knocked down every tent in the row and we had to start again; later, they only knocked the tent we were working on. We had to mow the grass in the company street with bayonets and small knives. We worked from reveille to drill time, with only a brief time out for breakfast. When we returned from training in the field, we were set to our chores again, working until it was too dark to see what we were doing, with a brief break for dinner. When it was over, we had the nicest looking company street in the regiment.

But we weren't to enjoy it long. Construction work had progressed in another part of the camp and new quarters were ready for us well before Christmas. We were still to be under canvas, but with a significant difference. The pyramidal tents were supported by wooden frames with screened siding; there were wood floors and the tents were equipped with metal cots (you know, the ones with flat springs), and a Sibley coal stove. We were given mattresses, pillows, sheets, pillowcases! The mess hall was a solid wooden structure with modern stoves and wooden tables with benches, and we were soon to eat "family style" with bowls of food set on the table. The latrines were enclosed wooden structure with flush toilets, a wash sink room, and a shower room, both with hot and cold running water. Paradise enow!! Officers' row was located in the regimental headquarters area with each officer or two, having a smaller tent over a wooden frame, which the troops referred to as "dog houses."

Even our division service club was special. Our division commander, Major General Robert S. Beightler, considering the stock service club designed by some one in the War Department for cookie cutter application in all camps to be a barn-like apparition, totally unsuited to meeting the moral needs of his troops, had the division service club especially designed and constructed, including guest house accommodations as part of the structure. His efforts, and the end product, were greatly appreciated.

For Christmas 1940, it was decided that as many as could be spared would be permitted leave to go home, and the railroads granted a special fare which made it easy for all who wanted to take advantage of the leave offer. Except, three men per company and at least one officer per regiment had to remain in camp to sustain basic operations and security. Three of us with weak family ties volunteered to remain in camp so there would be no need to have straws drawn and those eager to see their families would be able to do so; besides, we figured there would be no drill and we could just laze around in camp. WRONG!

The camp had to be guarded, so there was a guard to be mounted and guard posts to be manned. There were men to be fed, so food had to be prepared and the kitchens cleaned. There was only one kitchen per battalion open in the beginning, but later, even though other kitchens were open, all meals were taken in just one mess hall in each regiment. Then there were miscellaneous details: garbage had to be moved, supplies had to be moved from point to point, and the camp had to be kept clean. There was the morning "police detail" whereby a line of men walked down the company street picking up every cigarette butt, scrap of paper, and whatever other trash settles in an area. Further, as our Quaker fathers have admonished us early on "Idle hands are the devil's workshop." So, even though certain work generated itself, other work was created to keep us busy and out of mischief. But mischief has its own ways of creating itself. We devised ways to keep from being spotted for work details; we would hide in empty, unlocked tents. But we were easily found. So we adapted. Pyramidal tents had a double flaps for a doorway in order to provide some protection against the elements. The flaps are secured with rope ties. So one or two of us would climb up on the frame, untie the top flaps, drop inside through the top opening, and re-tie the flaps from the inside. Then we would pull covers from the cots so they draped to the floor, then crawl under the cot, behind the cover, and take a little snooze. Even with search parties peering through the flaps with flashlights, that ruse lasted almost until the end of the leave period.

But we were to be rewarded with little excursions, so that at one time or another each of us would have an opportunity to get out of camp for some diversion. With the luck of the draw, I drew an overnight trip to Biloxi, Mississippi. But I also drew guard duty on a shift that ended just before the truck was scheduled to leave. My relief was late. I was frantic. By the time I had raced back to my tent the truck was ready to leave. I had to change from field uniform to Class A, or a parade equivalent attire. Before I could get fully changed, the truck started to leave, but I was determined not to miss the trip. I ran after the truck, clutching an un-

USS American Legion carried GIs of Co. B and the 3rd Bat., 147th RCT and other personnel of Task Force OO51-13 to Nuku'alofa, Tongatabu via Panama April-May 1942. (Courtesy Chaney)

buttoned pants fly, with my shirt half buttoned, my tie draped loose around my neck, my blouse open, and clutching in my hands my pants belt, my blouse belt, and my garrison cap; my buddies dragged me up over the tail gate of the truck, and I made the trip to Biloxi.

But there was still mischief to be done in the camp. Of course, there was an enterprising bootlegger who made trips into Hattiesburg and brought back rotgut whiskey that should never have had a label attached to its bottle. Lemon extract had not yet been modified to eliminate its alcohol content and each mess hall was raided for that delightful commodity, with water being added to the bottle to make up for what was taken out. And our bootlegger also made friends with some females who were happy to come into camp and liven up our mess hall nightclub, disporting themselves lewdly, and accomodatingly, on mess hall tables.

One entrepreneur decided such female companionship should not come without some comfort and surcharge attached, so he commandeered a tent, ensconced a local lovely inside and proceeded to collect admission at the door. Soon there was a short line of callers that drew the attention of our ever present officer-of-the-day who wondered who could be issuing what from a tent having no special attribute, such as a supply or orderly room. He braced a departing customer and learned enough to put him onto the scheme. He got in line, which soon evaporated in front of him. The host, just inside the doorway and busy counting his cash, did not see the arrival of his upgraded clientele and, at the appropriate moment muttered, "Next," only to have the officer reach over, take the cash, and inform the greeter he was out of business and that the money was going into the officers' mess fund, although I suspect it went into a unit fund instead. The poor girl was barred, permanently, from the camp, and the entrepreneur drew additional duties quite unrelated to his latest endeavors. From that point on all our parties suffered from an absence of any local lovely.

Soon after the holidays were over, we were informed we would be receiving new companions. A selective service draft had begun and we would be brought up to a new strength, established by a newly devised Table of Organization and Equipment (TO&E). We were also instructed, and after some grumbling, ordered, directed, and commanded to greet the new arrivals hospitably, to the point of having their beds made for them when they arrived. Given our own experience in the "Old Area," we thought that a bit much. But a compromise was reached; no more than two beds per tent were to be 'short-sheeted.' You know, the old camp trick where only one sheet is used and is folded back on itself halfway down the bed so that when one crawls into bed he finds a fold that has moved the bottom of the bed halfway up and he can only get halfway in. Of course, the amusement was going from tent to tent watching the newcomers getting ready for bed and delighting in watching the reactions of the victims. One poor fellow from West Virginia who wore his shoes with no socks and who had no electricity in his home was made the butt of a lamp bulb joke. He was told to put out the light, which was an electric bulb suspended from cross members, and when he asked one sergeant how to do it, he was told to "blow it out." He kept huffing and puffing at it trying to blow it out until the sergeant finally took mercy on him and turned it off.

With the inductees came the problem of blending them into a homogenous unit, establishing morale, and motivating them to accept the role of soldiers. Many had never been away from home before and most had no experience with group living. It wasn't easy. Many factions abroad in the country remained unconvinced as to the extent of the Nazi threat, and some pockets of isolationism were influential and vocal in their protests against the draft. Even the term of federal service for the National Guard was to be only for one year. Later, as that year of service was coming to a close, two forces, with diametrically opposing aims, came into play. The National Guardsmen on federal duty were approached to apply for a transfer to the Regular Army; a friend and I participated in that aborted effort. And mothers of the guardsmen started petitioning the Congress against a proposal to extend the period of federal service. Because the Ohio National Guard was one of the first units to be federalized, the acronym "OHIO" (Over the Hill in October) became a battle cry and was reported in the national press. Some personnel over a given age were released from duty only to be returned to their units after the declaration of war.

With the infusion of inductees, duty rosters were expanded, work and guard details came around less frequently, and we received more essential training. But the routine was not to the liking of some of the new men and malingering, or goldbricking became a growing problem. Many began to "ride the sick book," feigning ailments and illnesses in order to make the sick call to the dispensary in the morning and to miss at least one-half day of duty in the field. If there were no extended field training exercises or day-long hikes, the company training day usually was broken into two periods of training in nearby field locations, with the unit returning to camp at noon for a regular meal in the unit mess hall, then returning to the field in the afternoon. The sick book malingerers thus would evade a half day in the field and, in the case of day-long hikes would evade an entire day in the field. In time that changed as they were brought out to the field with the mess truck whenever it served lunch in the field. Driving them out at noon with the mess truck, or otherwise driving them out to the field location, did not seem to discourage their malingering habits. The core cadre was still smarting under admonitions not to abuse or harass the newcomers. The more brazen malingers scented the weakness and exploited it shamelessly. The more conscientious inductees resented what was thought to be a lack of evenhanded treatment until morale was on the decline.

Clearly something had to be done. The 1st Sergeant of our company gathered a small contingent of the Old Guard for a conference and swore them to secrecy. Among them was a grizzled, alcoholic artist, who later was to do a beautiful job of painting landscape murals in our mess hall in return for all the beer he could drink as he was painting; we were dunned for contributions to pay for his beer. His best work was always done "under the influence." The "Top" had him paint a flag with a rooster in the lower corner strutting away from a pile of excrement. The Top said the company had become a "chicken-shit" outfit what with so many riding the sick book and he intended to fly the flag over the company street until the goldbrickers were shamed into performing their proper duty. Who would volunteer to be part of the project? A buddy of mine and I volunteered to go into a nearby woods to fell and trim a pine tree for the flag pole and to set it in the middle of the company street. Not much question was raised when we brought the 20 foot pole back to the unit, but when we started digging the hole we underwent a constant barrage of questioning in efforts to learn the secret of a very inappropriate hole in the company street and later of what obviously was a crude flag pole once we had attached a pulley and halyard. The pole stood starkly in the middle of the company street, halfway between the orderly room and the mess hall. It stood without action for two days as its mystery grew. Clearly something special was afoot; no other company street had such an embellishment. Why was it here, in this company? Did it have anything to do with the company being adjacent to the paved road that formed a perimeter of the regiment? Why the secrecy? And the secret held; only a few knew what was in the offing.

The scheme was set, but there had to be a fitting ceremony to raise the flag. It was decided we would have a flag-raising ceremony with a color guard and a cannon; nothing less would do! We rigged stove pipe next to the flag pole in the guise of a cannon and stuffed newspaper soaked with kerosene into it. Then after a regular formation, the company officers left the company street. The company was held in formation as four of us broke away, and out of sight of the rest, formed into a color guard with one carrying the flag and we marched smartly to the flag pole. A match was thrown into the "cannon" and flame and pieces of burning paper belched forth and the flag was hoisted to the top of the pole. The Top then brought the company to "Parade Rest" and delivered a scathing address to the malingerers, declaring they were making us a "chicken-shit" company and until they changed their ways, the chicken-shit flag would fly as a constant reminder of their weakness and lack of manhood for all of Camp Shelby to see. The Top urged the others in the company to point out to the sick book riders the error of their ways as the long the flag flew, the more the entire division would know of this gutless, chicken-shit company.

Thereafter, every day for a week, at formal formations, the flag was raised in the morning at reveille and lowered in the evening at "retreat," flying over the company throughout the day.

The regimental commander made daily trips around the perimeter of the regiment in his command car and could not help but note the flag as our company street bordered the perimeter road. Nothing was heard from for a week, then word came down through channels, after a weekly regimental officers meeting, the point had been made; take down the flag and the flag pole.

Indeed, the point had been made. The malingerers came into line and sick call returned to legitimate complaints.

Another division, the 38th was brought into camp and a rivalry was formed between the two divisions, sometimes developing into minor conflicts. The military police of the two divisions alternated on patrol in the local community, Hattiesburg, and on camp gate control.

The bus service between camp and town was strained on paydays and weekends. Men on pass would wait until the last minute to return to camp and often there would not be enough room to get all the men on the buses that would arrive back at the camp gate by midnight, the expire time of most day passes, although some lucky favorites were given passes that expired at reveille the following morning. The MPs at the gate usually would let men of their own division pass through, but would detain and send to the camp stockade late arrivals from the other division; it was an ongoing game of hazing.

Normally the camp stockade housed those convicted by courtmartial and serving sentences in terms of months, but the exceptional numbers of those not getting back into camp by the deadline time for day passes, and those attempting to smuggle a bottle or two of whiskey into camp (often tucked into the top of a sock), especially on paydays and payday weekends, posed special problems. These miscreants had to be detained until they could be turned over to a proper authority, usually unit commanders, for a fitting disposition of each case, more often than not "company punishment" involving restriction to the unit area and extra detail work not exceeding seven days, unless the offense was flagrant or repetitive, in which case a courtmartial might be invoked.

So a special area was set aside within the stockade for those transients who usually would be released to their units sometime the following morning once their units had been notified. Pyramidal tents were set up with four or five canvas cots in each, totally inadequate for the crowded conditions on paydays. Early detainees enjoyed the dubious luxury of getting a spot to sit on the edge of the cot; eight to 10 could sit around the edge of the cot, leaning against one another and dozing fitfully, while late arrivals either strolled around aimlessly or napped on the ground. Usually there was trading for a spot on the cot and the trading was more intense when one negotiated to have his spot saved when he had to go to the "can." By noon, most had been released to unit commanders, although some commanders, to make a point of displeasure, would not arrive until mid-afternoon, and there were no arrangements or facilities to feed these transients. To a point, it became amusing when a vehicle could be heard approaching the gate, to watch the slow wave of humanity roll to the fence, casually straining to see if one's unit designation could be read on the vehicle, with that wave turning to a rush as the hour grew late and anxiety rose.

In the early days, some one inaugurated a "quart a day club." To qualify, one had to drink a quart of whiskey a day for seven days. This was supposed to make one a rough, tough, fighting soldier, but I suspect it was a ploy on the part of the company bootlegger to increase sales. The routine was simple; a pint was put into your pack when you went out for field exercises in the morning. The whiskey was sipped intermittently during the morning and finished by the time the troops returned for lunch. Another pint was put in the pack for the afternoon and what wasn't finished in the field was nursed through the evening until taps. Out of over 200 men in the company only a dozen or so ever aspired to membership and qualified. It wasn't long before the practice was discovered and outlawed.

Promotions caused psychological problems and some strain on the feeling of camaraderie. It was felt that putting on your stripes too soon was an indication of "lording it" over your buddies and that you were more concerned about your promotion than you were about them. So, a common practice developed that one didn't sew on his stripes after his promotion until after about five or six days, or until a weekend had intervened. This affected operations and control as without wearing stripes, one was reluctant to assert the authority required in good military discipline. Part of the problem was the jealousy felt by those who did not get the promotion. As a rule, sergeants sewed their chevrons on faster than new corporals as they had already moved into the noncommissioned ranks. Plainly the tail was wagging the dog. So word came down from regimental headquarters that chevrons had to be sewn on no later than sundown of the day following the promotion announcement; if one didn't think enough of the promotion to display it, the promotion would be revoked. The policy was tested by inattention and after about three promotions were revoked, the authority of the position was assumed immediately and chevrons appeared overnight.

There was also a problem of assuming the responsibilities that came with authority, such as looking after the welfare of your men. Later, on maneuvers, non-commissioned officers would be reduced to private and lieutenants and captains would have letters of reprimand placed in their files for failing to see to the welfare of those under their commands. There would be periodic shoe and blister inspections and woe be unto the officer or non-commissioned officer who had a man with no socks, holes in his socks or shoes, or unattended blisters! But there was one incident, while we were still under a brigade organization, that raised the morale of the troops and inculcated a sense of responsibility in many. The brigade commander, a brigadier general, believed in attending to the welfare of his men and also in discharging his responsibilities. During late night and early morning hours he would ride around his brigade perimeter, assuring all was in order and that all guard posts were properly manned. (Whether he was partially motivated by the fiasco in the "old area" I will never know.) One rainy night while making his rounds he found a guard with no raincoat, drenched from the rain. Asserting his authority as high commander of the

Members of the 145th Inf, 37th Div. awarded Purple Hearts. Chaplain Hockwald; PFC Charles McLaughlin, PFC Nicholas Galante, Lt. Frank Lutze. (Courtesy Hochwald)

guard, the brigadier, who was wearing his trench coat, relieved the guard of his post, placed him in his command car, and had his driver return the guard to the guardhouse to get a raincoat while the general walked the post. The guard was returned to his post, the brigadier went to the guardhouse, reduced the corporal and sergeant of the guard to privates, and reprimanded the officer of the guard. After that, one pretty much went on guard duty with a raincoat folded over the back of his cartridge belt.

To call your weapon a "rifle" was to bring the wrath of the sergeants down upon your head. Your weapon was a "piece;" a "rifle" was a weapon of artillery. If you dropped your "piece" you took it with you wherever you went, to the mess hall, the latrine, and you slept with it, one night or more, depending on the offense and the whim of your sergeant.

We lived in a coupon world with coupons for the Post Exchange and coupons for the theater, all obtained on credit until payday which was the day of reckoning, not only for paying for the coupons but also for paying back the $7.00 for $5.00 money lenders who stood beyond the end of the pay line and collared the debtors before they had a chance to spend any money that might be left.

We finally went through two major maneuvers, the second of which really developed us into a formidable, cohesive, fighting force with a high esprit de corps and camaraderie which we took with us to Indiantown Gap and onto the Pacific where an exceptional record of high performance was established.

But between the maneuvers and the move to Indiantown Gap there was a recruiting effort by the Regular Army for transfers to Regular Army units in anticipation of a move to de-mobilize National Guard units. A buddy of mine and I volunteered and went through the screening process. His eyesight was as bad, or worse, than mine so we both had the eye chart memorized. Everything went well until we had to submit a urine sample. My buddy was so tense he couldn't urinate. We ran water and stalled as long as we could until we could stall the medical staff no longer and I urinated in his bottle for him. We passed the examination and we were discharged from the National Guard and assigned to Camp McCoy. The discharge was recorded on our service records. Before we could be shipped out, the Japanese attacked Pearl Harbor, war was declared, and the division was shipped out to guard bridges, textile plants (which would be manufacturing uniforms), pine forests (which would be generating raw material for turpentine) and processing plants, and other strategic locations in Mississippi and Louisiana; the two of us were left behind to await shipping orders. In a few days the word came: forget the discharge and the transfer; we were now all one Army and a big "X" was drawn against the discharge page of our respective service records. The following day we rejoined our unit out on the guard detail.

Signs proclaiming "Soldiers and dogs not allowed" came down, and people who would previously cross the street to prevent meeting a soldier face to face came to the guard camp sights to invite groups of soldiers to their homes for dinner; so many families came to the camps that a waiting list had to be established, not for the soldiers, but for the inviting families.

Mobilization - A trying time uprooting men and women from familiar, peaceful surroundings and known associates and casting them into a cauldron of humanity of mixed temperaments, social backgrounds, and mores and producing a homogeneous, effective fight force. Camp Shelby was certainly that "cauldron" and the 37th Infantry Division was certainly an effective fighting force.

Old Smash and Drive
Submitted by Marshal Chaney (To the tune of the "Men of Ohio")

From the bomb - er strip at Koli Point
Up to Mt. Austin's bloody knoll
Across the ridges down to Kukum Bay
Dodging Zeroes in from Munda all the way
And fighting thru the jungle down to the sea
Drive the smashing infantry
And with our colors highty and mighty
To show the victory
That we have won

Maj. Gen. Robert S. Beightler, July 13, 1948.

MG Leo M. Kreger, CO 37th Division, Korean Conflict era.

Hats off to Old Smash and Drive
To all the men of that infantry
To loyal sons of the one four seven, hooray.

To the flag that stands for freedom
We sing our praises one and all
And to our comrades left in the fields beyon
Whose our age drives us on and on
And we will fight, fight, until we have won
For that trust we'll not betray
and with our colors highty and mighty
To show the victory that's on the way
Hats off to Old Smash and Drive
To all the men of that infantry
To loyal sons of the one four seven, hooray.

Smash and Drive in it's original version was written by Colonel William B. Tuttle, (RA) USA, who commanded the 147th Regiment Combat Team (RCT), in the Asiatic-Pacific Theater for (28) months during World War II.
Smash and Drive has been revised several times since World War II. WMC

A Pacific Coincidence

As big as the Pacific theater was and with hundreds of thousands of soldiers there during WWII, my brother and I were able to find each other—not once, but twice!

Having reached our objective in Baguio, we were relieved by the 6th Division. We settled down for a much needed rest at San Fernando and finally had a mail call for news from home. In my packet of mail was a letter from my older brother, who was in the Navy Armed Guard. I figured out from the date it was sent and received it that he must be nearby, but where? How could I locate the family member I hadn't seen in two years?

The first choices were Manila Harbor or Lingayen Gulf. Manila was closer and had been secured, though you could still hear the artillery from the battles still being waged in the mountains. I was lucky on my first try. The Navy Post Office had his shipped marked in the harbor and I arranged for LCVP transport out to him for a grand brotherly reunion and then a day partying around the city. He went back to his ship which was headed back to the states; I headed back to my division and back to the war.

I remember the day very well. We were just a few miles outside the small town of Illagen in the Cagayan Valley, a bright sunny afternoon, when our gun crew which, in the lead, was hit. We'd been moving to our new position to support artillery units and had been informed that the Japanese were somewhere along the road and waiting for us. Four of our crew ended up in ambulances to the field hospital and back to the states.

A Red Cross volunteer at Letterman Hospital asked if there was something I needed. By some outside chance, could my brother's ship have gotten back to San Francisco? It had. the volunteer found him and within a day I had another reunion with him not very long after our tour in Manila.

Serving God and Country

Chaplain Heindl with the 37th Div. Clockwise from top left, Confession Time, May 1944, Bougainville. Easter 1944, 148th Inf. Regt. 148th Inf. Regt. Chapel, Bougainville. Christmas Mass, 1943, Bougainville.

37th Infantry Division—47

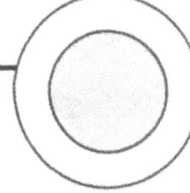

Christmas- Menu - 1940
Camp Shelby, Mississippi 147th Infantry

Christmas Dinner

Tomato Juice Cocktail
Roast Turkey with Oyster Dressing
Mashed Potatoes
Buttered Asparagus
Rolls
Currant Jelly
Coffee
Cigars

Celery
Ripe Olives
Candied Yams
Cranberry Sauce
Ambrosia
Mints
Nuts
Cigarettes

Company B
1st Lieutenant Dale A. Emery
Commanding Company B

2nd Lieutenant Edward E. Rosendahl   2nd Lieutenant Russell E. Cook

Captain Marion F. Rattermann
Special Duty with Selective Service Co. #2

FIRST SERGEANT
Emory M. Gregg

STAFF SERGEANT
Guy H. Merritt

SERGEANTS
George H. Fogle
Harry E. Gittinger
Charles W. Kistner

Michael S. Kreco
John A. Russell
Lonnie E. Robbins

Richard J. Schwarb
Samuel S. Sloan

CORPORALS
Wallace O. Allison
John R. Cory Jr.
Robert C. Goshorn
John B. Wilcox

Roy C. Hammond
Ronald H. Huff
Lawrence L. Lay

George E. McCann
Myron H. Murley
Walter Rowin

PRIVATES FIRST CLASS
Lee Bell
Lloyd A. Kelley
Ronald Lunsford
Lawrence L. Mains

Wesley L. Moore
Edward C. Petty
Frank Russell
James Shroyer

Jack Sizemore
James H. Snow
Earl N. Wall
James P. Walton

PRIVATES
Raymond N. Buschard
Marshall Chaney
Orville Calhoun
William Fisher
Edward L. Folz
Cordell G. Glass
Ralph R. Hasenbein
Thomas N. Huff
Eugene C. Hass
Richard T. Kattine
Edsel G. Mason

Larry J. Lombardi
Joseph A. Losito
Hardin Middleton
John E. Sargent
George Scott
Glenn W. Boanos
Samuel T. Carr
Robert Gregg
Karl E. Harris
Christian B. Holtmann

Charles L. Moss
Jesse H. Nichols
John F. Nolan
Walter M. Patterson
Willard R. Potter
Joseph C. Rettig
Ralph L. Robinson
Louis D. Schwing
Howard Wall
Kenneth E. Whiteford

Colonel Smith Retires

Colonel Ralph G. Smith - author of "approved solutions" for legal study and guidance by JAG officers in Ohio and throughout the nation - retired last month at age 60, after 26 years of military service.

Soldier, judge, lawyer, father, friend and respected gentleman - all of these terms are appropriate in a description of Colonel Smith, an outstandingly successful officer who made unique and notable contributions to the Ohio Militia which he joined as a private in 1942.

Respectfully known to Guardsmen as "The Judge," Colonel Smith built his military reputation on sound judgement, leadership, and willingness to serve. He achieved notable success as the individual responsible for Ohio Legislator's adoption of important legislation in support of military interests. Two recent examples of gains in this area are laws that insure Ohio Guardsmen are subject to almost identical military law as their active Army counterparts and the 1970 law providing $25 minimum salary for Guardsmen on riot duty.

A former Judge of Columbus' Municipal Court, in civilian life Colonel Smith has served as a member of the Board of Governors of the Columbus Bar Association while holding memberships in the Ohio State and American Bar Associations and many other legal organizations. After receiving an LLB degree from Ohio State University, Colonel Smith maintained his law practice while building a military reputation as an outstanding JAG officer whose service will be missed by Guardsmen throughout the nation.

In 1943 Ralph G. Smith, attorney-at-law, Columbus, Ohio, was elected president. The war was in progress and he was drafted in December of 1943 as a private in the U.S. Army. He recalls that getting members for the club was very difficult because of the large number of young people being drafted. His has been a most distinguished career. In 1954 and 1955, he served as a Judge of the Columbus Municipal Court. Prior to that from 1938 to 1943, he rendered yeomen service as Public Defender of the City of Columbus. In a long and steady rise since the days when he was an Army private, he has risen steadily until today he holds the rank of full Colonel and Judge Advocate, Ohio National Guard. He is secretary of the Workmen's Compensation Advisory Council.

USS George Clymer (APA-27)

George Clymer (AP-57) was laid down as *African Planet* on October 28, 1940 by Ingalls Shipbuilding Company, Pascagoula, Mississippi; launched September 27, 1941; renamed *George Clymer* on January 9, 1942; acquired by the Navy June 15, 1942; and commissioned the same day, Captain Arthur T. Moen in command.

She embarked 1,400 men of the 9th Infantry Division and departed October 23 for the amphibious invasion of French Morocco. At midnight on November 8, she debarked assault troops on special net-cutting and scouting missions against garrisons at Mehedia and the fortress Kasba. Just before dawn, the first wave of troops hit the beach and encountered resistance from the Vichy French. Enemy shore batteries fired on the assembled transports and straddled *George Clymer* before she opened the range. She sailed to Casablanca to complete off loading cargo. She departed for the United States the 17th, arriving Norfolk November 30. After embarking more than 1,300 Seabees, *(George Clymer* sailed December 17 for the Pacific. She reached Noumea, New Caledonia, January 18, 1943. Redesignated (APA-27) on February 1), Redesignated (APA-27) on February 1, she sailed in convoy February 5 for Guadalcanal, Solomons, where she arrived the 7th. She sailed the Southwest Pacific, carrying cargo and rotating troops from bases in New Zealand, New Caledonia, the New Hebrides, and the Fijis to Guadalcanal. *George Clymer* departed Guadalcanal October 30 for the invasion of Bougainville. *George Clymer* continued troop-carrying and supply runs in the Southwest Pacific until June 4 when she departed Guadalcanal for the invasion of the Marianas. She remained at Guam until August 20; steamed via Saipan to Hawaii; and arrived Pearl Harbor on August 31.

Underway again September 15, *George Clymer* steamed via Eniwetok and Manus, Admiralties to the Philippines. She sailed November 11 for the United States and arrived San Francisco December 3 for overhaul. Sailing January 26, 1945, she reached Guadalcanal February 11 and for more than a month trained for the invasion of Okinawa. She departed Ulithi, Carolines, in convoy March 27; arrived off Hagushi April 1. Steaming via Saipan and Pearl Harbor, she arrived San Francisco May 9. After conversion to a transport squadron and relief amphibious force flagship, she transported 1,200 Seabees to Pearl Harbor from July 21-27. After returning to San Francisco August 5 with wounded veterans embarked, she sailed August 12 for the Philippines. She made a similar voyage from Leyte to Japan; then as part of the "Magic Carpet." She conducted training operations along the Pacific Coast until December 15, 1947 when she departed San Pedro for the Far East. She arrived Tsingtao, China, on January 20, 1948.

George Clymer returned to San Diego on October 4. She departed San Diego July 14 and carried units of the 5th Provisional Marine Brigade to Pusan. *George Clymer* departed San Diego on June 4, 1951. She departed Yokosuka on April 1, 1951. She returned to the United States for seven months. On July 27, 1953, as the armistice which brought on uncertain peace to Korea, she arrived San Diego on August 22. Since the termination of hostilities in Korea, George Clymer has deployed to the Far East on numerous occasions as an important unit of the always-ready force for peace, the 7th Fleet. In August 1964 she cruised the South China Sea. During the summer of 1965, she deployed to South Vietnam, where she participated in amphibious landings at Da Nang and Chu Lai. *George Clymer* was placed out of commission.

George Clymer received five Battle stars for World War II and seven for Korean Conflict service.

Pearl Harbor Day December 7, 1941

The "day of infamy"

Pearl Harbor Day, Sunday, December 7, 1941, the troops of the 147th Infantry, 37th Infantry Division, USA, were stationed at Camp Shelby, Mississippi, where they had undergone cycle after cycle of extensive training since October 1940 in an effort to prepare for war. In the meanwhile, they had sincerely and fervently prayed for peace.

The majority of the GIs had been reared in Christian homes and communities, with wide and varied degrees of denominational differences. There was also a sprinkling of Jews among them. But whatever one's faith, chaplains were in abundance to assist the soldiers with their spiritual problems and worship, especially so in the States; however, in the combat zones the Catholic chaplains seemed to be more prominent.

When the GIs arrived at Camp Shelby, they found themselves in the Bible belt. Going to church on Sunday morning was very stylish, and those on the post, if not on detail, were encouraged to attend either Protestant or Catholic services. Those of the Jewish faith, small in number, were free to seek out their own worship services.

On arrival at Camp Shelby, generally speaking, the Protestant services were conducted outdoors under the southern pines. As a rule, the Catholics from two or more regiments would have joint services in a regimental recreational hall. However, the troops met en masse at the post theater for their 1941 Good Friday services.

On the heels of the mobilization of the National Guard and the reserve components in 1940-1941, and with the introduction of the draft of selectees in 1941, the Congress of the United States became acutely aware of the spiritual needs of the troops and of the lack of chapels on U.S. military bases.

In the early spring of 1941, a bill was introduced in both houses of Congress to appropriate funds for the construction of regimental chapels at Camp Shelby. The military brass of the 147th Infantry showed much interest in the bill. The off-duty troops who were on the post were urged to attend Sunday morning worship services. It was hoped that the powers-that-be would take notice of the general interest and that there would be a speedy enactment of the appropriation measure.

At Camp Shelby in the spring of 1941, attending church services wasn't a matter left to the election of the GIs' free will (especially not in B Company), 147th Infantry under the command of Captain Charles E. Beach, who was a strong disciplinarian and demanded that all of the troops in the quarters respond to church call. (Captain Beach later rose to fame and the rank of full colonel with Merrill's Marauders.) Protestant services were first on the schedule. The men were formed in company formation, and the captain marched them to services under the southern pines. After the services, the troops were returned to the company area and held in formation while the captain personally inspected the quarters to ascertain whether all the Protestant GIs had responded. Following the Protestant services a second church call was given for those of the Catholic faith. They were formed in formation and usually a sergeant marched them to the 145th Infantry recreational hall for services.

After two or three weeks of compulsory church attendance, there was a rumble and much griping in the rear ranks. This writer, who had been reared as a Baptist (and Baptists since before the days of Roger Williams have been renowned independent thinkers), felt that church attendance was a personal matter and should be left to the personal election of the soldier. The following Sunday morning, this writer, who was then a corporal and squad leader of an eight-man rifle squad, disregarded Protestant church call and remained in his quarters. Following Protestant services, Captain Beach made his regular inspection of the quarters. On entering the corporal's quarters "Attention" was called and all present assumed the position of a soldier and/or "Attention." Captain Beach addressed the corporal and inquired why he didn't fall-out for Protestant services. The corporal readily weighed the captain's stern voice, made a quick projection of potential disciplinary action, and without hesitation decided to be "a Catholic for a day." In responding to the captain's inquiry, the corporal advised that he was attending Catholic services. The captain with a firm smile told the corporal to be sure he did. And that is what he did.

The priest on opening the services flashed a friendly smile which put everyone at ease and spoke a few words in English, then went off into an unknown tongue (Latin). This writer was aware that he had ventured into uncharted waters. Shortly, those on his right and left were slipping in and out of their pews, kneeling and making crosses. The corporal made an effort to follow suit, but found that everyone was out-of-time except him. Private Raymond Witterstaetter sympathetically suggested that the corporal remain in his pew. This advice was well taken, but made the corporal conspicuous. He felt like a country bumpkin with two left feet standing on the sideline at a hoe-down.

The following Sunday morning found the corporal a firm believer. When the bugler sounded church call for the Protestant services, the corporal fell-out of his quarters on the double and was among the first of the GIs in formation.

Congress lost no time in approving the Military Chapel Construction Measure. Construction was immediately started on the regimental chapels at Camp Shelby. The finished products were beautiful and inspiring.

The 147th Infantry Regimental Chapel was erected on Second Avenue facing the junction of 25th Street. It was built on the pattern of an oblong square (rectangular). The exterior was weather boarded and painted white; there was an inspiring steeple rising from the roof above the front entrance. The auditorium seated approximately 1,100 people. The ceiling was high and afforded good acoustics. The sidewalls and ceiling were of native pine and had been stained with a clear varnish, retaining the wood's natural color. The hardwood floor was highly varnished with rubber runners covering the aisle ways. The alter and pulpit showed a glowing gleam of luster from the radiation of the swinging overhead lights. The pews were constructed of 1X4 yellow pine, also highly varnished to retain their natural color. The chapel was constructed to accommodate the services of the three major faiths (Protestant, Catholic and Jewish) with offices in the wings for the chaplains.

On Sunday, December 7, 1941, some of the troops of the 147th Infantry were wrapping-up weekend passes in Camp Shelby's surrounding communities, and a few were on furloughs. But for those GIs on the post, it was "Dedication Day" for the 147th Infantry Regimental Chapel, which meant it was a day of spit, polish and precision. The following was the Order of Service: assembly of troops; call "To the Colors;" invocation; hymn *America*; responsive reading led by Lieutenant Colonel Edwin Woellner, CO 1st Battalion; scripture lesson read by Lieutenant Colonel James Glore, Regimental Executive Officer; solo *The Lord's Prayer*, by Sergeant William Nimmo; presentation of chapel keys by Major Henry A. Ratterman, Regimental S-4; acceptance of chapel keys by Colonel John A. Blount, Commanding Officer, 147th Infantry; representing Men of Regiment, Master Sergeant Charles C. Daniels, Regimental Sergeant Major; hymn *Onward Christian Soldiers;* sermon by Captain Clifford Chadwick, Senior Chaplain, 147th Infantry; dedicatory prayer taken from *Book of Common Prayer,* by Major Frederick Kirker, Assistant 37th Division Chaplain; prayer for the Army, recited in unison as follows, "O Lord God of Hosts, stretch forth, we pray thee, thine almighty arm to strengthen and protect the soldiers of our country. Support them in the day of battle, and in the time of peace keep them safe from all evil; endue them with courage and loyalty; and grant them in all things that they may serve thee without reproach; through Jesus Christ our Lord. Amen." This was followed by the Benediction and then the Recessional.

Upon returning to their quarters, the troops turned on their radios and learned of the Japanese sneak attack on Pearl Harbor. President Franklin D. Roosevelt called it a "day of infamy." The attack was devastating. The U.S. Army and Navy were hit hard. Eight battlewagons were sunk or damaged. Three light cruisers, three destroyers and five other vessels were either sunk or seriously damaged, and nearly 200 planes were destroyed. Military and Naval casualties were high: 2,403 were killed while 1,178 were wounded. The Nips lost less than 100 men, 29 planes, five midget submarines and one large submarine. Chiefly, due to the element of surprise, the attack was a one-sided victory for Japan.

The tenor of the prayers of America's God-fearing people changed as they harmoniously prayed for total victory over their enemies with a lasting peace to follow.

"Hats off!" to Harry S. Truman, Commander-in-Chief, who had the courage to use the "Atom Bomb" which brought World War II to a speedy and victorious conclusion, that of saving millions of lives and abruptly ending the hardships and suffering of further battle casualties.

Let the faint-hearted and sob-sisters in our midst remember that had there been no Pearl Harbor, there wouldn't have been a Hiroshima nor a Nagasaki! As Americans, let's keep everything in its proper perspective.

```
               STATION AND RECORD OF EVENTS

                        APRIL 1942
                  ─────────── O ───────────

  2.  Indiantown Gap Military Reservation, Pennsylvania.  Detachment
         assembled.  1st Lt. Joseph E. Tritschler designated Commander
         of Troops.

  3-8 Indiantown Gap Military Reservation, Pennsylvania.  Usual camp
         duties.

  9.  Indiantown Gap Military Reservation, Pennsylvania.  Detachment
         inspected by Major General Robert S. Beightler.

 10.  Indiantown Gap Military Reservation, Pennsylvania.  Detachment
         entrained at 7:00 PM enroute to new station.

 11-14 Fontana Staging Area, San Francisco, Calif., Detachment detrained
         at 8:15 AM., at Oakland, Calif., and proceeded by ferry boat
         to San Francisco, Cali., thence by motor convoy to new station.

 15-19 Fontana Staging Area, San Francisco, Calif.  Usual camp duties.

  20  Aboard U.S.A.T., ARGENTINA, Pier, #38, San Francisco, Calif., Detach-
         ment embarked at 8:00 AM.

  22; At sea on U.S.A.T., ARGENTINA, enroute to new station. Sailed from
         San Francisco Bay at 6:20 PM.

 23-29 At sea on U.S.A.T., ARGENTINA., enroute to new station.

  30. At sea on U.S.A.T., ARGENTINA, enroute to new station, Equator cross-
         ed this date
```

The Iwo Jima Campaign

by LTC James J. Ahern, USAR RET, Co. F, 2nd Bn., 147th Inf. Regt.

The 147th Infantry Regiment of the U.S. Army had just reached the island of Eniwetok on March 11, 1945, after successfully completing its first two campaigns of WWII. Commanding Officer, Colonel Robert Johnson, opened the radiogram from his Task Force Commander that read: "Request Task Force commander carrying 147th Infantry be directed proceed Iwo Jima earliest practical date."

Rather than the originally planned two-day stopover, the regiment set sail for Iwo Jima after only several hours in the harbor. The original mission, to garrison and secure the island in three days from the 100-300 Japanese believed to be occupying it, had quickly changed.

Shortly after arriving off the West Coast of Iwo Jima on March 20, all units of the regiment were informed of the new combat mission. It was imperative to provide a safe haven for battle-damaged B-29s to land and be escorted by the Air Force VII Fighter Command to Tokyo. The regiment would remain under the command of the 3rd Marine Division for operational purposes until April 4, when the Marine Division was scheduled to leave the island and the 147th would be on its own.

Iwo, the Japanese word for sulfur, and Jima, the word for rock, describes the central portion of the island, which is a large sulfur field. On its southern tip is Mount Suribachi, an extinct 564 foot volcano. It was the northern half of the Iwo Jima, a high rocky plateau, that proved to be the greatest challenge for the 147th Regiment in securing the island.

General Tadamichi Kuribayashi, commander of all Japanese forces, artfully utilized the terrain of the island by nearly turning it into an impregnable fortress. His plan was to fight a war of attrition, killing as many of the enemy as possible by stopping the American forces on the initial landing and then falling back to a main line of resistance—the treacherous foothills of the now infamous northern rocky plateau.

The 1st Battalion was responsible for the northwestern sector, the 2nd Battalion, for the northeastern sector and the 3rd Battalion, the southern third of the island.

At first, it wasn't known how extensive and sophisticated the tunneling system was and how each position was inter-connected. But it soon became obvious that Marine General Harry Schmidt's estimate of 100 to 300 remaining Japanese on the island was much too optimistic.

This was revealed after the Japanese made their last organized attack on the night of March 26. The Japanese attacked through part of the 1st Battalion area, into a Marine unit. Over 250 Japanese casualties were counted, leaving 53 American men dead and 119 seriously wounded. The attack was aimed at the #1 Airfield, where many skilled mechanics and technicians were killed or wounded. The assault severely impaired the "safe haven" vision, but it also served to fuel the regiment with more determination to seek and destroy the enemy.

The regimental staff devised a coordinated plan of attack: Daylight patrolling, night ambushes, and establishing strong points in strategic areas of the island. It is hard to believe that it took 55,000 Marine infantrymen 35 days to accomplish their mission on the eight square mile island. It would take 2,700 men of the 147th Infantry almost 70 days to accomplish their mission, killing over 1,600 enemy soldiers and capturing over 800. Not included were a large number of enemy soldiers who died in their caves rather than surrender.

The average monthly conduct of daylight patrols and night ambushes by the Regiment from the period March 20 to May 31, 1945 was as follows: March-400 daylight patrols and 700 night ambushes; April-1,200 daylight patrols and 2,100 night ambushes; May-900 daylight patrols and 900 night ambushes.

An integral part of the Japanese defenses on Iwo Jima consisted of elaborate cave and tunnel systems. While the existence of these caves had been suspected prior to the operation, no information as to the extent and location was available until after D-day. Interrogations of prisoners of war indicated that the Japanese went underground early in December 1944, abandoning all surface installations except gun positions. Gradually, it became evident that the tunneling system was much more extensive than previously believed. The total amount of tunneling by the Japanese on Iwo Jima was approximately 13 miles.

Needless to say, the infantrymen of the 147th were impressed with the Japanese's skillful use of camouflage. Every rifle company sent out daily daylight patrols to search and seal the caves where the Japanese had skillfully disguised their presence. On one occasion, a smoke generator was aimed into a cave entrance to smoke out a Japanese position. To the surprise of the patrol leader, the smoke exited from at least 20 different sites.

Construction of the caves, which seemed to be individually planned varied from small holes to intricate tunnels. Some consisted of enlargements of natural caves, while others were hand-carved from soft, volcanic rock. Still others were lined with reinforced concrete. Most caves had more than one entrance, and were effectively closed only after several openings had been blasted. In some instances, the enemy was able to dig out of one entrance while others were being closed.

The caves were used for various functions, including headquarters installations, radio stations, supply and ammunitions dumps, hospitals, engineer depots, and warehouses and living quarters. One of the most interesting cave systems was the headquarters cave that housed sections for ordnance, intendance, finance and communication and was separated from another cave system housing the adjutant's section.

The most striking portion of the headquarters cave was the war room and the commanding general's room. From a former garden in a rugged part of the terrain, a concrete passage, complete with steps and hand rail, led down a 25 foot passage to a small anteroom. Below this room was another room of about the same size, accessible through a trap door in the floor. Adjoining the anteroom was a somewhat larger second and connecting third room. Three square foot openings with six foot thick walls connected the rooms.

In many of the caves, passageways were at several levels. The size of the passages, most likely dug out by hand, varied from 4 x 5 feet to 13 x 6 1/2 feet. The passages had numerous curves and turns, featuring various levels connected with wide steps.

The intricate nature of the caves made capturing the enemy extremely difficult. Removal attempts included smoking the enemy out. However, the fact that the smoke could be blocked with blankets and canvas often prevented the smoke from infiltrating the cafe.

Efforts were also made to talk the enemy out, but this was most often futile. Shooting the enemy was also unlikely since guards were posted at the entrances who fired on anyone entering. Consequently, in the largest cave it was decided to force the Japanese out by starting a fire within the larger caves.

Hundreds of gallons of salt water were pumped into the entrance of the headquarters cave with hundreds of gallons of gasoline and oil. The fire set off explosions of large amounts of ammunition. As a result of the smoke and heat, 29 Japanese were killed or committed suicide; 54 prisoners were taken, two of whom committed suicide.

The tactics developed by the 147th Regiment, which included the killing and capture of 2,469 Japanese, had a profound effect upon the rapid decrease in enemy activity. The combat mission of the regiment was complete. This proud old regiment (with a combat history that dates back to the Civil War) was very successful in providing a safe haven for the B-29s. By the end of the campaign, over 2,500 of these bombers had landed safely, thereby saving the crews which totaled 25,000. In June, the regiment then fulfilled its original mission to garrison Iwo Jima.

It is noteworthy to point out that Japan's "war of attrition," which began in Pelelieu, Iwo Jima and Okinawa, was extremely successful for them. The battle of Okinawa was the bloodiest battle ever fought. Its casualty rate of American soldiers was over 50,000 and the Japanese army and civilian casualties amounted to almost 200,000. This would have a profound effect on Pres. Harry Truman's decision to drop the atomic bomb on the cities of Hiroshima and Nagasaki, thus bringing an end to the horror that began Dec. 7, 1941-a date that will live in infamy.

The interiors of many caves have never been fully investigated as the presence of a belligerent enemy within necessitated their being closed with explosives to avoid casualties. This report describes those caves which were either cleared of the enemy during mopping-up operations by the 147th Infantry or which were closed by blasting and reopened at a later date. Many additional caves were closed after great difficulty, by both Marines and Army troops, and lie buried under tons of rock and rubble. Airfield and other construction projects on the island have also eliminated traces of numerous caves.

Material for report on caves was gathered from descriptions and diagrams furnished by battalions, A&P Platoon leaders, demolition teams and patrol leaders.

Cave Systems

Headquarters Cave-One of the most extensive and interesting cave systems on Iwo Jima is located in TA 235-A. This cave is reliably reported as having been the headquarters of Lieutenant General Kurabayashi, the Army group commander responsible for the defense of this base.

The cave system included space for ordnance, intendance, finance and communications sections and was separated a short distance from another cave system housing the adjutant's section. This cave consisted of numerous tunnels which were inter-connected. Forty-six prisoners were taken from this network and 20 dead Japs were counted when the cave was explored after having been blasted with TNT and bangalore torpedoes.

The most interesting portion of the headquarters cave is the war room and the commanding general's room. From a former garden in a rugged draw, a concrete passage complete with steps and hand rail, leads down approximately 25 feet to a small anteroom about 5x5x5 feet. Below this room is another of about the same size accessible through a trap door in the floor. Adjoining the anteroom is a second room about 10x5x5 feet and another of the same size is directly connected to this one. Access between rooms is gained through openings about 3 foot square. These openings reveal the strength of the construction. The walls are approximately 6' thick. From there concrete chambers, two passages extend. These two exits have been boarded shut for safety reasons.

Headquarters
3rd Marine Division, Fleet Marine Force in the Field

Secret
From: The Commanding General
To: The Island Commander, APO-86
VIA: Commander Forward Area, Pacific
Subject: Commendatory performance, case of the 147th Infantry Regiment, USA

1. During the period from March 21 to April 4, 1945, the 147th Infantry Regiment, USA, was attached to this division for operational control during operations against the enemy on Iwo Jima, Volcano Islands.

2. Throughout the period their performance of assigned duties and missions was outstanding and reflected great credit on their planning, training, and professional skill. The 147th Infantry Regiment displayed in their debarkation, movement into positions and execution of assigned missions a fine spirit of cooperation and a commendable eagerness for combat.

3. The commanding general takes this opportunity to commend the officers and men of the 147th Infantry Regiment for their splendid performance and devotion to duty. Their keen understanding and ready execution of missions assigned was an inspiration to all hands.

G.B. Erskine

Navy Unit Commendation

The Secretary of the Navy takes pleasure in commending the Support Units of the V Amphibious Corps United States Fleet Marine Force for service as follows:

For outstanding heroism in support of military operations during the seizure of enemy Japanese-held Iwo Jima, Volcano Islands, February 19-28, 1945. Landing against resistance which rapidly increased in fury as the Japanese pounded the beaches with artillery, rocket and mortar fire, the Support Units of the V Amphibious Corps surmounted the obstacles of chaotic disorganization, loss of equipment, supplies and key personnel to develop and maintain a continuous link between thousands of assault troops and supply ships. Resourceful and daring whether fighting in the front line of combat, or serving in rear areas or on the wreck-obstructed beaches, they were responsible for the administration of operations and personnel; they rendered effective fire support where Japanese pressure was greatest; they constructed roads and facilities and maintained communications under the most difficult and discouraging conditions of weather and rugged terrain; they salvaged vital supplies from craft lying crippled in the surf or broached on the beaches; and they ministered to the wounded under fire and provided prompt evacuation to hospital ships. By their individual initiative and heroism and their ingenious teamwork, they provided the unfailing support vital to the conquest of Iwo Jima, a powerful defense of the Japanese Empire.

All personnel attached to and serving with the following support unit of the V Amphibious Corps, United States Fleet Marine Force, during the Iwo Jima Operation from February 19-28, 1945, are authorized to wear the Navy Unit Commendation Ribbon.

Headquarters and Service Battalion; Medical Battalion; Signal Battalion; Motor Transport Company; Detachment, 1st Separate Radio Intelligence Platoon; Detachment, Signal, Headquarters, Air Warning Squadron 7, Army Fighter Command; Detachment, 568th Air Warning Battalion, Army; Detachment, 726th Signal Air Warning Company, Army; Detachment, 49th Signal Construction Battalion, Army; Detachment 44, 70th Army Airways Communications Service, Army; Detachment, Communications Unit 434 (Group Pacific 11); Landing Force Air Support Control Unit No. 1; 2nd Separate Engineer Battalion; 62nd Naval Construction Battalion; 2nd Separate Topographical Company; Detachment, 23rd Naval Construction Battalion (Special); 8th Field Depot (plus Headquarters Shore Party); 33rd Marine Depot Company; 34th Marine Depot Company; 36th Marine Depot Company; 8th Marine Ammunition Company; Detachment, 8th Naval Construction Regiment; Corps Evacuation Hospital No. 1; 2nd Bomb Disposal Company; 156th Bomb Disposal Squad, Army; Company B, Amphibious Reconnaissance Battalion, Fleet Marine Force; A and C platoons, 38th Field Hospital, Army; Joint Intelligence Corps, Pacific Ocean Area, Intelligence Teams Nos. 22, 23, 24 and 25; Detachment, Joint Intelligence Corps, Pacific

S/Sgt Forrest E. Lacy, Jr. Platoon Guide of the 1st Platoon, Co. B, 147th Inf. was killed in action as he attempted to rescue one of his wounded GIs. A GI kneels at Lacy's grave. (Courtesy Chaney)

Ocean Area, Enemy Materiel and Salvage Platoon; Detachment, 1st Platoon, 239th Quartermaster Salvage and Collection Company, Army; Detachment, Headquarters, Army Garrison Forces, APO 86; Detachment, Headquarters, 147th Infantry, Army; Detachment, Headquarters, VII Fighter Command, Army; Detachment, 47th Fighter Squadron, Army; Detachment, 548th Night-Fighter Squadron, Army; Detachment, 386th Air Service Group (Special) Army; Detachment, Group Pacific II; Detachment, Port Director; Detachment, Garrison Beach Party; Headquarters & Service Battery, 1st Provisional Artillery Group; 2nd 155mm Howitzer Battalion; 4th 155mm Howitzer Battalion; 473rd Amphibian Truck Company, Army; Detachment, Headquarters & Headquarters Battery, 138th Antiaircraft Artillery Group, Army; Detachment, 506th Antiaircraft Gun Battalion, Army; Detachment, 483rd Antiaircraft Air Warning Battalion, Army; 28th and 34th Replacement Drafts (less Advance Groups and those assigned assault units); Headquarters Battalion, 3rd Marine Division (less Reconnaisance Company); 3rd Marine War Dog Platoon; 3rd Service Battalion (less detachment); 3rd Pioneer Battalion (less 2nd Platoon, Company C); 3rd Medical Battalion (less Company C); 3rd Motor Transport Battalion (less Company C); 12th Marines (less detachment); Marine Observation Squadron 1 (less detachment); Headquarters Battalion, 4th Marine Division (less Reconnaissance Company and 1st, 2nd and 3rd Platoons, Military Police Company); 4th Motor Transport Battalion; 4th Medical Battalion; 133rd Naval Construction Battalion; 4th Tank Battalion (less Companies A, B and C); 4th Engineer Battalion (less Companies A, B and C); 4th Service Battalion; 4th Pioneer Battalion (less Companies A, B and C); 442nd Port Company, Army; 14th Marines (less detachment); 4th Marine Amphibian Truck Company; 476th Amphibian Truck Company; Marine Observation Squadron 4 (less detachment); Detachment, 726th Signal Air Warning Company, Army (4th Marine Division, Reinforced); 24th and 30th Replacement Drafts (less Advance Groups and those assigned assault units); Headquarters Battalion, 5th Marine Division (less Reconnaissance Company and 1st, 2nd and 3rd Platoons, Military Police Company); 5th Medical Battalion; 13th Marines (less detachment); 5th Marine Amphibian Truck Company; 471st Amphibian Truck Company, Army; Marine Observation Squadron 5 (less detachment); Detachment, 726th Signal Air Warning Company, Army (5th Marine Division, Reinforced); 5th Pioneer Battalion (less Companies A, B and C); 31st Naval Construction Battalion; 592nd Port Company, Army; 5th Motor Transport Battalion; 5th Service Battalion; 27th and 31st Replacement Drafts (less Advance Groups and those assigned assault units).

John L. Sullivan
Secretary of the Navy
September 26, 1947

Press Release

Date: June 1945 (apparently, inasmuch as Colonel Robert F. Johnson was relieved of command of the 147th Infantry Regiment, USA on May 31, 1945; by Lt. Col. Walter N. Davies on Iwo Jima).

Cincinnati's 147th, Best Known Regiment in the Pacific Area

The 147th Regiment, USA, originally composed of southwestern Ohio men, "is probably the best known individual regiment in the Pacific and Cincinnati men have proved their worth in every operation." This statement came from Colonel Robert F. Johnson, who returned to Cincinnati after being with the regiment throughout the Pacific War, and in command for a year.

Colonel Johnson said he could not reveal the present location of the regiment, but reported it was in the Western Pacific, its job virtually finished. (It was on Iwo Jima) (WMC).

The regiment, originally a part of the 37th Ohio Infantry Division, was separated from it when it went into action.

"Only two officers and 35 enlisted men of the originally 147th Infantry, that went into action in 1942, remain," Colonel Johnson said. "It is not so much a Cincinnati group as before, but it still is Cincinnati's own regiment."

The 147th Infantry has traveled more than 27,000 miles in the Pacific Ocean, from Tonga Tabu to the New Hebrides, Guadalcanal, British Samoa, New Caledonia, Northern Solomons and, finally their present location in the Western Pacific. (Iwo Jima) (WMC).

The Combat Infantryman's Badge and three Battle Stars are worn by men of the 147th Infantry, and they have been commended for their fighting ability in the battles they have participated in by the commander of the South Pacific, Colonel Johnson reported.

A native of Napoleon, Ohio, Colonel Johnson was an electrical engineer with the Cincinnati office of the Federal Civil Service Commission before the war. He is on leave for the first time since 1942, and expects to be out of the Army soon. He said he hoped to make his home in this city (Cincinnati) when he returns to civilian life.

Copied and submitted by William Marshal Chaney, September 24, 1985.

Iwo Jima Incident

By Lyle D. Guyer

It was on the morning of March 26, 1945 at Iwo Jima where the accident happened. I was standing up on a cliff and a shot went over my head. I saw a Jap in a cave down below. There were two cliffs about ten to 12 feet apart with a cave in the middle. I went down to the cave and threw a hand grenade into the cave. The Jap threw a grenade back at me. I don't know if it hit my gun or not, but it hit me in the chest area. It injured my eye and the blood was rushing and I couldn't see. Sgt. Lacy came to my rescue. I put my arm around him and as we were walking away he stepped on a land mine and was gone. This was a very sad and depressing experience. I felt Lacy's death was my fault.

I was flown to Honolulu immediately and was in the hospital there for six weeks. From there I was flown to Letterman Hospital in San Francisco and from there transferred to a hospital in El Paso, TX from where I was discharged in September 1945. I lost the sight of my left eye.

Years later I found out through some buddies that they had killed the Jap who threw the grenade.

My thoughts have been with the Lacy family ever since that tragic. day.

Ed. Note: Sgt. Lacy and PFC Guyer were members of Co. B, 147th Inf. reg. See S-2 Journal, dated 3/26/45 at 1815 hours.

A Pacific Coincidence

As big as the Pacific theater was and with hundreds of thousands of soldiers there during WWII, my brother and I were able to find each other—not once, but twice!

Having reached our objective in Baguio, we were relieved by the 6th Division. We settled down for a much needed rest at San Fernando and finally had a mail call for news from home. In my packet of mail was a letter from my older brother, who was in the Navy Armed Guard. I figured out from the date it was sent and received it that he must be nearby, but where? How could I locate the family member I hadn't seen in two years?

The first choices were Manila Harbor or Lingayen Gulf. Manila was closer and had been secured, though you could still hear the artillery from the battles still being waged in the mountains. I was lucky on my first try. The Navy Post Office had his shipped marked in the harbor and I arranged for LCVP transport out to him for a grand brotherly reunion and then a day partying around the city. He went back to his ship which was headed back to the states; I headed back to my division and back to the war.

I remember the day very well. We were just a few miles outside the small town of Illagen in the Cagayan Valley, a bright sunny afternoon, when our gun crew which, in the lead, was hit. We'd been moving to our new position to support artillery units and had been informed that the Japanese were somewhere along the road and waiting for us. Four of our crew ended up in ambulances to the field hospital and back to the states.

A Red Cross volunteer at Letterman Hospital asked if there was something I needed. By some outside chance, could my brother's ship have gotten back to San Francisco? It had. the volunteer found him and within a day I had another reunion with him not very long after our tour in Manila.

The Greatest Conflict, The Greatest Compromise: Rodger Young

by Cynthia S. Snyder

No one would have ever suspected that Rodger Wilton Young would become a hero. He was a rather ordinary young man from Clyde, Ohio, a typical small town. There wasn't anything particularly outstanding about him; but one day, while fighting with the enemy in the greatest conflict ever, Rodger made himself known to the entire nation when he gave the greatest compromise possible. He gave his life.

I learned about Rodger, who lived from 1918-1943, several years ago through my father, Lieutenant Colonel Daniel M. Snyder, commander of the 148th Infantry Battalion, the same battalion that Rodger fought in so many years ago. Dad played the song, *The Ballad of Rodger Young*, which instilled in me a drive to tell Rodger's story. I realized that his story would be an excellent topic for History Day.

I began by going to the Rutherford B. Hayes Museum Library in Fremont, Ohio, where the Rodger Young Collection is located. I found scrapbook upon scrapbook of documents, newspaper articles, citations, magazines, his Purple Heart and numerous other items. His Congressional Medal of Honor was not there because it is on loan to the USS *Intrepid*. I learned much from this collection and gained many ideas for my entry.

Then I visited the Archives at the Ohio Historical Society, Columbus, Ohio, and looked through many document books, federal records and books about the Congressional Medal of Honor. I also obtained books from the Findlay-Hancock County Public Library which helped me understand the battle on the Solomon Islands and the Pacific War.

Next I wrote letters to friends and relatives of Rodger and conducted interviews with Rodger's former commander, Colonel Francis B. Folk, and other military men who were near Rodger on New Georgia, Solomon Islands during World War II. They gave me interesting eyewitness accounts of Rodger's military career and events and conditions on the Solomon Islands and in the South Pacific during World War II.

At that point I wasn't sure whether to do a media performance or an individual performance, as both seemed to be good ways to portray my topic. As I assimilated all of the information I had collected, it became evident that an individual performance would be the best way to utilize my abilities.

After consulting with several teachers, my mother, and my father, I began to develop my performance using slides in the background. I obtained an Extagraphic Visual Maker from my school's audio-visual department, and I used this machine to make slides from pictures in books that I obtained from my public and school libraries.

Finally I began to put my performance together using the slides, music, correct props, and final script to best tell Rodger Young's inspiring story.

Rodger's sacrifice was not unlike many sacrifices made by countless soldiers during World War II and other wars, but it was the key to winning the battle of New Georgia; part of the Solomon Islands chain. When Rodger ignored the order to retreat and made the decision to destroy that Japanese machine gun, he knew he would be giving the greatest compromise to resolve his unit's conflict.

Rodger Young became an inspiration to all infantrymen who served and will serve their country, and in keeping with the motto of the 148th Infantry, "We'll Do It;" he did it.

XXXX

An oft made quote attributed to Major General Charles Willoughby, G-2 Intelligence Chief of MacArthur's Command: "The Nisei saved countless lives and shortened the war by two years."

Clifford Uyeda, President, National Japanese American Historical Society: "The direct impact of the MIS linguists on the outcome of the Pacific War was considerable. Timely and accurate tactical intelligence obtained by the MIS Nisei through prisoners-of-war interrogations and document translations gave the American and Allied forces impressive advantage over enemy troops."

It may be apropos to include in your record of WWII additional information about the Nisei Language Teams who served with the 37th Division at New Georgia, Bougainville, and Luzon.

The secretive nature of our mission being what it was, our very existence or service in WWII was classified for 30 years. The 442nd Regimental Combat Team got considerable publicity as an all Japanese-American outfit which ended up as the most decorated U.S. Army unit in U.S. history. Not so for the Military Intelligence Service Nisei.

By the time WWII ended, 6,000 graduated from the MIS schools from the Presidio of San Francisco, Camp Savage, Minnesota, and Fort Snelling, Minnesota. Today, its successor is known as the Defense Language Institute at the Presidio of Monterey. Its facilities and curriculum is a far cry from the original Army School at the Presidio of San

Francisco: 60 students, four instructors, housed in an abandoned airplane hangar at Crissey Field which began November 1, 1941.

Some of the members who served with the 37th are: Gilbert B. Ayres, Newton Stewart (Navy), Larry Farber, Austin W. Bach, Susumu Toyoda, Seian Hokama, Joe Yoshiwara, Yukio Kawamoto, Taro Asai, Bill Ishida, Keiji Fujii, Tad Uriu, Maxie Sakamoto, Haruo Ota, Kazuo Komoto, Dye Ogata, Jerome Davis. There were more but my memory fails me and documents are limited. A typical team was comprised of two officers and 10 enlisted men (mostly sergeant grades). Seven Nisei were assigned to Division Headquarters and the other three were sent to each of the regimental S-2s.

The MIS Nisei participated in every landing and assault in the Pacific War with Marines and Army Air Corps as well as Army units. They served in the China-Burma-India operations. Some served with British and Australian units as well. They were present at the surrender ceremonies on the Battleship *Missouri* and did much after the war during the Occupation of Japan. This is their unwritten history.

We also translated Lieutenant Masatane Kanda's pep talk to his troops which was to avenge the defeat at Guadalcanal. Kanda was CG of the famous or infamous 6th Division. The overseas edition of *Newsweek*, April 3, 1944, included it in its coverage of the Battle of Bougainville although liberally edited to polished form:

To avenge our mortification since Guadalcanal
Will be our duty true and supreme.
Strike, strike, and strike again
Until our enemy is humbled forevermore.
Brighten with the blood of American devils
The color of the renowned insignia on our arms.
The cry of our victory at Torokina Bay
Shall resound to the shores of our beloved Nippon.
We are invincible
No foe can equal our might.
To attain our aims we must always attack
And our enemies we must smite.
Danger comes soonest when it is despised.
Caution and prudence will bring no grief.
Serve in silence and bear all pain.
The shame of our souls will give us strength
To preserve our nation and our glory.

Rhyme and Reason

By Col. Rayman C. Spalsbury, AUS, Ret.

As with thousands of other service members who were thousand of miles from home in some jungle or strange land, I asked myself, "What am I doing here?' As we made our way onto the beach at Lingayen Luzon (the Japanese did not defend the beach) and walked into the village of Lingayen, a group of 9-12 children stood on the side of the street and, as we passed by, sang "God Bless America." It was then that the rhyme and reason for being there was very clear to me.

An Experience While On Bougainville

by Anton "Tony" L. Kadrmas

One time we were told to go on a patrol quite a ways ahead of the line on top of the hill to see if we could find out where the Japs were. This was after a few weeks on the island; we were told to stay there on that hill all night. I walked away to look around and one of the other men turned the dial on my radio and we were getting this strange voice. We had picked up the Jap's frequency, I called our 2nd Battalion Headquarters and gave them the number on the radio dial. It wasn't long until they called us back with orders to get off that hill as fast as we could as the Japs were making their way over the mountain. I have wondered many times that if that GI had not turned my radio dial, that maybe none of us would have made it back alive.

On another occasion, there were four of us runner/messengers in one pillbox and there was a small draw to our right and that's where our Army placed a 50 caliber machine gun and the crew was given orders not to fire until they were given orders to do so. The gun was so well camouflaged that the Japs were walking right into it, but since the Japs had cut our telephone wires there was no way to reach the machine gun crew. That's when us runners got a call to get to the gun and tell them to start firing. There was a lot of barbed wire in front of our pillbox and it was also dark. We drew straws to see which of us four would run the message and one of my good friends, Arthur Gibbons, drew the short straw and we opened the barricade and off he went. I saw a Jap sniper firing right back of Arthur's feet, I still don't know how he made it through the barbed wire so fast. In just a few seconds, we heard that gun start firing and Arthur even made it back to our pillbox; we were sure glad to see him.

The second night was even worse as the Japs had taken some of our pillboxes and almost made it to regimental headquarters. Two of us runners were chosen to find out which pillboxes had our men in them. There was no communication as the wires had all been cut. I ran from tree to tree as fast as I could and when I got close to one of the pillboxes and was hiding behind a banyon tree, when one of our men noticed me from his pillbox. This GI saw me and knew my name, he called me to come in as he opened the barricade, so I just dove in and skinned both of my elbows. He showed me the Jap that had a bead on me as I made the jump into the pillbox; he also told me that the next pillbox to the left was taken over by the Japs. Then I was ready to run the message back to our company headquarters, I could feel the lead flying all around me, but I never got hit.

While on Philippine Island we had to swim across a river that was covered with oil and the Japs let us cross the river then opened fire with everything they had. What saved a lot of us was some metal buildings, and the bank sloped a little and we hugged the ground. After that we got orders to get back across the river and somehow we managed to do it. A few days later, I was put on guard duty on one of the bridges that remained and still dirty with oil. A GI truck came down the road, the driver happened to be a black GI and as he got closer to me, he kept looking at me, I guess he wasn't sure if I was a GI or a Jap. There was a tall wooden rail on each side of the bridge and he kept nudging me against the rail. I thought I'd better get on top of the rail; about that time, a hook of some kind on the truck caught my right pant leg and tore it off, bruising me. Just at that time an MP happened to be coming across the bridge and saw what happened. He stopped the truck driver and raised hell with that driver, but he finally let him go. Someone brought me a meal at noontime and said they would get me some clothes. I was eating my meal and I saw this man coming down the road; it was hard to tell if he was GI, Jap or Filipino, but he kept on coming toward me. He had on a heavy overcoat and when he came up to me, he just stopped and kept looking at me. I thought that maybe he had a gun under his coat, but he wouldn't go away or say a word, then he opened his coat and I saw that he was a Filipino priest. I asked him if he was hungry and he said "Yes," that's the only word he said, so I gave him my meal. He ate it, prayed for me, then went on his way. I finally got clean clothes and a lot of soap and washed the oil off myself. I still say I was a lucky guy through the whole war, because there was one time I got a piece of shrapnel in my right arm, but I saw a lot of men get killed right next to me. I did pray a lot, and I had seven sisters, Mother and Dad in Dickinson, ND that said they prayed for me all the time I was gone, which was about three and a half years.

USS George Clymer, APA-27. (Courtesy Chaney)

Fiji, September, 1942. (Courtesy Atkins)

Burial in temporary cemetery. (Courtesy Hochwald)

Anton L. Kadrmas on duty, Fiji. (Courtesy Kadrmas)

37th Calvary Reconnaissance Troop, 3rd Platoon. (Courtesy Lawless)

New Caledonia. 1944-45. French-New Caledonian Mademoiselle under a banana plant. (Courtesy Chaney)

Recher and Seibert, Emirau, 1944.

Engine running from Noumea docks to nickel ore mines in New Caledonia. (Courtesy Chaney)

Mess Hall and kitchen, Fiji, 1942. (Courtesy Atkins)

William F. Rodgers, Vazenskie?, George Johnson, Hill 700, Bougainville, 1943. (Courtesy Rodgers)

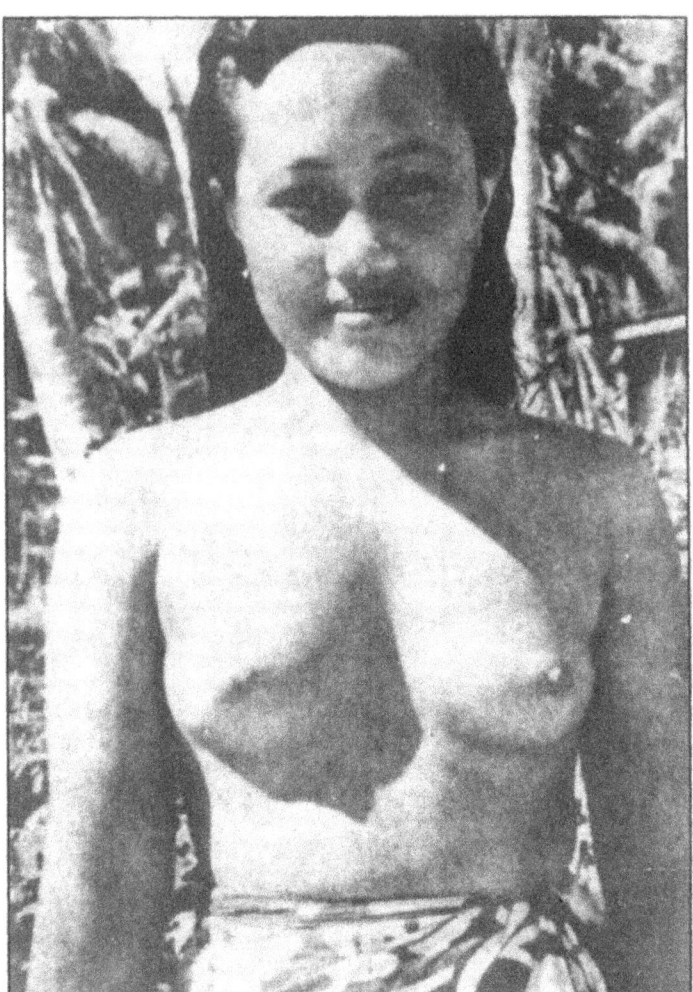
British Samoa maiden following the customs of the island. (Courtesy Chaney)

WWII Sherman tanks, which, where possible, spearheaded infantry rifle squad and platoon attacks in Bougainville. (Courtesy Chaney)

Guadalcanal, 1942-1943. Jap on the right side of the barbed wire. (Courtesy Chaney)

Jimmy Nargi, left, shortly before being wounded, and Joseph X. McGinn, Jr. in New Georgia pothole. (Courtesy McGinn)

PFC Thomas C. Sikes, Aug. 5, 1945, Camp Livingston, La. (Courtesy Sikes)

MAJOR U.S. COMBAT UNIT CASUALTIES IN WWI

The Units listed below account for the vast majority of the Americans killed by hostile action in WWI. Wounded in action include only those actually hospitalized.

The unit patches illustrated here (the total is far too numerous to display all) represent the divisions which suffered the highest casualties. All the divisions listed are infantry.

	DIVISION/BRANCH	KIA	WIA
ARMY	1st Division	4,996	17,324
	3rd Division	3,401	12,000
	32nd Division	3,028	10,233
	4th Division	2,903	9,917
	28th Division	2,874	11,265
	42nd Division	2,810	11,873
	2nd Division	2,683	9,063
	26th Division	2,281	11,383
	5th Division	2,120	6,996
	77th Division	2,110	8,084
	27th Division	1,829	6,505
	30th Division	1,641	6,774
	78th Division	1,530	5,614
	79th Division	1,517	5,357
	90th Division	1,496	6,053
	89th Division	1,466	5,625
	91st Division	1,454	4,654
	82nd Division	1,413	6,664
	35th Division	1,298	5,998
	80th Division	1,241	4,788
	37th Division	1,066	4,321
	29th Division	1,053	4,517
	33rd Division	993	5,871
	93rd Division	591	2,943
	36th Division	591	1,993
	7th Division	287	1,422
	81st Division	248	856
	92nd Division	182	1,465
	85th Division*	145	281
	41st Division	93	315
	6th Division	68	318
	83rd Division*	67	257
	88th Division	20	58
	76th Division	4	22
MARINES	(4th Brigade)	2,461	9,520
NAVY		431	819
ARMY AIR SERVICE		235	130
COAST GUARD	133		

*The 332nd Infantry Regiment (83rd) and 339th Infantry Regiment (85th) served in Italy and North Russia, respectively.

SOURCE: The Doughboys: The Story of the AEF, 1917-1918 by Laurence Stallings.

37th Infantry Division Association

Guadalcanal Campaign Vets Memorial Tribute, Winter Haven. (Courtesy Pierce)

Ladies 37th Auxilliary Officers, Rita Mathie, installing officer. (Courtesy Smith)

37th Division return to Manila, 1982. (Courtesy Heindl)

148th Inf. at Linguyan Gulf, 1982. (Courtesy Heindl)

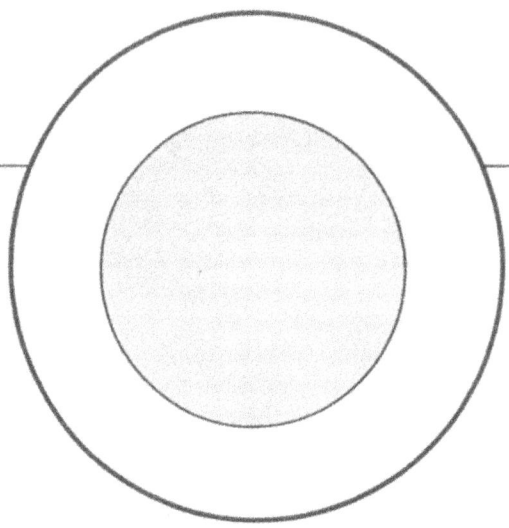

37th Division Veterans Association
Past National Presidents
1919 to 1994

Year	President	Year	President
1919	*Charles C. Chambers	1962	*John Howk
1920	*William V. McMaken	1963	Ward Ankeny
1921	*A.W. Reynolds	1964	*Chester W. Wolfe
1922	*Frank Gerlach	1965	*Herbert A. Lewis
1923	*John A. Buehrle	1966	*Ralph W.E. Gall
1924	*Ralph D. Cole	1967	*Charles Miller
1925	*Victor Heintz	1968	*Ralph DiNucci
1926	*Ralph R. White	1969	*Harry Romer
1927	*John S. Shetler	1970	*Michael Dancull
1928	*Arthur D. Hill	1971	Earl Buffington
1929	*Robert S. Roberts	1972	*Howard Perathaner
1930	*Claude Rhoads	1973	*Marvin D. Girardeau
1931	*Thomas H. Morrow	1974	Nicholas Perovich
1932	*James H. Secombe	1975	*Edwin P. Baer
1933	*Harry L. Dickey	1976	*Fred Gioglio
1934	*Chalmers R. Wilson	1977	George B. Nolt
1935	*Wade C. Christy	1978	Percy W. Lehr.
1936	*Clifford H. Sommers	1979	Lloyd T. Winters
1937	*Paul D. Meek	1980	Merle B. Sickmiller
1938	*E.H. Ellis	1981	*Ray Dysterhouse
1939	*Harold E. Snell	1982	Thomas E. Jones
1940	Harold O. Roth	1983	Nicholas J. Scarpa
1941	*Warren D. Williams	1984	*Joseph N. Wendling
1942	*Kenneth Little	1985	James W. Wallace
1943	*Clarence W. James	1986	Charles E. Miller
1944	*Harry Romer	1987	Jesse M. Knisely
1945	*Joseph A. Juenker	1988	*Dominic J. Anzevino
1946	*Glenn L. Bierly	1989	Herbert G. Kehr
1947	*Richard D. McCloskey	1990	Rossiter J. Chappelear
1948	*Robert A. Billups	1991	James E. McGinnis
1949	*Rudy Ursprung	1992	James F. Beatty
1950	*A.C. Mundew	1993	Edgar E. Davis
1951	*Floyd Reed	1994	Frank Niehaus
1952	*Elmer R. Krueger		
1953	*George F. Graf		
1954	*Allen Brown		
1955	*Frank Walker		
1956	*John McSweeney		
1957	*Sam Salzman		
1958	*Stanley Brown		
1959	*Allan Magid		
1960	John Hale		
1961	*Roscoe Flowlr		

Honorary Presidents

M/G *Robert S. Beightler
M/G *Leo M. Kreber

*Deceased

Ladies of the 37th Division Auxilliary

Past Presidents

Year	President
1934	*Jeanette A. Little
1935	*Pearl Sommers
1936	*Garnet Oxley
1937	*Grace Hetzel
1938	*Mae Dingledy
1939	*Alpha Leggett
1940	*Marie Simlik
1941	*Betty Blackburn
1942	*Otillie Bell
1943	Elizabeth G. Conner
1944	*Lola Bennett Olds
1945	*Ethel Green
1946	*Bessie Scain
1947	*Adele Stiles
1948	*Nellie Brown
1949	*Norma Hagberg
1950	*Pearl Leuthner
1951	*Sarah Murphy
1952	Mildred Beels
1953	Betty Walker Klein**
1954	*Daisy Mikesell
1955	*Margaret Foster
1956	Ruth Pollock**
1957	*Helen McGuire
1958	*Ozella Sanderson
1959	*Hazel Pelton
1960	Jane Wolfram
1961	*Mary Olendorf Sigler
1962	*Letha Hageman
1963	Evelyn King**
1964	*Dorothy Gall
1965	*Bette Langerman
1966	Helen Glesen
1967	Julia Landles
1968	*Ethel Miller
1969	*Helen Popp
1970	*Mary Macfadyen
1971	Margaret Perathaner
1972	*Esther Weidner
1973	Betty Jones
1974	*Kay Perrin
1975	Cora Gioglio
1976	Doris Wander**
1977	Marcells Grgich**
1978	Stefanie Perovich
1979	Opal Lehr**
1980	Marlene Lynn**
1981	Cindy Nupp
1982	Ann Sickmiller**
1983	Genevieve Miller
1984	Marge Jones
1985	Genevieve Piwowar**
1986	L. Jean Wendling**
1987	Rose Boticke**
1988	Genevieve Miller
1989	*Kathryn Gross
1990	Mary Bartholomew
1991	Rita Mathie**
1992	*Arlene Scarpa
1993	Ruth Knisely**
1994	L. Jean Wendling
1995	Mrs. Evelyn King

* Deceased

Evelyn King, Pres. 1992-1995.

Rita L. Mathie, Sgt. at Arms, 1994-1995

Marcie Grgich, Sec./Treas. 1994-1995

Doris M. Wander, Assistant National Secretary

Rizal Monument, Manila, 37th Anniversary of Liberation. (Courtesy Heindl)

Philippine Medals given to men of Youngstown Chapter. (Courtesy Smith)

Christmas Dinner, 1991, Dante's, Cincinnati, OH. (Courtesy Chaney)

1986 Christmas Dinner, Cincinnati, OH.

147th Inf. Chapter Reunion, 1994. (Courtesy Neihaus)

1986 Officers of the Association.

Rocco and Mary Bartholomew, Installation Banquet.

Christmas Dinner, 1991, Dante's, Cincinnati, OH. (Courtesy Chaney)

37th Infantry Division—65

37th Infantry Division Veterans

All 37th Infantry Division Veterans Association Veteran's Association members were invited to send a personal vignette and photos for inclusion in this book. All received were included as submitted. The Publisher and Association cannot guarantee the completeness or correctness of these personal stories.

JAMES J. AHERN, Lieutenant Colonel, enlisted as a private, Troop A, 104th Cav. in 1937. Re-enlisted in the U.S. Army in 1942; graduated from Officer Candidate School at Ft. Benning, GA; commissioned a 2nd lieutenant, Infantry, in March 1943; served with Cannon Co., 262nd Regt., 66th Div. and transferred to 147th Inf. Regt. in December 1943 on Samoa.

He participated in Northern Solomons Campaign on Emirau and Iwo Jima Campaign from March to May 1945. Transferred to Co. F, 381st Inf. Regt., 96th Inf. Div. in Battle of Okinawa from May to August 1945. Was evacuated to mainland stateside to Army hospital in August 1945.

In post-war years from 1946-1971, he served with 79th Inf. Div. and 1st U.S. Army as assistant G-2. Retired in 1971 as lieutenant colonel, USA, with total of 31 years active and reserve duty. Among his proudest decorations are the Combat Infantryman Badge and Bronze Star.

Married in 1946 and has two sons and a daughter. One son and a daughter are physicians and the other son is corporate executive officer. From 1962-1985 Col. Ahern and his wife operated a publishing company. They currently reside in Bethlehem, PA.

LEONARD L. ALLEN, Tech Sergeant, was born Feb. 15, 1925 at Kansas City, MO. He trained at Camp Roberts and joined G Company, 148th Inf. Commanded by Francis Folk the best combat officer ever at Guadalcanal in September 1943. Went on to Bouganville and Luzon.

After a long siege of malaria, he was discharged at Ft. Lewis in January 1946. He re-enlisted in the U.S. Army Corps of Engineers and attended school at Ft. Belvoir. Assigned to 370th Engr. Heavy Equipment Co. and promoted to master sergeant. His unit was sent to Germany during the Korean War. Met a master sergeant who was POW at Bilbid. Discharged in June 1954.

He worked on DOD Missile projects in Midwest and Cape Canaveral. He was excavating superintendent on shuttle runway. The last 14 years he was Florida manager for a large heavy earth moving company and retired with his wife Vyrle (who was his office manager) on Dec. 31, 1992.

DANIEL E. ATKINS JR., Captain, was born in Georgia. He was ordered to active duty and assigned

to the 129th Inf. Regt. at Camp Forrest, TN; transferred to HQ Sp. Troops, 37th Inf. Div. in June 1944, where he remained until the division was deactivated late in December 1945. He returned to Reserve status.

Was sent to Asiatic-Pacific Theater in September 1942 and served in Fiji, New Hebrides, Bougainville and Luzon. His awards include the Combat Infantry Badge, Bronze Star with one cluster, Bronze Arrowhead for Luzon invasion, Bronze Battle Stars for Northern Solomon and Philippine campaigns.

Atkins served as a civilian with the federal government from February 1946 until retirement in 1972. He remained in the Army Reserves and was recalled in 1961 to active duty for one year in the grade of lieutenant colonel for the Berlin Crisis.

He and his wife, Grace, reside in Holmes Beach, FL and have two sons; one born in 1943 and the other in 1947.

RICHARD A. AULT, 1st Lieutenant, was born Jan. 9, 1918 in Akron, OH. He joined the Ohio National Guard and served with M Co. 145th, 37th Div. Left M Co. 145 in 1942 from Indiantown Gap to go to OCS at Ft. Benning.

Later transferred to USAF for pilot training. He left the service in December 1945 as 1st lieutenant pilot. He is now retired and spends winters with his wife in Naples, FL.

MARVIN V. AYERS, Lieutenant Colonel, enlisted in Service Company in October 1937. Stationed at Camp Perry from 1938-1939; Wisconsin maneuvers, 1940; federalized Oct. 15, 1940, sergeant, Camp Shelby, MS; Louisiana Maneuvers, June and August 1941; Indiantown Gap, PA in February 1942.

On April 7, 1942, he departed NYPE for Tongatabu via Panama Canal, Guadalcanal Nov. 29, 1942 to May 12, 1943. Total of 165 days combat, Jan. 20, 1943, Lesage Trail, Kokumbona, Bonegi River, Western Samoa, New Caledonia, April 1944, Emirau Island, closest troops to Tokyo, between Rabaul and Truk.

New Caledonia again, short leave in New Zealand, Iwo Jima March 20, 1945. Command 2nd Bn., lieutenant colonel at age 26. Departed Sept. 9, 1945, total 172 days. Left Okinawa in October 1945 for States.

Discharged at Camp Shelby in November 1945 after 43 months overseas. He received the Combat Infantry Badge and Bronze Star.

Helped reorganize 147th Inf., Ohio National Guard in December 1946; he resigned in June 1950. Was in management with Proctor and Gamble until March 1976 when he retired to the beautiful Mississippi Gulf Coast. His wife is from Biloxi, MS, and they have five children and nine grandchildren. Three sons were in the service: USMC, USA, USAF.

ALFRED BARR, Private First Class, was born Dec. 6, 1918 in Syracuse, NY. He entered the Infantry, 37th Div. on Sept. 20, 1944. Served in Asiatic-Pacific, Philippines and Luzon.

Discharged Dec. 25, 1945; he received the Soldier's Medal (by Maj. Gen. Robert S. Beightler), WWII Victory Medal, Asiatic-Pacific Ribbon, Philippine Liberation with Bronze Star and Combat Infantry Badge.

Married and raised five children. He is currently retired and lives in Redding, CA.

ROCCO BARTHOLOMEW, Technician Fifth Grade, was inducted into the service Jan. 25, 1941 and assigned to Co. D, 112th Med. Bn. as an ambulance driver. He trained at Camp Shelby, MS. On May 26, 1942, he went overseas and crossed over the equator and time zone. He headed for the Northern Solomons Luzon Island then to Guadalcanal. Received honorable discharge in October 1945 after three years, four months and one day overseas. He received the Atlantic-Pacific Theater with two Bronze Stars, Philippine Liberation and Manila with one Bronze Star.

Married Sept. 7, 1946 to Mary Zupp. They have two sons, Dennis and Kenny; daughter, Linda Schulte; and five grandchildren: Scott, Erin and Alexis Schulte and Travis James and Tyler Shick Bartholomew.

THOMAS T. BARTLETT Tech 5, was born March 26, 1920 at Santa Rosa, CA. He entered the service Oct. 23, 1942 and was assigned to HQ Btry., Div. Arty., 37th Inf. Div., Wire Section. Basic training was at Camp Roberts, CA.

Served overseas at Guadalcanal, New Caledonia, Bougainville, Luzon, Lingayen Gulf, Manila, Baguio, and Cagayan Valley. His memorable experiences include on the *Westrailia* during the kamikaze attack and laying line at night during the capture of Clark Field.

Bartlett was discharged Oct. 9, 1945. He received the Asiatic-Pacific Ribbon, WWII Medal, Bronze Star, Philippine Liberation and Good Conduct.

Retired from the U.S. Post Office after 30 years of service. Married 48 years to Ruth; they have two daughters, Patricia and Marjory, six grandchildren and one great-grandchild.

EARL J. BAUMAN, Sergeant, was born Nov. 20, 1918 in Cleveland, OH. He served in the 37th Inf. Div.,

Co. E, 112th Engrs. from April 1937 to April 1940. He re-enlisted in 1940 and trained at Camp Shelby, MS and at Indiantown Gap, PA.

He left San Francisco in May 1942 for New Zealand and then on to the islands of Fiji and New Hebrides. The 37th Div. mopped up Bougainville and went on to Lingayan Gulf, P.I. and participated in the battle of Manila, Baguio and through the Caygayan Valley to Appari. His Army tours of duty were as a company clerk.

He was discharged October 1945 at Indianapolis, IN. Then went to work for the Cleveland Post Office. He married in 1949 and later moved to Colorado in 1957. He retired from the post office in June 1972. Moved with his wife in 1982 to Dumont, CO and now enjoys a mountain view. He has two daughters, Donna Darrow and Kathleen Martinez, and two grandsons, Eric and Benjamin Martinez.

KENNETH E. BEAUDOIN, Private First Class, was born June 17, 1921 in Kankakee, IL. He joined the service on Dec. 1, 1942; was assigned to K Co., 129th Inf., 37th Div.; and served in Bougainville and Luzon.

Honorably discharged, he received the Purple Heart with one cluster and Combat Infantry Badge.

He married Beverly Strauss in 1949; they have two daughters and eight grandchildren. He is retired from A.O. Smith Corp., Water Heater Div.

ROBERT S. BEIGHTLER, Major General, was a native of Marysville and received his education there and at Ohio State University. He enlisted in the Ohio National Guard in 1911 and retired in 1953 after 42 years of outstanding military service. During his military career, he received many decorations including the Distinguished Service Cross, Silver Star, Legion of Merit, Distinguished Service Medal with OLC, Bronze Star Medal with OLC and the Purple Heart. He also was the recipient of the Legion of Honor from the Philippine Government.

Gen. Beightler is well known for his outstanding career in WWII for leading the 37th Div. through 43 months of training and combat in Guadalcanal, New Georgia, Bouganville and Manila. His final command was as commanding general of the Ryukus Command on Okinawa, retiring from there in 1953 for physical reasons.

Maj. Gen. Beightler in civilian life was a registered professional engineer and was appointed executive director of the Ohio Turnpike Commission and continued during the construction and until the turnpike was opened.

He was a member of the Columbus First Community Church and a 33rd Degree Mason. He passed away in 1978, but will long be remembered for his leadership and concern for others.

WILLIAM E. BIGWOOD, Sergeant, was born on the farm at St. Thomas, ND on March 17, 1917. He served Feb. 21, 1941 to Oct. 9, 1945. Sent to Camp Forrest near Tullahoma, TN and Co. K, 129th Inf. for basic training. Spent the rest of his time in the service with the same unit which enabled him to make many close and lifelong friendships. He has treasured that most for all these years since.

Departed San Francisco on Sept. 1, 1942; arrived Suva, Fiji on Sept. 19, 1942; New Hebrides on March 13, 1943; Guadalcanal on Nov. 3, 1943; and Bougainville on Nov. 13, 1943, after an all night sea battle. The 129th Inf. was then at full strength and he would see his first combat. A practice landing was made at Lae, New Guinea. He arrived at Manus in the Admiralties on Dec. 21, 1944, and left Manus with the huge task force for Luzon in the Philippine Islands on Dec. 31, 1944. He landed with the first wave in Lingayen Gulf early on the morning of Jan. 9, 1945 and participated in battles at Clark Field, Baguio, and Cagayan Valley. He was wounded on a lower incline of "Top of the World," known as Mount Pinatubo.

He was awarded the Infantry Combat Badge, Asiatic-Pacific Medal with two Bronze Service Stars, Philippine Liberation Medal with one Bronze Service Star, Good Conduct Medal and Purple Heart.

He retired from farming in the Red River Valley of North Dakota in 1990, but still resides on the farm with his wife, Mildred, at St. Thomas, ND.

WADE A. BLANKENSHIP, 1st Lieutenant, was born Feb. 10, 1916 in Stopover, KY. He joined the service March 15, 1940 and served with Co. G, 148th Inf. Regt., 37th Inf. Div., USA. He was stationed at Camp Shelby, MS; Indiantown Gap, PA; Fiji Islands; Guadalcanal; Russell Island; New Georgia; and Solomon Islands.

His memorable experience was meeting John F. Kennedy on Banika, Russell Islands and meeting Mrs. Eleanor Roosevelt in a hospital in New Zealand.

Discharged Feb. 11, 1945 as 1st lieutenant. His medals/awards include the Silver Star, Combat Infantryman Badge, Purple Heart and Asiatic-Pacific Theater Ribbon.

He is married and has three children and three grandchildren. Retired from USDA, SCS National Soils Laboratory at Lincoln, NE in March 1976.

WILLIAM H. BLEACHER, Private First Class, was born June 23, 1922 at Lancaster County, PA. He served from Aug. 31, 1942 to June 25, 1946 and trained at Camp Wheeler, GA. In the beginning of 1943 he went to Fiji Island to join with the 37th Div., Co. D, 148th Inf. He went to Guadalcanal, Russell Island and then to New Georgia where he fought in the battle of Munda Airfield.

He was involved in the Battle of Bougainville and with the beach landing at Luzon. He fought also at the battle of Manila and the battle at Bagiuo where he was wounded in the leg by shrapnel. His memorable experience was the night that the Jap 6th Div. of Nanking was virtually obliterated.

Bleacher was awarded the American Theater Medal, Asiatic-Pacific Theater Medal with three Bronze Service Stars, Philippine Liberation Ribbon, Purple Heart, Bronze Star, Combat Infantry Badge and Guadalcanal/Solomon Islands 50th Anniversary Campaign Medal.

He was a chemist with RCA. He and his wife, Shirlee, live in Cranbury, NJ; they have three children: John, Gary and Sheri Lynn, and four grandchildren: Michael, Tonya, Jarrett and Jamie.

JOSEPH BONFIGLIO, Lieutenant Colonel, was born in Upper Sandusky, OH on Dec. 10, 1912. He enlisted in Co. E, 145th Inf. Regt. in October 1930, while still in high school and was still a member and its company clerk when the unit was federalized on Oct. 15, 1940.

At Camp Shelby, MS, where an earlier generation of soldiers from Co. E had trained during WWI, Bonfiglio trained through the Louisiana Maneuvers but was separated from the unit in February 1942 to attend OCS at Ft. Benning, GA. While with the 37th Div., Bonfiglio mainly handled public relations duties, co-editing with the 138th Inf. Div., the Camp Shelby *Reveille*, a soldiers' newspaper and writing news and human interest stories for Ohio Papers.

He was commissioned a 2nd lieutenant of Infantry in June 1942 and assigned to the Office of Strategic Services, an international espionage, intelligence and Special Operations organization. He served in North Africa, Sicily, Corsica, and the French-Italian Alps. While in the Alps Bonfiglio worked with Italian Partisans and French Resistance Fighters.

He was honorably separated from the Army in November 1945. For two years Bonfiglio was a foreign corespondent based in Italy and in June 1948 was recalled to extended active duty, retiring in June 1962.

A partial list of his military awards include the Legion of Merit Medal with OLC, Bronze Star Medal, Knight Order of the Crown (Italian Award), the South Vietnamese Civilian Service Medal, Special Forces Tab and the Combat Infantry Badge with Star. Bonfiglio retired in the grade of lieutenant colonel.

JOSEPH A. BOOKHAMER, Colonel, was born and raised in Columbus, OH. He attended Ohio State University and New York University, NYC. Enlisted in the 37th Inf. Div. in April 1938 and remained with them until 1945. Departed overseas to South Pacific in May 1942 and served in the Fiji Islands, Guadalcanal, New Georgia and Bougainville, Solomon Islands and participated in the Invasion of Luzon, Philippine Islands and the battle for Manila.

Later served in the occupation of Japan, China, two times in Germany, and in Alaska. He was wounded on two different occasions in the Solomon Islands and received the Purple Heart with OLC. Other awards include the Combat Infantry Badge, Bronze Star Medal with two clusters and the Army Commendation Medal with one cluster.

The Colonel after retiring from military service in 1966, entered the Life Insurance business as a general agent with several different companies. He is a past member of the Million Dollar Round Table and is a life member of the Life Insurance Leaders of Georgia. He is a life member of the DAV and life

37th Infantry Division—69

member of the Military Order of the Purple Heart.

The colonel and his wife, Marie, reside in Augusta, GA.

ALBERT J. BOSNYAK, Sergeant, was born April 1, 1922 in Akron, OH. He joined the service on July 26, 1940 and entered active duty Oct. 15, 1940. He served with Co. I, 145th Inf. Regt., 37th Inf. Div. He participated in the action at Luzon, Philippine Islands. One of their objectives was Mt. Pacauagen, east of Manila. He received two concussions while overseas.

Bosnyak was discharged Aug. 10, 1945 as sergeant squad leader. His awards include two Bronze Stars, two Purple Hearts, Combat Infantry Badge, Philippine Presidential Unit Citation Badge, Asiatic-Pacific Theater Ribbon with two Bronze Stars, American Defense Service Medal, Philippine Liberation Ribbon with one Bronze Star, Good Conduct Ribbon, Victory Medal, Expert Badge with Rifle Bar, Sharpshooter Badge and Marksman Badge.

On Jan. 16, 1976, a piece of shrapnel worked its way out of his ear. He has vestibular dysfunction, tinnitus, headaches and hearing loss due to concussion and went on total disability in November of 1978.

THOMAS F. BOTICKE, was born Oct. 18, 1919 in Ohio. He joined the service on Aug. 16, 1946 at Cleveland, OH and was assigned to the 37th Inf. Div.

He was discharged Aug. 18, 1949 at Camp Atterbury, IN with the rank PFC.

Boticke is active in the 37th Div. Assoc., Youngstown Chapter and attends the conventions every year.

Married to the former Rose Perno since May 2, 1949; they have a son, daughter-in-law and granddaughter who reside in Aurora, CO. Boticke is retired from the Republic Steel Co. and enjoys roller skating and dancing with his wife and friends and taking a few trips each year to visit his son and family.

JOSEPH G. BOWMAN, was born Dec. 11, 1919. He was drafted Dec. 8, 1941 and trained at Camp Croft, SC. He was assigned to the Infantry, 148th, 37th Div. as wireman. He was sent to Indiantown Gap, California, Fiji, Guadalcanal, New Georgia combat, Russell Islands, back to Guadalcanal to regroup, then combat on Bougainville, Lingayen Gulf, where he drove jeep with trailer under water to beach. Went on to Paco, Manila, Baguio and Cagayan Valley.

Memorable Experiences: while unloading ship at Bougainville and a 500 lb. bomb hit the hatch rim above their heads and the fantail broke six drums of gas, but there was no explosion; at Bougainville when Jap torpedo plane was shot down and hit 100 feet from their foxhole, it burned but never exploded; and when Manila Jap artillery cut their wire reel on rear of jeep and a second shell flattened both front tires, but they continued to drive it.

Got lucky on rotation and was sent home two weeks before the war ended. He is married and has six children and 15 grandchildren.

BYRON WINFIELD BROWN, Lieutenant Colonel, was born and raised in and around Greenville, OH. He enlisted in Co. M, 148th Inf. at Covington, OH in October 1940. In April 1941, he transferred as corporal to Service Company and became staff sergeant before transferring to Division Headquarters Co. in August 1942.

He was assigned to IGD and promoted to tech sergeant and then to master sergeant. In July 1943 he accepted appointment as warrant officer and assistant division inspector general. He served with the 37th at Camp Shelby, MS, Indiantown Gap, PA; Fiji; Guadalcanal and New Georgia before returning to medical administrative OCS at Camp Barkeley, TX in September 1943. He later served five years at the Medical Field Service School, Ft. Sam Houston, TX, and also served at installations in Missouri, Washington, Colorado, Ohio, Europe, Japan and Korea, before retiring in July 1963 at Ft. Belvoir, VA where he was a hospital administrator. During this active duty, he attended night school on three continents and received an undergraduate degree in military science from the University of Maryland in 1960.

For the next 14 years, Brown became involved in environmental health and in July 1977, he retired as supervisor from the Dept. of Health, Commonwealth of Virginia, with concurrent retirement from the Health Dept. of Alexandria, VA. During that time he authored numerous articles for national and international trade and professional publications and served as president of the National Capital Area Association of Sanitarians. He was a member of the Royal Society of Health of London, Diplomat in the American Academy of Sanitarians and Fellow in the American Public Health Assoc.

Since his full retirement, he has compiled a seven-volume family history on the ancestors and descendants of his great-grandfather, Ahijah Brown and related lines. He is a member of the 37th Div. Veterans Assoc., National Assoc. of Civilian Conservation Corps Alumni, a life member of the VFW, a member/officer in numerous local and national genealogical and historical societies and a regular contributor of articles and features to periodicals published by those groups.

On Dec. 7, 1944, he married Eleanor Jean Comolli of Piqua, OH and they have three sons. One was an Air Force navigator who turned lawyer and is in practice in California. The other two are Army M.I. officers, one in Washington and the other in Georgia. Eleanor passed away Oct. 31, 1990 and Byron subsequently moved from Virginia to Ohio.

LEO BUCSA, was drafted into regular duty on Jan. 25, 1941. His company, the 37th all-Ohio Division of the National Guard, including three outfits from Youngstown, went through basic training three times because the government and Army higher-ups didn't know where to send them. They were eventually assigned to New Guinea, Bougainville and three chains of islands in the Lingayen gulf of the Philippines, along with the 40th Div. to which his infirmary unit was attached. Included among the 37th Div. were many Americans of Japanese ancestry. "Without the Japanese Americans, we would have had a rougher time fighting the war," Bucsa said. "They listened to the radio and translated messages."

He remembers the time he spent overseas and all of the people he met during those years. Once he and a group of men were watching movies in a recreation hall in Tokahoma, Japan (a city conquered by the U.S.) when they heard Japanese planes above them. They left the rec-room and the planes hit exactly where the movie screen was.

At the time of the bombing of Pearl Harbor, Bucsa was on guard duty at the motor pool at Camp Shelby, MS. Every year since the service, he attends the memorial service for those lost at Pearl Harbor. He says, "It was an event that changed the lives of many people."

After six years in the service, Bucsa worked for the U.S. Postal Service. He is now retired and enjoys sponsoring high school girls baseball teams in the summer, as well as Boardman and Austintown sports and the Youngstown State University Penguin athletic programs.

AMOS CHANEY JR., Corporal, was born March 16, 1931 in Pulaski County, Somerset, KY. He enlisted in the USN on March 30, 1948 to Jan. 18, 1950; NTC at Great Lakes, IL; USS *Albany* (CA-123); Receiving Station, Naval Base, Philadelphia, PA. Left Navy as seaman CR. Received the Naval Occupation Service Medal (Europe).

Inducted in U.S. Army Nov. 29, 1951; assigned to Co. I, 148th Inf., 37th Inf. Div., USA; Co. C, 19th Inf. Regt., 24th Inf. Div., Camp Polk, LA and Korea. Discharged Nov. 23, 1953 as corporal E-4. His medals include the Korean Service Medal with one Bronze Campaign Star, United Nations Service Medal and National Defense Service Medal.

Chaney was married and had three children and nine grandchildren. He passed away April 4, 1991.

WILLIAM MARSHAL CHANEY, Staff Sergeant, was born July 22, 1922, Pulaski County, Somerset, KY. Graduated from high school in Mt. Victory, KY and Washtenaw Community College, Ann Arbor, MI. He enlisted in the OHNG on July 5, 1940; mobilized into federal service Oct. 15, 1940; assigned to 147th Inf. 37th Div. and stationed at Camp Shelby, MS; Indiantown Gap Military Reservation, PA; Camp Howze, TX; and Camp Atterbury, IN.

He served in the Asiatic-Pacific Theater with the 147th Inf., RCT, USA from April 7, 1942 to Dec. 31, 1944. His memorable experiences include the Bonegi River Battle on Jan. 30, 1943; and Guadalcanal.

Chaney earned the Combat Infantry Badge, Bronze Star Medal, Asiatic-Pacific Theater Ribbon with three Bronze Campaign Stars (Guadalcanal, Northern Solomons and Bismarck Archipelago campaigns), American Defense Service Medal, Good Conduct and WWII Victory Medal. He was honorable discharged on June 23, 1945, at Camp Atterbury, IN with the rank of staff sergeant, Infantry. Married the former Mae Marie Smith of McCreary County, KY on Dec. 1, 1945. They have three children: Helen Berneta Warner, Janet Sue Warner and William Marshall II, who have given them a total of seven grandchildren, all residing in Johnson County, IN. Chaney resides in Indianapolis, IN and was coach operator for the Indianapolis Public Transportation Corp. until retirement in August 1990.

He is a Shriner, member of American Legion, VFW, DAV, Non-Commissioned Officers Association, Guadalcanal Campaign Veterans Assoc., 37th Inf. Div. USA Veterans Assoc. and the USA Non-Commissioned Officer Museum Assoc., Americal Div. Veterans Assoc. and the Society of the 1st Inf. Div. Served a two year term as National Secretary of the Guadal Campaign Veterans and a three year term as National Executive Committeeman of the 37th Inf. Div. Veterans Assoc.

ROSSITER J. CHAPPELEAR, Captain, was born Dec. 25, 1928 at Columbus, OH. He joined the 37th Div. Band as a trumpet player on Feb. 17, 1947. Activated Jan. 15, 1952 in the Korean War; rejoined the 37th Div. Band on Jan. 15, 1954 and was commissioned 2nd lieutenant ARTY, 137th AAA Dec. 24, 1957.

Attended Basic Officer Transportation School, Infantry Company Officers Course, Advanced Engineer School, RIF 1972, joined 122nd Army Band until Dec. 25, 1988. Retired as captain with over 41 years service. He has played taps over 4,500 times at funeral and memorial services.

Past national president, 37th Div. Veteran Assoc.; past commander, Franklin Post #1, American Legion; AM LE Voiture #15 40&8; past commander Capital City #3 DAV; past commander, 10th Dist. DAV; president, Columbus Chapter 37th Div. Vets. Assoc.; member of AMVETS Post #89; Sojourner #10, Reserve Officers; past president State Commanders and Adjutants Assoc. of Ohio; past president Retired Officer of Central Ohio; past president Armed Forces Community Relations Council; past chancellor, Champion Lodge #518 K of P; member of Community Lodge #684 F&AM; Hilliard Grange #2715; Classic Car Club of America; Buckeye Packard Club; 16th Ward, Republican Committeeman.

Chappelear is the administrative assistant to the Franklin County Coroner, Columbus, OH.

ARTHUR CHRISTENSON, Staff Sergeant, was born May 24, 1916. He joined the service Nov. 7, 1941; assigned to Co. G, 148th Inf., 37th Div. and was stationed at Camp Wheeler, GA, Indiantown Gap, PA, San Francisco, Guadalcanal, New Georgia, Luzon, Philippines and Bougainville.

His memorable experience was Feb. 13, 1945, Manilla, Philippines, when a sniper bullet went through his helmet and creased the right side of his head.

Discharged May 21, 1945 as staff sergeant. He received the Infantry Combat Badge, Purple Heart, Silver Star, American Defense and Pacific-Asiatic Campaign with four Battle Stars.

Christenson is retired from farming but still living on his farm in Montevideo, MN. He is married and they have seven grown children.

ERSHEL C. CONRAD, T-5, was born March 19, 1921 at Wheeling, WV. He joined the Army Oct. 15, 1940; assigned to HQ Co., 1st Bn., 145th Inf. Regt., 37th Div.; stationed at Camp Shelby, MS; Indiantown Gap, PA, Fiji Islands, Guadalcanal, New Georgia, Bougainville, Luzon, Philippines.

Memorable Experiences: New Georgia Island-coming back from water pick-up with five gal. water can on his back and a sniper shot a hole in water can; Bougainville-in a foxhole with three members of his unit when a mortar shell landed at the edge of hole, he was the only one not wounded; Luzon Island, Lingayen Gulf-first boat, first wave to hit the beach; Clark Air Center, a 90mm shell hit within 10 feet and tore up stock of his rifle, put dents in his helmet; Manila, crossing the Pasig River, took part in battle for the walled city, advance patrol to secure Bilibib prison and released Filipino Nationals held there.

Discharged Oct. 3, 1945 as T-5. Received the Asiatic-Pacific with two Bronze Stars, American Defense Medal, Philippine Liberation Ribbon with one Bronze Star, Good Conduct with two Knots and Victory Medal.

Conrad is married and has three sons. He is a retired Mfg. eng/tool engineer.

JAMES P. COONEY, Staff Sergeant, was born Feb. 21, 1913 in Cleveland, OH. He joined the Army Jan. 21, 1941; assigned to 135th FA, Btry. B, 37th Div.; stationed at Camp Shelby, Indiantown Gap, Illinois, Oklahoma and Northern Solomons.

Discharged Sept. 26, 1945 as staff sergeant. Awards/Medals include WWII Victory, Good Conduct, American Defense, American Campaign and Asiatic-Pacific Campaign.

Cooney has been married 49 plus years and has three children and one grandchild. He is retired and lives in North Olmsted, OH.

DEAN H. COUPER, CWO, was born in Littleton, MA on March 4, 1913. He served Jan. 21, 1941 to Dec.

17, 1945; trained with the 121st Combat Engrs., 29th Div. at Ft. Meade, MD until April 1942 when he joined the 117th Engr. Combat Bn., 37th Div. at Indiantown Gap, PA.

Departed San Francisco in May 1942 for New Zealand, then to Fiji Islands, and Guadalcanal. On Sept. 28, 1942 in Fiji Islands, he accepted appointment as warrant officer, supply. On June 16, 1943, he witnessed over 100 Japanese planes shot down off shores of Guadalcanal.

Returned to the States in July 1943 and was assigned to 253rd Engr. Combat Bn. Trained at Camp Crowder, MO and Ft. Campbell, KY. Departed for England in October 1944, then to France and Germany as the 253rd Engr. Bn. was assigned to 7th Army. They were in Ulm, Germany when the European Conflict ended.

He was awarded the American Service Medal, EAME Medal and Asiatic-Pacific Service Medal.

Couper retired from the U.S. Government as accountant and auditor in 1970. He and his wife, Daphene, reside in Kensington, MD.

LACY B. CROUCH, Tech 5, was born Nov. 24, 1916 in Rockingham, NC. He joined the service Nov. 6, 1941; assigned to HQ Co., 1st Bn., 145th Inf., 37th Div. and was stationed at Camp Croft, SC for basic training; joined 37th Div. at Indiantown Gap; then to New Zealand, Fiji, Guadalcanal, New Georgia, Bougainville, etc.

Memorable Experiences: landing and battle on New Georgia; Hill 700 Bougainville; and time spent in Fiji Island.

Rotated to the States in September 1944 and was discharged Oct. 5, 1945 from Camp Blanding, FL. Received the Sharpshooter, Good Conduct, Combat Infantry Badge, Asiatic-Pacific Theater Medal and American Defense Service Medal.

Married since 1951 to Rosell; they have two daughters and each one has a son. He retired after 47 years in textile industry.

EDWARD F. CROZIER, Sergeant, was born Sept. 18, 1914 in Buffalo, NY. He joined the service Feb. 1, 1941; assigned to Co. G, 145th Inf., 37th Div.; stationed at Camp Shelby, MS; Indiantown Gap, PA, New Georgia, Bougainville and Philippines.

Memorable Experiences: when his name was drawn out of the hat to go home for a 45 day furlough (after cleaning up Manila) and when the soldier who was to go home with him was killed in action.

Discharged May 15, 1945 as sergeant. Received the Good Conduct Medal, MDS Ribbon, Asiatic-Pacific Theater Ribbon with two Bronze Stars, Philippine Liberation Ribbon and one Bronze Star.

Married over 51 years to Verna; they have two daughters and three grandchildren. He retired 16 years ago and is loving every minute of it.

ROBERT W. CURTIS, Sergeant, was born Feb. 1, 1925, in Windsor, VT. He served from July 31, 1943 to Jan. 15, 1946, and trained at Camp Wheeler, GA. In

37th Infantry Division—71

January 1944, he was sent to the South Pacific, landing on New Caledonia, then assigned to Co. K, 148th Inf. which he joined on Bougainville.

He participated in battles for the Cagayan Valley and Baguio and the invasion of Luzon. Contacted malaria at Manila and was wounded in the back from shrapnel during battle for Manila.

Received the Asiatic-Pacific Theater Campaign Ribbon with one Bronze Star, Philippine Liberation Ribbon with one Bronze Service Star and the Purple Heart.

Curtis is retired from the U.S. Postal Service and resides in Claremont, NH.

DURWARD B. DAVIS, Staff Sergeant, was born Dec. 29, 1912 in Bayonne, NJ. He joined the service May 23, 1942, and was stationed at Ft. Dix, NJ; Camp Croft, SC; Ft. McDowell, CA; Guadalcanal, New Georgia, Bougainville and Luzon.

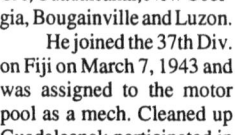

He joined the 37th Div. on Fiji on March 7, 1943 and was assigned to the motor pool as a mech. Cleaned up Guadalcanal; participated in battle for New Georgia; back to Guadalcanal; then Bouganville, Lingayen Gulf, Manila, Baggio, San Assidro, and was at Taggario when the war ended.

Discharged Dec. 30, 1945 as staff sergeant. He received the Good Conduct, Philippine Liberation, Bronze Arrowhead, WWII Victory Medal and Asiatic Victory Service Medal.

Married and has three children. He had his own business 26 years and worked 18 years as mech. in Bradley Beach, NJ. He retired in October 1990 and bought a house in Pennsylvania. He still keeps in contact with the widow of Dan Gerbrich (one of the drivers) and Louis Tobaz (went overseas together but then put in different companies).

EDGAR E. DAVIS, Private First Class, was born Aug. 6, 1921 in Youngtown, OH. He joined the National Guard in 1939; federal service in 1940, Army, rifle, machine gunner, BAR; assigned to Co. H, 145th Inf., 37th Div.; stationed at Camp Shelby, MS and Indiantown Gap, PA.

Participated in battles at Rendover, Munda, Bougainville and Manila. His memorable experiences include jungle fighting and beachhead at Lingayen.

Discharged June 15, 1945 with rank private first class. Received the Expert Infantry, Bronze Star, American Campaign, Good Conduct, Combat Infantry, National Defense, Asiatic-Pacific, WWII Victory, Unit Citation with Bronze Oak Leaf Cluster, Philippine Liberation and Philippine Presidential Citation.

Lives with his wife, Ruth, in Youngstown, OH; they have three children and 10 grandchildren. Retired from Teamsters in 1985, he drove 18 wheeler for 35 years. Enjoys fishing, does volunteer work at VA Clinic and belongs to AMVETS, DAV, VFW and CWV.

HAROLD E. DAVIS, Private First Class, was born in Tulsa, OK on April 14, 1923. He served from April 6, 1943 to Jan. 18, 1946; trained at Camp Roberts, CA; went to South Pacific in September 1943; landed at New Caledonia, New Hebrides and Guadalcanal, where he was assigned to the 37th Div., Co. F, 148th Inf.

Sent to Bougainville. Once across the river, Lt. Flood, Clyde Allen and Davis found a Japanese sending and receiving radio. Located inside, was the Japanese map of the entire island, including positions of antiaircraft. They turned these belongings over to their captain.

He participated in the invasion of Luzon and the battle of Manila, where he was wounded. He was hit in the left shoulder and arm by shrapnel.

Davis was awarded the Combat Infantry Badge, American Theater Ribbon, Asiatic-Pacific Ribbon with two Bronze Service Stars, Philippine Liberation Ribbon with one Bronze Service Star, WWII Victory Medal, Purple Heart Medal, Distinguished Unit Badge and one Bronze Arrowhead.

He is a retired painting and decorating contractor, and resides with his wife, Maxine, in San Leandro, CA.

HAROLD E. De FOREST, Private First Class, was born March 1, 1924, St. Catharines, Canada. He was assigned to Co. A, 129th Inf. 37th Div. and trained at Camp Wheeler, GA. Participated in battles at Bougainville, Solomon Islands, invasion of Luzon and the battle for Manila.

Discharged Nov. 30, 1945, with a disability from wounds received Feb. 10, 1945 in Manila. Obtained the rank private first class, mortar gunner. Received the Combat Infantry Badge, Bronze Star, Purple Heart, Asiatic-Pacific with two Campaign Stars, Philippine Liberation with one Campaign Star and Arrowhead, American Campaign, Good Conduct, WWII Victory and Presidential Unit Citation.

After discharge he took a job at Dodge Main Car Maker until 1947, then took a job with the *Detroit Times* newspaper, then Detroit News and retired after 30 years in 1989. He married May 24, 1947 and has four children, nine grandchildren and four great-grandchildren. They all reside in Michigan. He is a life member of DAV and the 37th Div. Assoc.

WILLIAM J. DEMMER, Tech Sergeant, was born and raised in St. Louis, MO. He entered the service in February 1942 and was assigned to Co. I, 129th Inf. and remained with them until December 1945.

He trained in Camp Forest, TN and served in the Fiji Islands, New Hebrides, New Zealand, New Caledonia, Guadalcanal, Bougainville and Luzon. He participated in the battles on Bougainville and Luzon. He was awarded the Combat Infantry Badge, Bronze Star Medal and was promoted to battalion sergeant major.

As an automatic rifleman, he was a member of a reinforced platoon which was assigned reconnaissance and combat deep in enemy territory on Bougainville in April 1944. The mission was made more intriguing since it was guided by a native over trails known only by the natives. The engagements encountered were successful.

He retired from electric and gas utility supervision and resides with his wife, Julie, in Hazelwood, MO.

JOSEPH E. DEWHIRST, Sergeant, was born in Cincinnati, OH on April 4, 1918. He served in Co. D, 147th Inf., 37th Div. from Feb. 1, 1941 until June 26, 1945. He trained at Camp Shelby, MS. In April 1942, he went to the South Pacific and served at Tongatabu, New Caledonia, New Hebrides, Guadalcanal, Florida, Tulagi, Upolu, Emirau and Iwo Jima.

Involved in the Battle of Guadalcanal from Nov. 4, 1942 through June 1943. Made landing with 4th Marines at Emirau in 1944. In the Battle of Iwo Jima from Feb. 26, 1945 until June 1945.

In March of 1945 at Iwo, his good friend Sgt. Paul Firecloud, a full-blooded Sioux Indian from the Fort Totten Reservation in North Dakota, saved his life by wrenching a heavy, water-cooled machine gun from it's position and coming to his assistance after he had been immobilized and deafened by grenades of the attacking Japanese. Firecloud, a very powerful man, fired the heavy weapon with it's tripod still attached on full automatic while holding it in his arms. He fired the entire 250 round belt cutting down the numerous attackers.

Sgt. Dewhirst was involved in the taking of over 100 POWs on Iwo. He was acting platoon sergeant and at times platoon leader for over two years and was offered a direct commission. Awards included Combat Infantry Badge, Theater Ribbons with three Battle Stars, etc. He is retired and is living on a farm near Morrow, OH with his wife, Sybil.

RALPH T. DILULLO, Tech 5, was born May 22, 1915 in Italy. He joined the USA Feb. 6, 1941 and assigned to Co. M, 145th Inf., 37th Div. Stationed at Camp Shelby, MS; Ft. Story, VA; Northern Solomons; Fiji Islands, Guadalcanal, New Georgia and Bougainville.

His memorable experience was staying alive during his nearly three years in the South Pacific Theater of Operations.

Discharged Sept. 21, 1945 as tech 5. He received

72—37th Infantry Division

the American Defense Service Medal, Good Conduct Medal, Asiatic Pacific Theater Service Medal with one Bronze Service Star and Combat Infantry Badge.

He and his wife, Rosa, raised five sons and three daughters. He retired from B.F. Goodrich in 1979 after 39 years of service. DiLullo passed away July 5, 1986 and is buried in Akron, OH.

JOHN H. DOCHERTY, Captain, was born Nov. 11, 1917 in Youngstown, OH. He joined the Army Sept. 1, 1944; basic training was at Camp Wolters, TX; assigned to the 5th Div., European Theater. Reassigned Office Military Govt. for Germany (Berlin).

Transferred from USAR to 37th Div., Co. D, 145th Inf., 2nd lieutenant, April 13, 1949. Participated in Korean Conflict and assigned to HQ Co., 1st Cav. Div., Japan as 1st lieutenant on Jan. 26, 1953.

Returned to the States and assigned company commander, Co. D, 145th, 37th Div. in August 1953. Retired from 83rd Div. H&H Co. on July 1, 1962. Attended two service schools, TIS ALOCC, Ft. Benning, GA.

Left the service in September 1964 as captain, AUS. He received the Combat Infantry Badge, Good Conduct Medal, WWII Victory Medal, EAME Theater Medal, Army of Occupation Medal (Europe), Korea and Japan.

Retired from the Dollar Savings and Trust Company and USA. Plays a little golf and travels with his wife, Jean. They have two sons and three granddaughters.

WILLIAM M. DUKE, Sergeant, was born March 4, 1920 in Arcadia, FL. He joined the service Jan. 28, 1942 and was assigned to the 136th FA HQ BTRY, 37th Div. His stations include Indiantown Gap, PA; New Zealand; Fiji Islands; Guadalcanal; New Georgia; Bougainville; and Luzon, P.I.

Discharged Oct. 12, 1945, as sergeant. He received the Purple Heart and Bronze Star with three OLCs.

Duke is a semi-retired doctor of optometry. He and his wife, Laurie, have three daughters: Lynn, Lisa and Leigh.

WILLIAM M. ENRIGHT (CPL) was born in Chicago, Il Sept. 13, 1924. Served March 18, 1943 to Dec. 23, 1945. Trained with the 75th Inf. Div. at Ft. Leonard Wood, MO, until September 1943. Departed San Francisco in September for New Caledonia, and then to Guadalcanal. Assigned to Co. H, 148th Inf. Landed at Bougainville Nov. 8, 1943. Landed at Lingayen, participated in battles at Manila, Baguio and Cagayan Valley. Blisters came with the rescue of Bilibid Prison prioners in February 1945, after our 125 mile march down from Lingayen. Met an Australian lieutenant who had been captured at Hong Kong in December 1941.

He was awarded the CIB, Asiatic/Pacific Ribbon, Bronze Star Medal, Philippine Liberation Ribbon, Good Conduct Ribbon, Distinguished Unit Citation, WWII Medal. He is a retired colonel after 34 years of active and reserve duty. He and his wife, Colleen, reside in San Leandro, CA.

CHARLIE B. ESTES, Tech 5, was born Aug. 21, 1916.

He joined the Service Co., 147th Inf. in 1941; trained at Camp Wolters, TX; and was stationed at Camp Shelby, MS; Indiantown Gap, PA; New Hebrides; Panama Canal; New Caledonia; Emirau; Gaudalcanal; etc.

His whole time in service was memorable. Discharged Aug. 30, 1945 as tech 5. He received all the usual awards/medals.

Estes is married and has four children. He is presently retired and lives in Avery, TX.

BYRON FARWELL, 1st Sergeant, was born June 20, 1921 in Manchester, IA. He joined the service May 1936 and served seven years in the Army in WWII and the Korean War. He was a first sergeant of a firing battery in the field artillery at the age of 20 and was commissioned in the Corps of Engineers, 10 days before his 21st birthday.

At 23 he was the youngest captain of engineers in the Mediterranean Theater. He took part in "Torch," the invasion of Morocco, and served three years in North Africa and Italy.

During the Korean War, he served in the Ordnance Corps and was commandant of the Ordnance New Vehicle Maintenance School.

Farwell earned a master's degree from the University of Chicago and is the author of 11 books, and of numerous articles and reviews. He has taught at the University College of Chicago, University of Detroit and has lectured at many colleges, including the National Defense University and the Army War College.

He is married to the former Ruth Saxby; they make their home in Hillsboro, VA and have three grown children.

AARON N. FEINMAN, Private First Class, was born March 10, 1919, in Kings County, Brooklyn, NY. He joined the service in September 1941; assigned to the 117th Engrs., C Co., 37th Div.; stationed at Ft. Belvoir, VA; Ft. Meade, MD; Indiantown Gap, PA.

Participated in battles in Northern Solomons and Luzon. Discharged Oct. 19, 1945 as private first class. He received the Good Conduct Medal, Philippine Liberation and American Defense Service Medal with one Bronze Star.

Hairstylist for 42 years, presently retired and makes his home in Pawtucket, RI. He has a son, daughter and three grandchildren.

WARREN FITCH, Staff Sergeant, was born May 20, 1916 in Belvidere, IL. He enlisted Nov. 25, 1940; basic at Ft. Snelling, MN; Rec. Center duty at Camp Robinson, AR; Ft. Leavenworth, KS; and Ft. Leonardwood, MO.

Sent to New Caledonia Nov. 6, 1943 and assigned to Abel Co., 145th Regt. at Bougainville on Dec. 4, 1943. He was wounded March 9, 1944 on Hill 700. Landed Lingayen, Philippines D+1 and wounded in Walled City, Manila, on Feb. 24, 1945.

Discharged Oct. 11, 1945 as staff sergeant. He received the American Defense Service Ribbon, Asiatic-Pacific Theater Ribbon with two Bronze Battle Stars, Philippine Defense Ribbon with one Bronze Star, three Overseas Service Bars, one Service Stripe, Good Conduct Medal and Purple Heart with two OLCs.

Fitch is single and lives in Poplar Grove, IL.

OSCAR FLATELAND, Private First Class, was born in Trail, MN. He joined the service in February 1942 and assigned to Co. G, 129th Inf., 37th Div. Stationed at Camp Forrest, TN; Fiji; Guadalcanal and Bougainville.

Flateland was discharged October 1945 as private first class. He received the Purple Heart for shrapnel wounds.

A retired carpenter, he makes his home in Oklle, MN. Both his parents came from Norway.

ROBERT F. FOOR, Warrant Officer (jg), was born Sept. 5, 1915 in Slough, OH. He joined the OHNG in September 1940; Army, Communications, 37th Div. He was stationed at Camp Shelby, MS; New Zealand; Indiantown Gap, PA; Fiji Islands; Guadalcanal; Solomons; Bougainville; New Georgia; Philippines.

Enlisted with HQ Co., 145th Inf. in 1940; left for the Pacific in 1942 and stayed with the same company until the war was over. He advanced from private to warrant officer in 1943, communications officer in 1944 until his discharge in 1946.

Awards/Medals: Combat Infantry Badge, two Bronze Stars, Asiatic-Pacific Theater, Philippine Liberation and WWII Victory.

Was a dairy plant manager until retirement in 1980. Married to Molly Lou Lowry for 47 plus years; they have three sons: James, Robert and Mike. They make their home in Manchester, MD.

GAIL E. FOX, Staff Sergeant, was drafted Jan. 25, 1941, Army, Co. K, 147th Inf., 37th Div. He and Vernon Pierce left Springfield, OH for Ft. Hayes, OH where they boarded the train for Camp Shelby, MS. While waiting for the train, Fox said he wasn't too happy about leaving for the Army. He soon made corporal and later was made sergeant.

On the way to the South Pacific, Fox said to Pierce, "I wonder how many of us will be making a one-way trip?" Fox was leading his platoon when the Japanese caught them in a crossfire of machine guns on Guadalcanal, Feb. 4, 1943, and he was killed. He received the Purple Heart. Pierce was proud to see Gail's name on the Honor Roll of KIAs at Springfield High School where he graduated in 1937. Rest in peace Gail, we miss you. *Written by Vernon Pierce, Co. K, 147th Inf.*

FRANK L. FRANCISCO, Corporal, was born March 18, 1918 in Gardner, IL. He joined the Army Jan. 19, 1942; assigned to Co. H, 145th Inf., 37th Div.; stationed in the Pacific Theater of Operations from May 1942 to September 1945.

Participated in battles in Northern Solomons and Luzon. Was discharged Oct. 12, 1945 as corporal. Received the Asiatic-Pacific Theater Ribbon with two Bronze Stars, Combat Infantry Badge, Philippine Liberation Ribbon with one Bronze Star and Bronze Star Medal.

Francisco is a retired electrical contractor. Married since April 20, 1968 to Lorraine; they have one son, Wayne and make their home in Pontiac, IL.

STANLEY A. FRANKEL, Major, was born Dec. 8, 1918 in Dayton, OH. He joined the service in January 1941; assigned to 148th Inf. Regt., 37th Div.; stationed at Camp Shelby, Fiji Islands, Guadalcanal, New Georgia, Bougainville, and in the Philippines: Manila, Baguio and Cagayan Valley.

Memorable experience was at the end of WWII when he wrote the history of 37th Div.

His awards/medals include the Combat Infantry Badge, Bronze Star with two OLCs and Presidential Unit Citation.

Frankel is a professor at Pace University and Baruch College; columnist for *This Week* paper; consultant to Ogden Corp. and manning Selvage Lee PR firm. Married 46 plus years to same wife; they have two sons (lawyer and CPA) and daughter is ATT PR director).

MILO FREY, Private First Class, was born Feb. 24, 1924 in Cambridge, WI. Army service time was from Feb. 10, 1943 to Jan. 6, 1946; basic training at Camp Roberts, CA; assigned to Co. C, 145th Inf. on New Georgia. The most despairing time in his life was the three or four days and nights spent on Hill 700, Bougainville in March of 1944.

Some better times remembered: Father Evans coming to their camp with a deck of cards for a good, enjoyable game of "500;" watching a sergeant from HQ play volleyball. That was a fun time; also, he was the best volleyball player in the world. If you really wanted an exciting time, you could volunteer to be an umpire between two company softball teams. WOW!

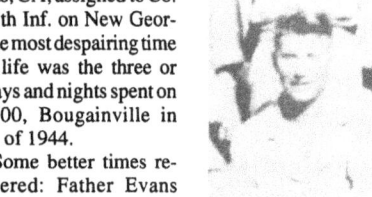

After reading many history books on the subject, he must admit they had the finest leadership of any division in WWII.

A. JAY FUGITT JR., Buck Sergeant, was born Oct. 2, 1924 in Long Beach, CA. He joined the service March 5, 1943 and was a truck driver with the 37th Div. QM Co. Basic training was at Ft. Francis E. Warren, Cheyenne, WY.

Overseas, he participated in battles at Bougainville and Lingayen Gulf. He was discharged Dec. 23, 1945 as buck sergeant.

Married for the second time and celebrated their 25th on Aug. 15, 1994. Between them, they have six children, 11 grandchildren and six great-grandchildren. He is a semi-retired accountant and lives in La Verne, CA.

IVERS LEONARD FUNK, Major, was born Wakatomika, OH on Sept. 15, 1911. He enlisted in Btry. F, 134th FA on Jan. 17, 1927, commissioned in 1939 and went to Camp Shelby. With the 140th FA BN, Indiantown Gap, San Francisco, left aboard the *Coolidge* to Fiji, Guadalcanal, Russells and New Georgia, where he was wounded as a forward observer with the 148th Inf.

Later went to Bougainville, where he was credited with more time as observer with the Infantry than any other artilleryman.

Returned to the States on a cadre with Lt. Cols. Haines and Shafer and Capt. Boldrick. After the Artillery Advanced Course, he commanded an 8" howitzer battery and went to Italy with it. He remained in the service, retiring in 1960 and earned nine medals. He had tours in Germany, Korea and many Stateside stations.

CARLOTT O. FUNSETH, Staff Sergeant, was born Jan. 4, 1918 in Northwood, ND. He joined the Army Feb. 21, 1942; assigned to 37th Div.; stationed at Camp Forrest, TN, Fiji Islands, New Hebrides, Guadalcanal, Luzon, Bougainville, Cagayan Valley, Clark Field, Ft. Stotsenberg, Manila and Baguio.

His memorable experiences: aiding in rescue of civilians inside Walled City of Manila; and first days in Manila when starving children watched them eat.

Discharged Oct. 8, 1945 as staff sergeant. Funseth is married and has three children and nine grandchildren. He is a retired farmer in Northwood, ND, but still active.

HARRY E. GAJEWSKI, Private First Class, was born in Milwaukee, WI on Sept. 20, 1921. He was drafted Oct. 20, 1942; inducted Oct. 27, 1942; entered into service at Fort Sheridan, IL and sent to Fort Sill, OK for basic and artillery training.

He was sent to Camp Stoneman, CA, then shipped overseas to New Caledonia to join the 37th Div. B Btry., 140th FA BN on Guadalcanal in August 1943. His first battle was at Bougainville on Nov. 8, 1943; sent to Philippines; and participated in battles at Lingayen Gulf, Clark Field, Manila, Baguio, Cagayan Valley.

He was wounded on June 21, 1945 at Cagayan Valley and flown back to the States. Awarded the Bronze Star, Purple Heart, Asiatic-Pacific Ribbon, Philippine Liberation Medal, Good Conduct Medal and WWII Medal. Discharged from Schick General Hospital on Jan. 31, 1946.

Retired and lives in Milwaukee with his loving wife, Anne.

EDWARD C. GILLETTE, born in Columbus, OH on Dec. 28, 1921 and passed away April 13, 1991 in Houston, TX. He joined the OHNG in 1937, 37th Div. HQ Btry., 136th FA. They were mobilized Oct. 15, 1940 and sent to Camp Shelby, MS.

He served in the battles of New Guinea and Luzon. Awarded the American Defense Service Medal, American Theater Ribbon, Asiatic-Pacific Theater Ribbon with two Bronze Stars, Philippine Liberation Medal and Ribbon, Good Conduct Ribbon, Meritorious Unit Award and Victory Medal. He was discharged on Dec. 7, 1945.

Retired as state examiner, Auditor's Office, state of Ohio and last resided in Katy, TX. He was rated 80% disabled by the Veterans Administration at time of his death, April 13, 1991, in Houston, TX. He is survived by his widow, Eleanor; daughter, Mrs. Scott (Cynthia) Johnson; and two grandchildren, Sherri and Scott Johnson.

JAMES A. GLOBE, Staff Sergeant, was born Jan. 7, 1923 at Columbus, OH. He joined the service in April 1938; assigned to HQ Co. Special Troops, 37th Div., Infantry; and stationed at Camp Shelby, MS; Indiantown Gap, PA; New Zealand, Fiji, Guadalcanal, New Georgia, Bougainville and Luzon.

Participated in battles at New Georgia, Bougainville and Luzon. His memorable experience was the day in September 1945 when the captain called him and said his bags were in the truck and he was going home.

Discharged in October 1945 as staff sergeant. Received the Combat Infantry Badge and Bronze Star.

Married Margaret and they have two married daughters, Marian (John Hurd) and Merry (Mark Whiting), and four grandchildren.

NORBERT J. GOODMAN, Private First Class, was born May 4, 1924 in Los Angeles, CA. He joined the Army March 19, 1943; assigned to Co. H, 129th Inf., 37th Div.; and stationed at Fort Leonard Wood,

MO. Participated in battles at Bouganville and Luzon. His memorable experience was receiving shrapnel in the face at cemetery near Baguio. He was discharged Dec. 19, 1945 as private first class.

Retired, he is married and has six children.

JOHN A. GREEN, Captain, was born June 19, 1922 at Auburn, IN. He joined the National Guard in 1939 and Federal Service in October 1940; assigned to Army Infantry, 37th Div., 148th Inf. Regt., Co. H&D; and was stationed at Camp Shelby, MS; Indiantown Gap, PA, Fiji Islands, Guadalcanal, New Georgia, Bougainville and Philippines.

Participated in the clean-up of Guadalcanal, New Georgia, Bougainville and Philippines. Was hit outside Baguio after getting field commission in Manila, March 1945 and spent two years in hospitals.

He had many memorable experiences; but the most vivid was the horror of Japanese bodies piled up like cordwood on Hill 700 (or maybe 500) in Bougainville.

Retired for physical disability on July 23, 1947 as captain. He received various theater ribbons, two Bronze Stars, Unit Citation and Purple Heart.

Retired as an officer in RCA and now does consulting. He and his wife Heide have two sons and one daughter.

DONALD D. GREFFE, Tech Sergeant, was born June 20, 1919 in Taylorville, IL. He joined the service April 18, 1941; served and trained with the 129th Inf. of the 33rd Div. at Camp Forrest, TN. He moved to Camp Stoneman, CA in August 1942 and left for overseas on Sept. 1, 1942, with I Co., 129th Inf.

Went to Fiji Island and the 129th Inf. joined the 37th Div. and moved to New Hebrides Island, then to Guadalcanal, Bougainville, Solomon Island. Participated in the invasion of Luzon and the battle for Manila.

He was awarded the Combat Infantry Badge, American Defense, Asiatic-Pacific Ribbon with two Bronze Service Stars and one Bronze Arrowhead, Victory Medal, Bronze Star with two OLC, Good Conduct Medal, Philippine Liberation Ribbon with one Bronze Service Star and pre-Pearl Harbor Medal. Was discharged June 1, 1945 as tech sergeant.

Joined the ILNG on Dec. 7, 1951 and stayed in until June 1, 1963. He and his wife, Grace, have one daughter Annette. They live in Taylorville and he has been farming since WWII to the present. Annette is married to Judge Ron Spears and they have a son Donald.

FREDERICK H. GROOMS, Sergeant, was born March 29, 1915 in Goes, OH. He joined the Army Jan. 25, 1941; assigned to 147th Inf., 37th Div.; stationed at Camp Shelby for basic training; and went by train to Indiantown Gap.

Left Indiantown Gap for Tonga Tabo on May 10, 1942. Boarded USS *President Hayes* in November 1942 for Guadalcanal front lines. He was on the front lines for three weeks. Remembers going three days without food and filling canteen with muddy water and adding iodine before drinking. After Guadalcanal went to British Samoa and New Caledonia for rest, then to Emirau, Iwo Jima and Saipan until release from service.

Discharged Sept. 24, 1945 as sergeant. He received the Asiatic-Pacific Theater Ribbon with three Bronze Stars, American Defense Service Medal and the Good Conduct Ribbon.

Retired from Hobart Corp. as shipping clerk. He lives with his wife, Evelyn, in Greenville, OH. He enjoys playing golf, bowling and traveling.

EUGENE R. GUY (BUD), Staff Sergeant, was born Dec. 14, 1927 in Youngstown, OH. He joined the USN on July 29, 1945; assigned to Co. D, 145th Inf., 37th Div.; squad leader machine gun platoon; stationed at USN Training Center, Great Lakes, IL and Guam, M.I.

He completed nine and a half years active and Reserve duty. Memorable experience was the Ohio National Guard. Left the service Feb. 12, 1958 as staff sergeant. He received the American Theater, Asiatic-Pacific and Victory Medal.

After 31 years, he retired as a crane operator. Spent six years with Culligan Water Conditioning. He lives in Hubbard, OH and has three daughters: Jane, Sandra and Diane, and one son George.

EDWARD TYLER HALSEY, Master Sergeant, was born in Dayton, OH on March 9, 1917. He served from July 1936 to Oct. 3, 1945 in the Army. Served in Btry. B, 136th FA of OHNG, which was mobilized Oct. 15, 1940. He trained at Camp Shelby, MS as supply sergeant. After Pearl Harbor was bombed, the 37th Div. (one of the oldest with training) was moved to Indiantown Gap to leave for the European Theater. The boat they were to ship out on was bombed, so they were sent to San Francisco, CA to leave for the Pacific Theater.

They sailed for 29 days, zig-zagging across the Pacific. Some of them were unloaded in New Zealand and others in Australia. They were in New Zealand seven weeks, then went to the Fiji Islands for six months of jungle training. The 37th was then moved to the Solomon Islands, where they were bombed almost nightly.

They were the first in Guadalcanal in 1943, next took the island of New Georgia. Their first sergeant was hit by shrapnel and sent back to New Caledonia to recuperate. He was appointed acting first sergeant of Btry. B, 136th FA along with his regular job as supply sergeant in the New Georgia Campaign. He then went back to Guadalcanal to rest. Next was moved into Bougainville, where they took only 10 square miles near an active volcano and a string of mountains. While on the island, he was selected to return to the States on a rotation plan.

In the USA, he was assigned to the Tank Destroyers Board in Camp Hood, TX. He was promoted to master sergeant in late 1944. After the war, the Tank Destroyer Board was deactivated and the soldiers discharged.

He returned to his parents' home in Dayton, OH and to work at Lau Blower Co. which was merged with Philips Industries. Retired on March 1, 1981 and now works part-time in a grocery to keep active. He is married and has seven children, 15 grandchildren and one great-grandchild.

EDWIN E. HANSON, Private First Class, was born and raised in Central Illinois (Urbana and Peoria). At age 17 in 1943, he enlisted in the Army Reserves for two semesters in college. After Combat Engr. basic training at Fort Leonard Wood, he was assigned to the replacement pool for the 37th Inf. Div.

Via New Caledonia and Bougainville, he reached the 148th Regt. in January 1945 in Manila. He served in F Co. in northern Luzon until the end of WWII. He was returned home with infectious hepatitis in December 1945 and discharged upon recovery in 1946.

Awards received include the Bronze Star Medal, Combat Infantry Badge, Asiatic-Pacific Theater Ribbon with one Bronze Battle Star, Bronze Service Arrowhead, Philippine Liberation Ribbon with one Bronze Battle Star.

After graduating from Purdue University, he had a 35 year career at Caterpillar Tractor Co., finishing as staff engineer, Research Dept. He and his wife, Lyn, live at Peoria, IL.

GEORGE LEWIS HANSON, Staff Sergeant, was born Feb. 8, 1924 in Ogden, UT. He joined the service Dec. 23, 1942; assigned to Co. I, 129th Inf. Regt., 37th Inf. Div.; stationed at Camp Wolters, TX, Espiritu Santo, New Hebrides, Bougainville, Solomons, Luzon and Philippines.

Most memorable experience was landing at Lingayen in Co. I; they were first men ashore.

Discharged Dec. 23, 1945 as staff sergeant. Received the Asiatic-Pacific Ribbon, Bronze Star, Philippine Liberation Ribbon and Good Conduct Ribbon.

He and his wife are currently in Australia as missionaries for the LDS Church and will be there for one a half years. They have three daughters.

FRANK L. HARROP, Sergeant, was born in Dayton, OH on Jan. 6, 1925. He served from March 22, 1943 to Dec. 23, 1945; trained at Fort Leonard Wood, MO; and on Oct. 21, 1943, went to the South Pacific.

Landed at New Caledonia, Guadalcanal where he was assigned to Co. B, 129th Inf., 37th Div. Landed at Bougainville where he was awarded the Bronze Star and Purple Heart Medals. Participated in the invasion of Luzon and was wounded the second time at Fort Stotsenburg where he received the Silver Star medal.

Also participated in the Battle of Manila, Cagayan Valley and Baguio.

Harrop was awarded the Combat Infantry Badge, Silver Star Medal, Bronze Star Medal, Purple Heart Medal with OLC, Meritorious Unit Badge, Good Conduct Medal, American Theater Ribbon, Asiatic-Pacific Ribbon with two Bronze Stars, one Bronze Arrowhead, Philippine Liberation Ribbon with one Bronze Star and Victory Medal.

Frank and his wife, Maryhelen, are retired and live in Dayton, OH. They have a daughter and son, Pamela and Steven, and two grandchildren, Melissa and Michael.

GERALD RICHARD HASTY, Lieutenant Colonel, was born on April 12, 1926 in Pekin Tazewell County, IL. He volunteered and entered the Army at Fort Sheridan, IL on Aug. 9, 1944. (His great-grandfather, Robert J. Hasty, served under Gen. Sheridan at the battle of Missionary Ridge in 1863.) Gerald Hasty completed infantry basic training at Camp Hood, TX.

After basic he was shipped to Hollandia, New Guinea then to Leyte, P.I. His first real taste of hostile action was on Luzon with the 37th Div. during a surprise, mid-night air raid. As the division continued its rapid drive to and the subsequent liberation of Manila, he saw the newly released prisoners from Bilibid and Cabantuan prisons.

Later, while moving up the Cagayan Valley, during a daylight recon patrol, he was captured; later freed by advancing U.S. troops. As a 19 year old corporal, he continued to fight with the 37th until the division returned home. They sailed under the Golden Gate Bridge just in time for Christmas 1945.

Infantry Officer's Basic Course at Fort Benning was next, then came his first station as a platoon leader with the 17th Constabulary Sqdn. (Separate) in Russian blockaded Berlin. He commanded the first replacement troops to be flown into the besieged city of Berlin. A cold-war experience of detention by Russian MPs while driving on the open Autobahn in the East Zone of occupied Germany (1950) will long remain a part of his memory.

Assignments of particular significance include the Army General Staff, the Office of the Secretary of Defense and the Joint Staff, UN Command. At this point in his career (1974), he requested retirement. He had advanced through the ranks to lieutenant colonel, Regular Army. WWII (Pacific): an M-1 rifle; blockaded Berlin (cold war); Platoon; Korea A Co.; Vietnam (19 months); A Bn., Stateside; an Army depot with a world-wide distribution mission of ammunition, POL, and heavy Marine equipment. He received Silver Jump Wings, Legion of Merit with OLC, Purple Heart with OLC, Good Conduct Medal and others.

Has Ph.D, LLB, DD (hon.) degrees; Armed Forces Staff College; Air War College; Mensa and he is listed in Who's Who in America Law. The year 1974 found him enjoying college level and graduate level teaching. He closed his new career during the summer of 1986 and was granted Professor Emeritus status in 1990.

MARTIN D. HEARST, Tech 5, was born Aug. 1, 1919 in Boston, MA. He joined the service Jan. 15, 1942; assigned to 140th FA, 37th Div.; stationed at Fiji, Guadalcanal, Russell Islands, New Georgia and Bouganville. Participated in battles at New Georgia, Bougainville and Luzon.

His memorable experience was leaving from San Francisco in 1942 and returning to States in 1945. Discharged Oct. 14, 1945 as tech 5. He received the Good Conduct, Asiatic-Pacific, WWII Medal and Philippine Liberation Ribbon.

Hearst is retired and lives in Framingham, MA. He is married and has three daughters and six grandchildren.

GEORGE W. HEIER, Sergeant, was born Feb. 9, 1925 in South Gibson, PA. He joined the service April 6, 1943; squad leader (sergeant) Co. D, 129th Inf.; stationed at Fort Leonard Wood, MO; New Caledonia; Guadalcanal; Bougainville and Philippines. Participated in battles at Luzon, Northern Solomons and Southern Philippines. Memorable experience was amphibious landing on Luzon.

Discharged Dec. 31, 1945 as sergeant. He received the Asiatic-Pacific Service Medal with Bronze Arrowhead, Bronze Star Medal, Good Conduct and Victory Medal.

Heier is retired, lives in Binghamton, NY; he is married, has four daughters and three sons.

CARL R. HEIL, Staff Sergeant, was born in St. Marys, OH on Nov. 21, 1918. He joined OHNG, HQ 3rd BN, 148th Inf., May 2, 1936. Went to Camp Shelby on Oct. 15, 1940 and departed San Francisco May 26, 1942 via *President Coolidge* for the Fiji Islands.

Sent to Espiritu Santo, New Hebrides to form the 1st Bn., 129th Inf., 37th Div., assigned to Co. A. and joined the rest of 37th Div. on Bougainville. Departed December 1944 and landed Lingayen Gulf on Jan. 9, 1945. Participated in battles of Camiling, Clark Field, Fort Stotsenburg and Manila.

He was wounded in battle of Manila on Feb. 12, 1945 and April 21, 1945 was sent back to the States. He was discharged from Newton D. Baker General Hospital on Feb. 16, 1946. Was awarded the Purple Heart, Bronze Star, Philippine Liberation, Combat Infantry Badge, Asiatic-Pacific Theater Ribbon, American Theater Ribbon, American Defense Ribbon, Good Conduct Ribbon and Victory Medal.

ELMER HEINDL, (Chaplain) Lieutenant Colonel, was born June 14, 1910 in Rochester, NY. He joined the Army on March 13, 1942, chaplain. (1942) BIRTC, Anniston, AL; Fiji Islands. (1943) 145th Inf., 37th Div., Fiji; 148th Inf., 37th Div., OHNG; Guadalcanal - New Georgia (combat); Bougainville (combat).

In 1944 he left for Philippines; (1945) Lingayen Gulf, liberation of Philippines (combat); liberation of Manila. (1946) Ft. Dix, NJ; Rhodes General Hospital, NY (suffered malaria attack); 2nd Army, Governors Island, NY; Aberdeen Proving Grounds, MD.

Retired from active service as major in July 1948. Was Reserve Chaplain, 98th Div., 391st Regt. in 1949; division chaplain, 98th Reserve Div. in 1958 and retired from Active Reserves in 1970. Still serving in retirement as chaplain of many veteran associations.

Life member of Military Chaplains Assoc., Legion of Valor (DSC), 37th Div. Veterans Assoc., ROA, TROA, VFW, and American Legion. Member of 40 and 8 - 111, United Veterans of Monroe Co. Chaplain, Memorial and Executive Council Chaplain, 7th District USA Retiree Council, 98th Div. Retiree and 391st Officers Assoc. He is honorary member of New York State Guard, Marine Corps League and MOPH.

His awards include the Distinguished Service Cross, Silver Star, Legion of Merit, Bronze Stars (valor), Distinguished Unit Emblem, American Campaign Medal, Asiatic-Pacific Campaign, WWII Victory Medal, Armed Forces Reserve Medal, Bronze Arrowhead, Philippine Liberation Medal with one Bronze Star and Philippine Presidential Commendation.

Single clergyman with Rochester Diocese, St. Charles Bomomeo, Greece, NY.

WILFRED D. HENDERSHOT, Tech Sergeant, was born 1918 in Malaga and graduated from high school in Beallsville, OH. He volunteered for the draft

on Jan. 23, 1941 and was assigned to Btry. H, 136th FA Camp Shelby. Assigned to HQ 140th FA, Indiantown Gap, PA and later transferred to adjutant general's office. He shipped from San Francisco May 1942 on the *President Coolidge*. Served in the Fiji Islands, Guadalcanal, Bougainville, New Georgia and Luzon.

As personnel technician, AG Office, he was awarded the Bronze Star Medal for meritorious service. He rotated from Luzon in June and was discharged on June 21, 1945. Was employed with War Manpower Commission Wheeling from 1945 until that service was returned to state control in 1946. Continued employment with the West Virginia Dept. of Employment Security as Veterans Employment Representative, manager and field supervisor.

He retired June 1980 after more than 34 years of service. He holds life membership in Wheeling Post #1, the American Legion.

He and his wife, Betty, reside in Wheeling and have four children and five grandchildren.

ROBERT H. HENIGAN, Tech 4, was born Aug. 20, 1924 in Fullerton, CA. He enlisted Dec. 15, 1942 at Fort Crook, NE. After training at Camp Kohler and Western Signal Corps School, Davis, CA, he departed Camp Stoneman on May 11, 1944 and arrived at New Caledonia on May 26.

In June, via Guadalcanal, he arrived on Bougainville and was assigned to the 37th Cav. Recon. Troop as radio operator and machine gunner. He participated in patrols to Kuraio Mission. In 1945 the Recon Troop spearheaded the 37th Div.'s drive to Manila, mopped up the northern suburbs, shuttled infantry on the road to Baguio, led the drive up the Cagayan Valley, and in July and August ran foot patrols into the Sierra Madre Mountains.

He was awarded the Distinguished Unit Citation and the Bronze Star. Discharged Dec. 20, 1945, Fort Logan, CO.

A retired college English teacher, he resides with his wife, Avis, in Springfield, MO.

CHARLES A. HENNE, Colonel, was born and raised in St. Mary's, OH. He enlisted in 1935 and was commissioned in February 1940. He served continuously with the 148th Inf. until December 1945. He held positions in the 37th Div. as platoon leader, company XO, company commander (Cos. K, M and L) and XO 3/148th and commander 1/148th.

His WWII overseas service included Fiji, Guadalcanal, New Georgia, Bougainville, Luzon, P.I. (Lingayen, Great Central Plain, Manila, Baguio, Balete Pass and the Cagayan Valley). He was never wounded.

Awards include the Combat Infantry Badge, five Bronze Stars, two Legion of Merits and numerous citations, ribbons and badges. He is a graduate of many service schools including the Army War College and he also served in West Germany and Vietnam.

After 32 years of continuous serve, he retired and resides with his wife, Jule, in Gilbert, AZ.

JOHN T. HERMAN, Staff Sergeant, was born March 31, 1923 in Vinton, IA. He joined the Army

April 25, 1944; assigned to Co. E, 147th Inf. Regt., rifleman 60mm, mortar leader; and stationed at Camp Roberts, CA; New Caledonia, Iwo Jima and Okinawa.

His memorable experience was when attached to the 3rd Marines on Iwo Jima.

Discharged April 10, 1946 as staff sergeant. His awards include the Combat Infantry Badge, Bronze Star Medal, Victory Ribbon, Expert Infantryman Badge, American Theater, Navy Unit Commendation on Iwo Jima, Asiatic-Pacific Ribbon and Good Conduct Medal.

Semi-retired, he still farms 235 acres in La Porte City, IA. His wife is deceased.

ALFRED J. HERVIEUX JR., Private First Class, was born in Lowell, MA on Jan. 10, 1920. He attended school in Lowell, MA and enlisted in the Army on Jan. 17, 1942. He took his training in Fayetteville, NC; joined the 37th Div.; and was assigned to the 136th HQ Btry. FA in March 1942 in Harrisburgh, PA.

Went overseas in May 1942 to New Zealand, Fiji Island, Guadalcanal, New Georgia, Bougainville and Solomon Island. He participated in the invasion of Luzon and the battle of Manila. He was discharged in October 1945 and while serving he received the Silver Star for Gallantry in Manila, along with the Asiatic-Pacific Campaign Ribbon, two Bronze Stars, Philippine Liberation Ribbon with one Bronze Star, Good Conduct and Victory Medals and the Philippine Presidential Unit Citation Badge.

His memorable experience was when half-way across a bridge in Manila, he saw a group of Japanese approaching. He opened fire with his submachine gun and held them immobile until a combat patrol arrived. His action prevented a surprise attack upon his artillery battalion's area and the enemy was denied the use of fortifications. For this he received the Silver Star Medal.

EARLE C. HOCHWALD, Major, was born Aug. 19, 1911 in Philadelphia, PA. He was assigned to the 37th Div. shortly after landing at Bougainville and served as a battalion chaplain with the 145th Regt. until the end of the war.

He remembers the hard-fought victory when the Japanese counter-attacked at Bougainville, the long fighting-march from Lingayen to Manila, and the fierce, courageous battle for the city. Discharged with the rank of major, his awards include the Purple Heart, Bronze and Silver Stars. A retired psychologist, he lives with his wife, Nancy, in Scottsdale, AZ.

BENJAMIN F. HOFFMAN, Private First Class, was born Nov. 13, 1918 in Toledo, OH. He joined the service Jan. 29, 1941; assigned to 148th Inf., Co. G, 37th Div. and was stationed at Russell Island, New Georgia, Fiji, Guadalcanal, Bougainville and Luzon.

Memorable Experiences: when liberating Bilibid prison, Luzon; Hill 700, Bougainville; and beachhead landing, Luzon.

Discharged Oct. 18, 1945 as private first class. His awards include the Asiatic-Pacific Theater Ribbon with two Bronze Stars, Combat Badge, American Defense Medal, Philippine Liberation and Purple Heart.

Retired 1979 after 27 years in auto sales, he makes his home in Sylvania, OH. He and his wife, Doris, have two sons, Jeffrey and Gregg.

MAURICE L. HOPE, Tech 5, was born Feb. 27, 1917 in Knoxville, TN. He joined the Army Nov. 23, 1942; assigned to 117th Combat Engrs., 37th Div.; and stationed at Fort Leonard Wood, MO. He participated in battles at Munda, New Georgia, Bougainville, Luzon and Manila.

His memorable experiences: witnessing a major "dog fight" on Guadalcanal in June 1943 near Henderson Field; and beachheads: Munda, Lingayen and Bougainville.

Discharged Dec. 24, 1945, Camp Chaffe, AR as medic tech 5. His awards include the WWII Victory Ribbon, Asiatic-Pacific Theater Medal, two Bronze Service Stars, Bronze Arrowhead, Bronze Star and D.V. Badge.

Retired locomotive engineer, Southern Railway, he lives in Knoxville, TN with his wife Dorothy. They have a son Edward and daughter Charlene.

GEORGE HOSEK, Tech Sergeant, was born June 19, 1921 at Comstock, NE. He joined the USA Sept. 20, 1944; assigned to Infantry, 37th Div., HQ Co., Special Troops. Basic training was at Camp Roberts, CA.

Overseas to Frankfurt/M, Germany, Baguio, Cagayan Valley and Luzon, Philippine Islands. His memorable experience was Luzon when shells burst in HQ area (estimated 300 to 400 caliber).

Discharged Jan. 20, 1946 as tech sergeant. He received the Purple Heart.

Retired from the U.S. Postal Service, he lives with his wife Margaret in Omaha, NE. They have two sons, one daughter, Gary and twins, Lynn and Linda; and five granddaughters.

GERHARD K. HOSUM (GARY), Tech 5, was born at Hamberg, ND on Aug. 21, 1915. He entered the service Oct. 2, 1942 and trained at Camp Wolters, TX. In May 1943 he went to the South Pacific and landed at New Hebrides. From there he was sent to Guadalcanal, Bougainville, New Guinea, Leyte, Philippines.

Participated in battles in New Hebrides, Guadalcanal and Bougainville. In October 1945, he went to Japan, then back to the States where he received his discharge at Ft. Lewis, WA on Dec. 29, 1945. Gary was in the 129th Inf. of Co. B, 37th Div.

He received the Combat Infantry Badge, Asiatic-Pacific Service Medal, Good Conduct Medal and was awarded the Bronze Star after his discharge. He received the rank of tech fifth grade.

Spent more than 25 years in the lumber business as manager before his retirement. He and his wife Martha are the parents of a grown son and daughter. Hosum is now residing in a nursing home after becoming disabled from strokes.

EDWARD R. HRUNEK, Private First Class, was born Nov. 7, 1923 in Oak Park, IL. He joined the Army in March 1943 and was assigned to the 37th Inf. Div. Stationed at Fort Sheridan, IL; Camp Robinson, AR and Camp Stoneman, CA.

Was with Co. I, 129th Inf.; first went to New Caledonia, then joined the 129th on Guadalcanal in November 1943. Participated in action at Bougainville, invasion of Luzon on Jan. 9, 1945, Manila and Baguio. His memorable experiences include: Fort Stotsenberg, Clark Field, Intramuros, Walled City and the fighting in the streets and buildings in Manila, a different warfare than the jungles of Bougainville.

Discharged Dec. 23, 1945 at Camp Grant, IL. Received the Combat Infantry Badge, Bronze Star and Combat Ribbon with Arrowhead.

Retired from AMP Inc. and lives in Cherry Valley, IL with his wife. They have one daughter, two sons and six grandchildren.

BARNEY F. JASEK JR., Corporal, was born Dec. 7, 1924 in New York City. He joined the Army in March 1943; Browning auto rifleman, Co. C, 148th Inf. 37th Div. He trained at Camp Croft, SC; Camp Stoneman, CA; then San Francisco POE, September 1943.

Overseas to New Caledonia, Guadalcanal, Bougainville, Luzon and Japan. Memorable experiences are the beach patrols to Kurio Mission area, Bougainville, crossing the Pasig River onto the Palace grounds under fire, Luzon and the fighting of Co. C, 148th Inf. on Feb. 9, 1945 at Manila.

Discharged in 1946 as corporal. He received the Asiatic-Pacific Ribbon, Purple Heart, Victory Medal, Philippine Liberation Medal, Combat Infantry Badge and Presidential Unit Citation. Retired, and lives with his wife, Marilyn, in Walden, NY. They have three daughters and three grandsons. He enjoys fishing and boating with his family.

GEORGE I. JENKS, Private First Class, was born Oct. 6, 1923 in Lenox, MA and raised in Pittsfield, MA. Entered the service March 17, 1943 at East Devens, MA; sent to Fort Leonard Wood for training and joined the 37th Div. in November 1943.

Served in Bougainville, the invasion of Luzon, battle for Manila, Baguio, Cagayan Valley to Aparri. He was wounded on Bougainville. Memorable experience was wiping out a Jap machine gun nest with his BAR team. Also memorable was the battle in the Walled City.

Discharged Dec. 28, 1945 as private first class. He received the Purple Heart, Combat Infantry Badge, Bronze Star, U.S. Presidential Citation and Philippine Presidential Citation. Member of VFW and 27th Div. Vets. Assoc.

A retired widower, he still lives in Pittsfield where he enjoys retirement and lots of hunting.

FRANK E. JOHNSON, was 1st sergeant of HQ Btry., 140th FA, 37th Inf. Div. in the Fiji Islands, Guadalcanal, Russell Islands, New Georgia and Bougainville. He was born in Pekin, IL on July 1, 1920. Entered federal service Oct. 15, 1940, starting with the 37th's 134th FA Regt.

He trained at Camp Shelby, MS and shipped out with the 140th FA in May of 1942 from San Francisco via Indiantown Gap, PA. His memorable experience was getting up from a cot just seconds before it was shredded by an enemy antipersonnel bomb.

Discharged June 28, 1945. His awards include the WWII Victory, Asiatic-Pacific, Good Conduct and American Defense Medal.

A retired newspaper editor, he lives with his wife, Louise, in Tucson, AZ. A son, John, died in 1980. Their daughter, Christia, lives in Riverside, CA and son, Frank III, lives in Tucson.

GILFORD JOHNSON (GIL), Sergeant, was born in Ft. Wayne, IN on Dec. 8, 1924. He was inducted into the Army in March 1943; basic training

was at Camp Joseph T. Robinson, AR. He departed September 1943 from San Francisco to New Caledonia, where he joined Co. A, 148th Inf.

At Bougainville in November 1943 and made landing at Lingayen Gulf in January 1945. He was wounded in Manila and sent to Hollandia, New Guinea. Returned to Co. A, 148th at Baguio and advanced to Cagayan Valley.

Discharged Dec. 26, 1945. His awards include the Asiatic-Pacific Ribbon, Bronze Star, Purple Heart, Philippine Liberation Medal, Good Conduct and WWII Victory Medal.

Retired after 41 years at International Harvester in Ft. Wayne, IN. Was married 40 years, wife passed away. He remarried in 1991; they reside in Brookville, OH and spend winters in Florida.

ANTON L. KADRMAS (TONY), Private First Class, was born in Dunn County, ND on Jan. 28, 1920. He served in the Army from Feb. 24, 1942 to Oct. 9, 1945. Basic training was at Camp Forrest, TN, and he was assigned to 37th Div., 129th Inf., F Co. He was the F Co. bugler and a radio messenger, carrying "backpack 300" radio. Departed San Francisco on Sept. 2, 1942 for the 18 day voyage to Viti Levu in Fiji Islands; went on to Espiritu Santo Island (New Hebrides); Guadalcanal, Bougainville and Lingayen Bay (Luzon, Philippines). He was in many battles on Bougainville and Luzon and spent many nights in foxholes and/or pillboxes, often in cold water that was waist deep.

His memorable experience was when he received a call from an officer to relay the message to Capt. Bettendorf "that the war is over." He was a very happy man.

Awards include the Asiatic-Pacific Ribbon, Combat Infantry Badge, Bronze Star, Philippine Liberation Medal, Good Conduct Medal, Pacific Service Distinguished Unit Badge and the Purple Heart.

He is retired after 30 years at Atlantic-Richfield Refinery and he and his wife, Annamae, live in Klamath Falls, OR.

YUKIO KAWAMOTO, Tech 3, was born Nov. 13, 1919 in Berkeley, CA; educated in public schools including the University of California. Inducted Presidio of Monterey on Feb. 25, 1942. Basic infantry training at Camp Robinson, AR; Camp Crowder, MO; Military Intelligence Service Language School, Camp Savage, MN.

Fall of 1943, USAFISPA, Noumea, New Caledonia; one month TDY COMSOPAC Combat Intelligence HQ. He joined the 37th in November 1943, participated in the second battle of Bougainville, Lingayen landing and recapture of Manila and Baguio.

Left Manila in May 1945 for emergency furlough to States to help his elderly parents resettle back to California (Government was going to close down the Topaz, UT Relocation Camp where they had been incarcerated during the war). One of his many memorable experiences was his language team's learning from a PW about one month before the beginning of the second battle of Bougainville that a massive attack was being prepared to begin on Japanese Army Day. The information was accurate and saved many lives.

Discharged Aug. 10, 1945, Fort Douglas, UT, a couple of days after Hiroshima (his parents came from there and two aunts were killed there). Received the Asiatic-Pacific, Philippine Liberation Ribbons with Battle Stars.

Occupation of Japan, 1946-48, International Military Tribunal, Far East. Returned to the States and did graduate studies at Berkeley. He joined the Department of State after serving two years at the Consulate General of Japan in San Francisco. He was primarily a Japanese specialist, but had a varied and interesting career. His last assignment was as American Counsul, American Embassy, Tokyo. He retired and returned to Washington in January 1980, credited with 34 years of service to the U.S. Government.

He is enjoying retirement: traveling, playing a little golf and trying to keep up with his 10 grandchildren (all at least 50% English, Scotsman, Irish, or German). He and his Tokyo wife, Sayo, raised three sons and one daughter. They all graduated college and are happily married. He and Sayo reside in Springfield, VA a suburb of Washington, DC.

EARL LEONARD KELLY, Private First Class, was born Nov. 15, 1918 in Spencer, IA. He enlisted in the Army on Jan. 27, 1942; took basic training at Camp Wolters, TX; went overseas May 16, 1942; and served in 37th Div., 147th Inf. Regt., Co. H.

Overseas duty at Fiji Islands, Guadalcanal, Western Samoa, Wallis Island, New Caledonia and Emirau Island. He was rotated back to the States in July 1944 and discharged Oct. 16, 1945. His awards include the American Campaign, Asiatic-Pacific Campaign, WWII Efficiency Honor, Rifle Badge and Combat Infantry Medal.

Worked for Minneapolis, MN Const. Co. for 35 years until a heart-attack that ended his working days. He is a lifetime member of the VFW, Richfield, MN. Married Verena Waldron on July 3, 1945; they have five children: Kathryn, Vanona, Donald, Howard (d) and Lynetta. Also has three grandchildren and four great-grandchildren.

LOYD J. KLASSEN, was in Co. H, 145th Regt., 37th Div. He sends his dues to Mahoning Valley Chapter, Youngstown, OH.

HERBERT L. KNIPP, Corporal T/5, was born in Carter County, KY on Oct. 29, 1921. From age two he was raised in Lawrence County, OH and graduated from Decatur High School in May of 1941. He was drafted into the service Aug. 3, 1942. After being issued clothing at Fort Thomas, KY, he was sent to Camp Wolters, TX for infantry basic training.

Was transported to the South Pacific from Fort McDowell at Angel Island, CA. Upon reaching the Fiji Islands, he was dispatched to the H&S Co., 117th Combat Engr. Bn. attached to the 37th Inf. Div. He served in the Fiji Islands as well as Guadalcanal, New Georgia and Bougainville in the Solomon Islands. He participated in the invasion of Luzon and was involved in the retaking of Clarks Field and Fort Stotsenburg, the battles of Manila and Baguio and the armored run up the Cagayan Valley.

One of his most memorable experiences was on the island of Luzon on an armored run. He was sent back to Santiago to pick up more supplies for bridges, and approached a group of seven men who he thought were Filippinos, but turned out to be Japanese who were sick with malaria and in need of medical attention. He left them at a check point set up in the road at the edge of Santiago.

His awards include the American Theater Ribbon, Asiatic-Pacific Theater Ribbon, Philippine Liberation Ribbon, two Bronze Stars, Good Conduct Medal, Bronze Arrowhead, WWII Victory Medal, Distinguished Unit Badge. Also during a special Philippine Independence Day celebration, June 14, 1991, he was awarded a Philippine Liberation Medal and Presidential Citation Medal by the Philippine Ambassador to the U.S. He was discharged Dec. 23, 1945 from Camp Atterbury, IN.

He began his civilian career with Allied Signal Corp. on Oct. 5, 1948 and retired from there March 1, 1984 as their area supervisor. He is a member of the Improved Order of Redmen and is a lifetime member of the VFW. He now resides with his wife Sue and family at their Lawrence County home in Pedro, OH.

FRANK A. KOTARBA, Tech 5, was born Jan. 28, 1916 in Chicago, IL. He joined the Army Dec. 2, 1941, assigned to 148th Inf. HQ Co., 37th Div. He was stationed at Fiji Islands, Guadalcanal and New Georgia.

Participated in battles in Northern Solomons and New Georgia Campaigns, where he was wounded in action on Aug. 5, 1943. His memorable experience was jungle warfare.

Discharged Dec. 10, 1944 as tech 5. He received the Purple Heart, Bronze Star for Northern Solomons Campaign.

Retired from GE after 32 years of service. He and his wife, Valerie, make their home in Chicago, IL. They have a daughter Christine.

GEORGE C. KRUEGER, Corporal, was born in Waukesha, WI on March 28, 1924. He attended schools in Waukesha, then enlisted in the Army in July 1942. Basic training was at Fort Sill, OK.

Went overseas to New Caledonia as a replacement in December 1942. He was sent to Guadalcanal in April 1943 to serve with the 37th Div., 135th FA. He took part in all the battles until the end of the war.

Memorable experience was firing on and knocking out a Japanese machine gun position by direct fire from the Tondo Railroad Station. An artilleryman doesn't have a chance to see the target too often. He returned home in December 1945.

Took an apprenticeship in patternmaking and retired from that profession in January 1990. He married Dorothy and they have two children, Peter and Mary. Peter joined the Peace Corps and served on Luzon from 1977 until 1979. Things seemed to be the same as they were during the war.

JOHN R. KULKA, Sergeant, was born Feb. 17, 1925 in Cleveland, OH. He joined the Army Feb. 1, 1941 and was assigned to the 37th Div. in 1941. Military stations include Camp Shelby, MS, Fort Dix, NJ and Camp Gruber, OK.

Overseas duty was at Normandy, Northern France, Rhineland and Central Europe. Memorable experience was their shakey landing into Normandy.

Discharged Oct. 4, 1945 as sergeant. He received the American Defense, American Campaign, EAME with four Bronze Stars, WWII Victory, Good Conduct and Marksman Badge with automatic rifle bar.

A retired school teacher, he is married; there are no children.

EDWARD P. KYSAR, Corporal, was born in Oakland, CA on Sept. 22, 1924. He served from Oct. 17, 1942 to Dec. 18, 1945, trained at Camp Hale, CO as a ski trooper in the 87th Mountain Inf. Regt. Was sent to the North Pacific and on Aug. 15, 1943 particpated in an assault landing on the Japanese held island of Kiska in the Aleutians.

On returning to the States, some of his regiment were earmarked as replacements for the South Pacific. Kysar was sent overseas for a second time, debarking at New Caledonia and from there to Bougainville in the Northern Solomons. As a member of D Co., 145th Inf. Regt., 37th Div., he landed at Lingayen Gulf on Luzon and participated in the battle of Manila, the fighting on Mount Pacawagen and the Cagayan Valley Campaign.

Memorable Experience: As his regiment walked south toward Manila, the Japanese proceeded to do what they were paid to do "kill the Yankee dogs." With the first burst of fire, he desperately sought a place of safety and found it. Lady Luck was indeed smiling upon him, for there, just a few feet away, was the grandest, deepest, Japanese crafted foxhole he had ever seen. Suddenly, he realized he was not alone; apprehensively, he looked about and met the two beady, black eyes of a large ugly rat who apparently had fallen into the foxhole and couldn't climb out. As he was pondering its fate: death by shooting or by stomping with rifle butt, a sense of pity welled over him and he decided on a third option—freedom. He took off his helmet and lowered it to the bottom of the hole; the rat, with rare insight, jumped in and he raised the helmet to the top of the hole and the rat took off.

He was awarded the Combat Infantry Badge, Bronze Star Medal with V, Asiatic-Pacific Medal with three Battle Stars and Arrowhead, Philippine Liberation Medal with one Battle Star, Philippine Distinguished Unit Badge, American Theater Medal and the Victory Medal.

37th Infantry Division—79

He is a retired graphic designer, now living in Tarzana, CA.

RAYMOND BERNARD LAWLESS, Colonel, was born Feb. 9, 1920. He holds BS degree from University of Maryland. Military education includes OCS (basic and advanced), Signal School, Command and General Staff College and Logistics Management Procurement School. He entered active service with the OHNG, 37th Inf. Div., 74th Inf. Bde., HHQ. Served at Camp Shelby, MS and Indiantown Gap, PA.

Departed for overseas in spring of 1942 to serve with 37th Recon Troop in New Zealand, Fiji Islands and Guadalcanal. He progressed through the enlisted ranks from private to 1st sergeant before departing the unit in April 1943 for OCS.

Upon graduating from OCS as a second lieutenant, Signal Corps, he returned overseas to serve in the Persian Gulf Command, Iran. Released from active service in December 1945 as 1st lieutenant, USAR. Was recalled in 1948 during the Berlin Airlift and served in various command and staff positions: 82nd Abn. Div.; Commander, STRATCOM LLBN; Office of Chief Signal Officer; Army Material Command; Office of Deputy Chief of Staff for Logistics, DA; senior advisor; and deputy commander, STRATCOM Group.

Also served in various commands worldwide: Okinawa, Hawaii, Korea, HQ USAREUR, Europe, Washington, DC, Lexington Army Depot, Fort Gordon, GA, Vietnam and Fort Monroe, VA.

Retired on July 31, 1975. Awards received were Legion of Merit with OLC, Bronze Star, Meritorious Service Medal, Commendation Medal with two OLCs and various service medals. Upon retirement, he worked in the field of education. He is married to the former Margaret (Peg) A. Buerger of Marietta, OH. Together 46 years, they reside in Augusta, GA and raised three sons.

WILBER R. LEE, CWO-1, was born Jan. 21, 1914 at Ada, OH. He joined the ARNGUS Oct. 30, 1930 and was assigned to Co. H, 2nd Bn., 148th Inf., 37th Div. Stationed at Ada, OH, Mississippi, Fiji, Guadalcanal, New Georgia, Bougainville, Luzon, Philippines and Camp Polk, LA.

Participated in battles in New Georgia, Bougainville, Luzon, Philippines and Manila. His memorable experiences include Hill 700 and the release of prisoners from Bilibib Prison in Manila.

Discharged from AD on Oct. 3, 1945 and from ARNGUS Jan. 22, 1974. His awards include the Combat Infantry Badge, Asiatic Pacific Ribbon, BSM, Philippine Liberation Medal, Philippine Presidential Unit Citation Badge, Ohio DM, Good Conduct Medal, WWII Victory Medal, Korea and ADSM. Retired after 44 years, 23 years as full time AST. Married 47 years to Iva Lee; they have three sons: Jack, Ronald and Randall.

LEONARD O. LINGENFELTER, Sergeant, was born Feb. 27, 1924, Canton, IL. He joined the service Feb. 27, 1943, assigned to 148th Inf., 37th Div., Co. C. Stationed at New Caledonia, Guadalcanal, Luzon P.I., Bougainville, Scott Field, IL and Camp Roberts, CA.

Participated in battles at Bougainville and Luzon, P.I. A memorable experience was when they found Japs hiding in a haystack and they burned it. The Japs had ambushed a patrol a few days before.

Discharged Dec. 12, 1945 as sergeant. His medals include the Combat Infantry Badge, Asiatic-Pacific Ribbon, Philippine Liberation Ribbon, Victory Medal and Purple Heart.

Retired, he lives in Wisconsin in the summer and winters in Texas. Married 51 years, raised six children and has 14 grandchildren.

VINCENT LO CURCIO, Staff Sergeant, was born in Passaic, NJ on Sept. 13, 1924. He served from March 15, 1943 to January 11, 1946; trained with 106th Div. at Fort Jackson, SC in the heavy weapons platoon (81mm mortar).

Arrived at Oro Bay, New Guinea Replacement Depot on Sept. 27, 1944; went to Bougainville and was assigned to the 37th Div., Co. A, 145th Inf. He participated in the invasion of Luzon at Lingayen Gulf and the Battle of Manila. Co. A suffered heavy casulaties at Manila and at one point was reduced to less than 100 men.

He is still active in the food market business and resides in Nutley, NJ with his wife Antoinette (Toni). They have four children and eight grandchildren.

HARRY L. LODGE, Tech Sergeant, was born June 6, 1919 in Steubenville, OH. He was inducted into the service on Jan. 23, 1941 in Cleveland, OH; sent to Camp Shelby, MS and assigned to Co. G, 145th Inf., 37th Div.

Stationed at Indiantown Gap, PA; San Francisco, CA; Auckland, New Zealand; Fiji; Guadalcanal; New Georgia and Bougainville. He is very proud to have served with the 37th Div. His comrades will always be with him. They were "family."

Discharged April 6, 1945. He received the Asiatic-Pacific Theater Campaign, three Bronze Stars, Combat Infantry Badge, Purple Heart and Good Conduct Medal.

Entered college on GI Bill in September 1945; received bachelor of arts degree, Geneva College, PA; master of education from Univesity of Cincinnati, OH; and juris doctor degree from Chase College of Law, Cincinnati.

Retired adminstrator and adjunct professor, Cincinnati Public Schools, University of Cincinnati, Xavier University and Chase College of Law.

Married and has one son; they reside in Cincinnati, OH.

GEORGE F. LYNCH JR., Staff Sergeant, was born Oct. 23, 1924 in Boston, MA. He joined the Army March 22, 1943; assigned to Co. G, 148th Inf. Regt., 37th Div.; and stationed at Fort Devens, MA and Fort Leonard Wood, MO.

Participated in battles in Bougainville, Solomon Islands, Luzon, P.I. Memorable experiences: sergeant of guard, home of Gen. MacArthur in Manila; after Battle of Manila and before Baguio. Discharged Dec. 27, 1945 as staff sergeant. He received the Bronze Star and Purple Heart with two clusters. Retired from U.S. Postal System, he is married, lives in Auburn, MA and has three children.

FRANK H. LYNN, Tech 5, was born March 9, 1920 in Maynard, OH. He joined the service Jan. 24, 1941; assigned to 37th Div., 112th Med. Bn., Co. B; stationed at Camp Shelby, MS, San Francisco, South Pacific and Indiantown Gap, PA.

Participated in battles in Northern Solomons and Luzon. Discharged Oct. 3, 1945 as Tech 5. He received the American Service Medal, Asiatic-Pacific Theater Ribbon with two stars, Philippine Liberation Ribbon with Bronze Star, Good Conduct Ribbon and Purple Heart.

Lynn passed away Nov. 8, 1993. His sister, Mary Mozden, lives in Salem, OH; brother, Albert Lynn, Cadiz, OH; widow, Marlene, in Worthington, OH; son Gene Allen, Bradenton, FL; and grandson, Jeremy Michael, in Hartsville, SC.

MARVIN H. MAHANNAH, Private First Class, was born March 11, 1921 in Cage, OK. He joined the service Aug. 19, 1942; served with Co. D, 129th, 37th Div., combat infantryman; and stationed at Camp Wolters, TX.

Sent overseas and participated in battles in Northern Solomons and Luzon. He was wounded in leg, later returning to active duty.

Discharged Dec. 17, 1945 as private first class. His awards include the Bronze Arrowhead, Pacific Theater, Victory Seal, Good Conduct, Asiatic-Pacific Ribbon, Victory Medal, Purple Heart, Silver Star and Philippine Liberation.

Retired, he enjoys gardening and fishing. He is married and has one son.

MICHAEL MALANDRINO, born Oct. 27, 1917 in Lawrence, MA. He joined the service in September 1941 and served with the 37th Div., Co. H, 148th Inf. and was stationed at Camp Shelby, MS.

Sent overseas to South Pacific and participated in New Georgia Campaign. Malandrino was discharged in 1944.

He is retired.

JOHN J. MAREK, Corporal, born March 11, 1924 in West, TX. He served in the Infantry with Co. G, 37th Div., 145th Inf., stationed at Camp McCain, MS, Fort Jackson, SC, New Guinea and Philippines.

Made landing at Luzon and participated in liberation of Manila and Mt. Pacajuan. He had many memorable experiences.

Discharged May 16, 1946 as corporal. His awards include the American Theater Service Medal, Purple Heart (3) and Philippine Liberation Ribbon with one Bronze Star.

Stockbroker for 33 years, he is married and has four grown children and grandchildren.

JOHN MARSHALEK, Sergeant, was born June 8, 1921 in Russellton, PA. He joined the Army Nov. 19, 1942 and served with Cannon Co., 148th Inf., 37th Div. Was stationed at Camp Roberts, CA.

Sent overseas to New Caledonia, Guadalcanal and participated in battles at Bougainville and Luzon. His memorable experience was being in a crew of six men (they were all wounded, plus two medics and radioman) and he came home without a scratch. Also memorable was meeting Father Elmer Heinol on Bougainville; he was a fine soldier and they are still friends.

Discharged Dec. 27, 1945 as sergeant. His awards include the Combat Infantry Badge, two Bronze Stars, American Theater, Asiatic-Pacific with two Bronze Service Stars, Philippine Liberation, Philippine Presidential Unit Citation, one Arrowhead, Good Conduct and Victory Medal.

Retired, he lives in Rural Ridge, PA and is a widower.

EDWARD J. MARTENS, 1st Lieutenant, was born Sept. 9, 1922 in Davenport, IA. He joined the service in February 1943, served in the Infantry, Co. F, 145th Inf., 37th Div. and was stationed at Camp Roberts, CA.

Sent overseas and participated in action at Solomon Islands, Luzon and Manila. His memorable experience was when mortar shell landed in foxhole and killed five soldiers.

Discharged in December 1945 as 1st lieutenant, USAR. His awards include the Combat Infantry Badge and three Bronze Stars.

Martens is a retired plumbing contractor. He is single and lives in Davenport, IA.

FRANK FURLONG MATHIAS, was born in the Ohio River town of Maysville, KY in 1925. He was drafted in 1943 and served two and a half years in the Army, most of which was in the 37th Inf. Div.

After the war, Mathias earned a BA degree at the University of Kentucky, then worked on a newspaper and played in a dance band in Mexico City. In 1953 he started a five year stint in sales promotion for Lorillard Tobacco Co. Meanwhile, he met Florence Duffy of Midway, KY and they were married in 1958. The same year he entered the University of Kentucky to work on a doctorate in history and earned his Ph.D in 1966.

Dr. Mathias taught his first year at West Virginia Tech, but in 1963 accepted an assistant professorship at the University of Dayton. He was twice elected professor of the year during his 25 years at UD. He taught American history to over 8,000 students during his career, yet he found time to author three books and parts of seven others, as well as publish some 30 articles in journals and magazines. His *GI Jive: An Army Bandsman In WWII* remains the only memoir by an enlisted man to issue from the Pacific Theater in WWII. Mathias retired in 1987.

JOHN W. MATZ, Sergeant, was born June 3, 1919 in Clyde, OH. He joined the Army Feb. 5, 1941 and served with the 135th FA, Btry. C, 37th Div. He trained at Camp Shelby, MS.

Sent overseas in 1942 to the South Pacific to New Zealand and Fiji. He participated in battles at Bougainville, New Georgia and Guadalcanal. Matz was discharged in 1946.

A retired gasoline semi-driver, he and his wife, Dorrine, live in the country near Republic, OH.

ROBERT E. McCOMBS, Sergeant, was born Nov. 9, 1922 at Wyandot, OH. He was inducted at Fort Benjamin Harrison, IN on March 9, 1943; and received 13 weeks of basic training at Camp Joseph T. Robinson, AR.

Embarked from San Francisco, CA in September 1943 for New Caledonia and joined Co. I, 148th Inf., 37th Div. on Guadalcanal. Landed at Bougainville in November 1943 and saw front line action. He participated in securing the island.

Was hospitalized with malaria and diphtheria; transferred to 3769th QM Truck Co. and transported food, ammo and fuel to front lines. Landed at Lingayen Gulf and hauled supplies and ammo to infantry and artillery companies on front lines. His memorable experience was transporting the first women and children from Bilibid prison to safety in Manila in Feb. 1945.

Was hospitalized and evacuated to Fletcher General Hospital in Cambridge, OH in August 1945. Received medical discharge on Oct. 23, 1945. His awards include the Good Conduct Ribbon, Distinguished Unit Citation, Rifleman Medal, Asiatic-Pacific Ribbon with two stars, Philippine Liberation, Sharpshooter Medal and WWII Medal.

Retired from the railroad in 1970 and motel management in 1985. He lives with his wife, Dorothy, in Palm Harbor, FL and they enjoy traveling. They have one daughter, one son and three grandchildren.

WILLIAM A. McGARRITY, Staff Sergeant, was born Oct. 21, 1910 at Osceola, AR. He joined the service and served with HQ Co., 136th FA BN, 37th Div. and was stationed in the Philippines, Cagayan Valley.

Discharged in 1945 as sergeant. He received the Philippine Liberation and Good Conduct Medal. Retired from the civil service, he lives with his wife, Bonnie, at East Point, GA.

JOSEPH X. McGINN JR., Tech 5, was born in New York City. He was inducted into the military on Aug. 14, 1941. After completing basic training, he was assigned to Co. H, 148th Inf., 37th Div. in 1942. Transferred to the Intelligence Section in BN HQ and then to Intelligence Regimental HQ.

Sent to the Pacific in 1942 and served in the Fiji, Russell Islands, Guadalcanal, New Georgia, Bougainville and Solomon Islands. He remembers a day on New Georgia when he could hear the mortars in the distance and the explosion of shells nearby. He went to the aid station for some aspirin for his headache and when he arrived there, he found that H Co. (his old squad) had been hit, the squad leader killed and several others were injured. He forgot all about his headache and returned to his foxhole. At this point he knew the war was real.

Discharged on Oct. 2, 1945. His awards include the Combat Infantry Badge, Bronze Star, Good Conduct Medal and South Pacific Campaign Medal.

He entered the food service industry as a food service consultant, designing commercial kitchens. Retired, he lives with his wife, Dorothy, in Bethpage, NY. They have a son, daughter-in-law and three grandchildren.

CHARLES F. McGINNIS, Corporal, was born Oct. 8, 1918 in Quinebaug, CT. He enlisted in the Army in 1937; served three years in 2nd FA, Fort Clayton, Panama, one year in 99th FA, then to B Btry., 6th FA at Fort Hoyle, MD.

Went to Fiji Islands in 1942, then to Espiritu Santo and New Hebrides. The 6th FA moved to Guadalcanal and was attached to 37th Div. in early 1943. He remained with the division until after Bougainville.

Rotated back to the States in August 1944. Went to MP Co. in Binghamton, NY until discharge in September 1945. His awards include the American Theater, American Defense, Pacific Theater, Good Conduct and Victory Medal.

Charles McGinnis was single; he passed away in 1966 from a heart attack.

JAMES E. McGINNIS, Sergeant, was born July 31, 1917 in Oxford, MA. He joined the Army July 7, 1940; served with the 99th FA and 603rd FA; stationed at Bora Bora and New Hebrides; transferred to 135th FA, 37th Div. on Guadalcanal. He was also stationed at Bouganville and Northern Solomons.

McGinnis was discharged July 11, 1945 as sergeant. His awards include the Pacific Theater with two stars, Victory Medal, Good Conduct, American Theater and American Defense. An accountant licensed by the state of Ohio, he works as comptroller for a large wholesale dist. He and his wife Catherine have been married since July 12, 1941; they have six children: Barbara, Kathleen, Patricia, James, John and Robert.

JAMES E. McGUIRE, Private First Class, was born Feb. 14, 1924 at Bloomington, IL. He joined the Army Infantry Sept. 10, 1942 and served with the 147th Regt.

Sent overseas to Samoa, Wallis, New Caledonia, Emirau, Iwo Jima, Tinian and Okinawa. Memorable experience was seeing the *Enola Gay* on Tinian after its return from Hiroshima.

McGuire was discharged Dec. 11, 1945. His awards include the Combat Infantry Badge, three Bronze Service Stars and Asiatic-Pacific Ribbon. A retired construction worker, he lives with his wife, Mary, in Bloomington, IL.

JAMES E. McINTOSH, T-4, was born in Oxford, OH on June 13, 1917. He served from January 1941 to September 1945. He trained with the 37th Inf. Div. at Camp Shelby, MS. In March 1943, he departed Suva, Fiji in cadre for San Francisco and then to Camp Robinson, AR where he trained with the 561st FA BN.

He departed New York for England in March 1944 and then on to Utah Beach in June. He participated in the Battle of Bulge in December 1944 and then went on to the Elbe River in Germany. In May 1945 he was sent to Munich for occupation duty and while there visited Dachau Concentration Camp.

He was awarded the Asiatic-Pacific Ribbon, EAME with five Bronze Service Stars, Army of Occupation Medal, Good Conduct Ribbon and WWII Medal. He achieved the rank of T/4 in Radio.

Retired from personnel department at Tampa Shipyards, he lives with his wife, Florence, in Thonotosassa, FL.

LEE MCKARNS, T-4, was born on March 4, 1915 in Williams County, OH. He served from Feb. 3, 1941 to July 31, 1945. Basic training was at Camp Shelby, MS. From there he went to Guadalcanal, New Georgia, Bougainville and the Philippines. Served with Co. H, 148th Inf. and 112th Engrs.

Returned to the States on rotation with 119 points. He participated in the battles of Northern Solomons and Luzon. He was discharged from Camp Atterbury, IN. His awards include the EAME Theater Ribbon, Bronze Star, American Defense Service Medal, Philippine Liberation Ribbon and Good Conduct Ribbon.

He is a retired crane operator and lives with his wife, Margaret, at Montpelier, OH. They have three children and four grandchildren.

CLARE A. MILLER, Private First Class, was born July 17, 1922 at St. Charles, IL. He was inducted Dec. 7, 1942 at Fort Sheridan, IL and went to Camp Wolters, TX for basic training, then to Camp Stoneman, CA for PTO, May 8, 1943. Assigned May 29 to Weapons Plt., B Co. in newly formed 1st Bn., 129th Inf.

Moved from Espiritu Santo to Guadalcanal (staging), Nov. 13, 1943, for Empress Augusta Bay, Bouganville landing and ensuing campaign of 1944. Participated in Lingayen Gulf landing, Jan. 9, 1945, from Dagupan, Fort Stotsenburg and "Top of the World." He was wounded in February in battle for Manila, but returned in June for the Cagayan Valley drive, Cabagan to Aparri.

Wars end would find the journey home from Cabanatuan, San Fernando, LA Union, Camp Santa Ana, CA to Camp Grant, IL for discharge Dec. 20, 1945. His awards include five Overseas Service Bars, Service Stripe, Combat Infantry Badge, Asiatic-Pacific with Bronze Arrowhead, two Battle Stars, Philippine Liberation with Bronze Star, Good Conduct, Purple Heart with OLC for meritorious service and WWII Victory Medal.

He resides with his wife, Beverly, in Batavia, IL, a short distance from where it all started.

EDWARD E. MILLER, T-4, was born in Great Falls, MT on Oct. 1, 1919. He served from Nov. 7, 1941 to June 16, 1945; trained at ORTC, Aberdeen, MD; Camp Shelby, MS; Indiantown Gap, PA; assigned to the 37th Div., 737th Ord. Co. He served with the best group of men a person could ask for.

In May 1942 he went to the South Pacific, landed at Fiji Island, then to Guadalcanal, New Georgia and Northern Solomons Campaign. He suffered malaria several times while on Guadalcanal and was hit in the knee with shrapnel (minor injury, no record made).

His awards include the American Defense Medal, Asiatic-Pacific Medal, Bronze Battle Stars, Sharpshooter Medal, Rifle M-1. He served as a small arms weapons repair technician with the 737th Ord. Co. and earned the rank of T-4.

A retired office machine repair technician manager, he resides at Great Falls, MT.

RALPH MISKO, Sergeant, was born in Struthers, OH on Oct. 18, 1921. He served from Jan. 21, 1941

through July 11, 1945. To 145th Inf., he participated in the North Solomon, New Georgia campaigns.

He was awarded the Bronze Star and Purple Heart at Bougainville in March 1944 against Nanking's 1938 Baptist of the 6th Imperial Japanese Div. Also awarded the Asiatic-Pacific Theater Ribbon, Good Conduct Medal, American Defense Service Medal, Combat Infantryman Badge, Pistol Marksman Badge and Rifle Marksman Badge. He was discharged at the grade of sergeant in Co. H, 145th Inf.

Ralph Misko passed away May 10, 1986, leaving his wife, Josephine, who resides in Campbell, OH, and three sons: Ralph and Jeffrey of Poland, OH and Wayne of Tempe, AZ.

FREDERICK MITCHELL, Tech Sergeant, was born July 7, 1924 in Scranton, PA. He joined the Army June 12, 1943 and served as antitank gunner with 129th Inf., 37th Div. Trained at Camp Wheeler, GA then went to the South Pacific.

Sent to New Caledonia, Bougainville, Luzon, Lingayen Gulf landing, Clark Field, Fort Stotensenburg, Manila, Baguio and Cagayan Valley.

Discharged Dec. 26, 1945 as platoon tech sergeant. His awards include the Bronze Star Medal with OLC, Good Conduct Medal, Asiatic-Pacific Campaign Medal with two Bronze Stars and one Bronze Arrowhead, WWII Victory Medal, Combat Infantry Badge, Philippine Liberation Medal with one Bronze Star and Philippine Unit Citation Ribbon.

EDGAR J. MOORMAN, was born May 11, 1919 at Frenchtown, OH. He joined the Army Jan. 22, 1941 and served with the 37th Inf. Div. He was stationed at Camp Shelby, Fiji Islands, New Zealand, Guadalcanal, New Georgia, Luzon and Bougainville.

Participated in battles in Northern Solomons and Luzon. Memorable experiences include: three years and four months survival in the South Pacific; being on the flagship *Mt. McKinley* on the trip to take back Luzon; and returning to the Solomons (Fiji, Guadalcanal, New Georgia) on 10 day tour in 1988.

Discharged Oct. 7, 1945 as tech 4. His awards include the Good Conduct Medal, American Defense Ribbon, Asiatic-Pacific Theater Ribbon with two Bronze Stars and Philippine Liberation Ribbon with one Bronze Star.

Retired, he does some gardening and plays bingo. He is married and has 12 children, 22 grandchildren and two great-grandchildren.

JOHN C. MORICOLI, Colonel, was born Nov. 9, 1920 at Orange, NJ. He served from Oct. 15, 1940 to Nov. 22, 1945 and from Aug. 15, 1950 to Aug. 15, 1952. Trained with Co. C, 112th QM Regt., HQ Co., 3rd Bn., 166th Inf. and Svc. Co. 166th Inf. at Camp Shelby, MS, New Orleans, LA and Ft Barrancas, FL through 1942, then attended OCS at Ft. Washington, MD.

Commissioned March 17, 1943; overseas assignment with HQ Co., 120th Replacement Bn. as classification and assignment officer. He was recalled in 1952 as CO 3582nd Trans. Trk. Co. ONG, assigned Ft. Sill, OK.

His medals/awards include the American Defense, National Defense, Asiatic/Pacific Medals, Good Conduct, WWII, NG/RES Service Medals with three devices, Meritorious Service Medal and Ohio and California State Service Medals.

Retired after 40 years of active and Reserve service. He and his wife, Lucille, reside in Tujunga, CA.

WAYNE L. MORR, T-5, was born in Cerro Gordo, IL on April 10, 1924. He served from March 12, 1943 to Dec. 23, 1945 and trained at Camp Roberts, CA.

Departed San Francisco in September 1943 for New Caledonia and then to Guadalcanal. Was assigned to HQ Co., 1st Bn., 145th Inf. as a telephone lineman. Landed at Bougainville on Nov. 8, 1943 and landed at Lingayen, Luzon on Jan. 9, 1945.

Participated in battles at Clark Field, Fort Stotsenburg, Manila, Mt. Pacawagon, Cagayan Valley. Came down with dengue fever in April 1945; hepatitis and malaria in June 1945; and evacuated to Biak Island near New Guinea to convalesce. Returned to his unit at Aparri, Luzon on September 1. Bivouacked at Camp La Croix near Cabanatuan during October and November.

His awards include the Combat Infantry Badge, Asiatic/Pacific Theater Medal, Bronze Star Medal, Purple Heart Medal, Good Conduct Medal, Philippine Liberation Medal, Philippine Presidential Citation Badge and WWII Victory Medal.

Retired after 34 years of federal civil service. He and his wife, Dora Faye, reside in Xenia, OH.

FOREST MORRISON, Sergeant, was born Sept. 18, 1919 at Alliance, OH. He joined the service Oct. 1, 1940 and served with 135th FA, Btry. C, 37th Div. Was stationed at Camp Shelby, MS, Indiantown Gap, PA, Fiji Islands, New Georgia Island and Bougainville.

His memorable experience was before the battle of Hill 700; they were out on patrol and trapped by a bunch of Japs, but were able to sneak away during the heavy rain. He also remembers a day during battle for Hill 700 when a patrol party arrived at camp and the men were gathering around to hear their story when an officer yelled "Don't gang up!" Then two shells landed in the middle of the group, killing five and wounding several others. Next morning going to chow, they were cutting body parts out of the vines.

Discharged Aug. 18, 1945 as sergeant. Morrison is married and lives in Wilmington, NC. He is retired.

HUBERT R. MORRISON, Sergeant, was born in Akron, OH on June 5, 1928. He served with Co. K, 3rd Bn., 145th Inf. ONG, May 1948 to May 1955. Was called to active duty Jan. 15, 1952 during the Korean Conflict. Trained at Camp Polk, LA; attended Infantry School at Fort Benning, GA from June to October 1952; returned to Camp Polk to instruct infantry communications until November 1952.

Departed from New York in November 1952 for Germany. Was assigned to D Btry., 73rd AAA (7th Army) in Karlsruhe, as Comm. Chief, Rhine River Patrol.

He was awarded the Army of Occupation Medal for Germany and the National Defense Service Medal. Returned to the States in December 1953 and reverted to ONG until discharge in May 1955.

Retired after 45 years in the typesetting trade. He and his wife, Grace Jane, are spending their retirement years between Akron, OH and Palmdale, CA.

ROBERT HOWE MOYER, served three years (1937-40) in M Co., 145th Inf. Regt. at Akron, OH. In the summer of 1941, he took a civil service exam for shipfitter first class at the Pearl Harbor Navy Yard and received orders and train tickets to report to the Mare Island Navy Yard at Vallejo, CA.

Left Barberton, OH on Nov. 11, 1941; arrived at Mare Island and was told to report on the USS *Henderon* at San Francisco. Arrived at Pearl Harbor Dec. 1, 1941 and was there when the bombing started. Returned to Barberton in July 1941, entered the Army in August with one thought in mind—to catch up with his old division, the 37th. Sent to Camp Wolters, TX and Fort Ord, CA.

Overseas to Noumea, New Caledonia and assigned to the 132nd Antitank Co. of the Americal Div. on Bougainville. The 37th was also there and finally a couple of weeks later, he was back in M Co., 145th Regt., 37th Div. Wounded Feb. 13, 1945, after several hospitals was discharged in September 1945.

VIRGIL MUELLER, Staff Sergeant, was born Jan. 9, 1925 in Sturgeon Bay, WI. He was inducted in the Army March 15, 1944, trained at Camp Wolters, TX; and joined the 37th Div. in the South Pacific.

Participated in the Luzon Invasion, Top of the Mountain, Fort Stottensburg, and Baguio. When the war ended, he was sent to Korea for occupation duty. Was discharged Feb. 25, 1946 as staff sergeant. Received the Combat Infantry Badge and Bronze Star.

Semi-retired from his own trucking company, he still operates 25 tractors and 40 trailers. Married since 1948, he has two sons and two daughters.

WILLIAM A. MULLER, Sergeant, was born May 10, 1919 at Chicago, IL. Joined the Army in January 1942, as clerk/typist, mechanic and truck driver. He was first with the 29th Div. and later transferred to the 37th Div., staying with them until 1945. Stationed at Camp Grant, IL and Camp Lee, VA.

He was sent to the South Pacific in May 1942 and served at Fiji Islands, Guadalcanal, Russell Islands, Pitty Lou, Rendova, Munda, Bougainville (Hill 700), Solomon Islands and in the Invasion of Luzon and battle for Manila and the Walled City. He remembers the bombings and strafing in daylight raids, wounded comrades and loss of his buddies on Hill 700. Discharged Oct. 12, 1945 as T-5. His awards include the Asiatic-Pacific Theater Ribbon with Bronze Battle Stars, Philippine Liberation with Bronze Battle Star, Overseas Service Bars, Service Stripes, Good Conduct Medal and Bronze Service Arrowhead. Retired, he is enjoying life with his family. Married 47 years and has two married daughters and three grandsons.

HOWARD F. MURPHY, Private First Class, was born and raised in Princeton, WV. He was drafted during WWII years and was sent to the South Pacific to serve with Co. G of the 145th Regt. of the 37th Div. as a scout and rifleman in the liberation of north Luzon Island.

At the end of WWII, he served with the 738th MP Bn. in Manila, then re-enlisted and was stationed at Stuttgart, Bayreuth and Lanshut, Germany with the 1st Inf. Div.

He was awarded the Combat Infantry Badge, Asiatic-Pacific Ribbon with one star and the Bronze Star Medal.

On leaving the military, he worked as a steam locomotive fireman for the Virginian Railway until dieselization, he then joined the U.S. Postal Service and retired with 30 years service. He and wife, Evelyn, still reside in Princeton and are active members of the Kee Street United Methodist Church.

DAVID W. MUSSER, Sergeant, was born May 19, 1919 at Lafayette, OH. He joined the service Jan. 4, 1940; served with Btry. D&S, 136th FA BN, 37th Div. as a mechanic; stationed at Camp Shelby, MS, Indiantown Gap, PA and Ft. Sill, OK.

Sent overseas to Bougainville, Aukland, New Zealand, Guadalcanal and New Georgia. Discharged Sept. 14, 1945 as sergeant. His awards include the Carbine Marksman, Good Conduct, American Campaign, WWII Victory, Asiatic-Pacific Theater and American Defense.

Retired after 45 years service at 5 Acre Auto Wrkg. Co. He is married and has five daughters, 13 grandchildren and 13 great-grandchildren.

ALEX NAGY, T-4, was born Jan. 28, 1925 at Akron, OH. He served in the Army from April 1943 to December 1945. Basic and advanced training was at Fort Knox, KY. Departed San Francisco for overseas duty in September 1943.

Duty at New Caledonia, Guadalcanal; assigned to a mortar squad in Co. M, 145th Inf.; landed at Bougainville in November 1943; attended Radio School on the island; then assigned to HQ&HQ Co. of the 145th Inf. Landed at Lingayen and participated at Clark Field, Manila and Cagayan Valley.

After being discharged, he studied journalism at Ohio University, worked on weekly and daily papers in Iowa and Wisconsin. He later did graduate work in journalism and mass communications at the University of Wisconsin. Madison is currently a professor of journalism at Middle Tennessee State University. He and his wife reside in Murfreesboro.

LAWRENCE WAYNE NEWELL, was sent to basic training at Camp Roberts, CA in March of 1943. He and Wayne L. Morr were in the same barracks and soon became best friends. Morr remembers a Sunday afternoon when Newell's parents and girl friend came to visit him at Camp Roberts. They were escorted to the orderly room and Newell asked Morr to go with him to meet his mom, dad and girlfriend. They were very nice people.

Newell and Morr were sent overseas where Newell was put in the 148th Inf. Regt. and Morr in the 145th Inf. Regt. They continued to visit whenever they had a chance. One day in Manila, Morr happened to be

37th Infantry Division—83

in Newell's area and asked a couple of soldiers if they knew where he was. They sadly said that the day before, Newell and a group of soldiers seized a two story building from the Japs, but the Japs counter-attacked and drove the men up to the second story and then set fire to the building. They were all burned to death. *Submitted by his buddy Wayne L. Morr.*

FRANK NIEHAUS, Mess Sergeant, was born in 1917 near Greensburg, IN. He moved to Cincinnati in 1927, attended parochial grade school and went to a printing trade school. He served his apprenticeship in several job shops until he was drafted on Feb. 1, 1941. His Army career was spent with the 147th Inf. of the 37th Inf. Div.. In May of 1944, after 26 months overseas and while on Emirau Island, he was rotated back to the States and assigned to Camp Blanding, FL IRTC BN. Promoted to mess sergeant until his discharge Sept. 1, 1945.

Returning home, he married his lovely wife, Dorothy. They have seven great children who have blessed them with 16 wonderful grandchildren.

Presently he is president of the 147th Inf. Chapter of the 37th Div. Veterans Assoc. This year he was highly honored to be elected their national president for the 1994-95 term.

VICTOR J. NORKA, Staff Sergeant, was born May 24, 1922 in Akron, OH. He enlisted July 15, 1940, Co. M, 145th Inf., 37th Div. National Guard and activated into federal service in November 1940. Trained at Camp Shelby, MS and departed from POE San Francisco on May 26, 1942 for Auckland, New Zealand, to Suva Fiji, then to Guadalcanal.

On July 4, 1942 with two battalions of the 145th and two battalions of Marine Raiders, they invaded New Georgia. When battle was over, he departed on USS *Lureline* with a group of volunteers later called Merrills Marauders for Bombay, India.

Was sent to Deogarh (Central India) where they trained with the British Chindits. Assigned to I&R Kahki Combat Team and sent to Ledo, India and from there marched 140 miles over the mountains into Burma. He engaged in battles for Walawbum, Ngagantawng, Nhpum Ga and was evacuated at Myitkyina.

Returned to the States via North Africa in September 1944. Was stationed at Camp Blanding, FL until his discharge on June 15, 1945. Besides all the usual awards, he received the Bronze Star and Presidential Unit Citation.

Norka is a retired HACV contractor. He married Violet on May 11, 1942; they have two sons and two daughters.

ALERT NOWJACK, born in Cleveland, OH on Nov. 18, 1916. He served in the 148th Inf. Regt. from Jan. 24, 1941 to Aug. 16, 1945 with Co. K, 3rd Bn. Aid Station, Antitank Co. and Co. G.

He was cited for gallantry in action during a bonzai attack on July 10, 1943 on New Georgia and for gallantry in action on Luzon, Philippines at Malolos on Feb. 1, 1945.

His memorable experience was entering the Bilibid in Manila on Feb. 4, 1945 to free about 800 prisoners and 400 internees. Also memorable was crossing the Pasig River (while under fire) in a rubber boat, Feb. 10, 1945.

Since retirement from teaching at Willard, New Athens and Cadiz, he has resumed full time operation of his farm at Cadiz, OH.

JOSEPH F. O'HARA, Sergeant, was born Aug. 3, 1919 in Cleveland, OH. He enlisted Feb. 5, 1941 in the 37th Div., C Btry., 135th FA. Was stationed at Camp Shelby, Indiantown Gap, New Zealand, Fiji, Guadalcanal, Munda, Bougainville and Ft. Sill, OK. A memorable experience was having Thanksgiving dinner with the hospitalized men back from Guadalcanal on Nov. 11, 1942.

Discharged with the rank of sergeant on Sept. 23, 1945. His awards include the American Defense Medal, Good Conduct, South Pacific and one Battle Star.

Married Jackie in 1949; they have four daughters: Karen in Nova Scotia; Sheila in Miami; Eileen in Big Bend National Park; and Rita Ann in California. They also have seven grandchildren.

He was a police officer in Cleveland, OH for 30 years and retired in 1976. Lived in California for 13 years and has lived in Florida for the past five years. He enjoys golfing, fishing and traveling. He is a national executive committee member of the 37th Div. Assoc.

GLEN I. OLSON, Private First Class, was born Nov. 15, 1925 in Crosby, ND. He joined the Army Oct. 25, 1944 and served in the Infantry, Co. G, 145th Inf., 37th Div. He was stationed at Camp Robinson, Little Rock, AR and Fort Ord, CA. Participated in Philippine Liberation and Luzon. He served some time with 209th MP, Yokohama, Japan.

His awards include the Combat Infantry Badge, Philippine Liberation with one Bronze Service Star, Victory Medal, Asiatic-Pacific Service Medal, Army of Occupation and Good Conduct Medal. Was discharged Nov. 13, 1945 as private first class.

He and Arlene were married in 1959; they have two daughters, three grandchildren, one son deceased. He is a member of American Legion and Legion Color Guard for last 48 years; member of VFW and 37th Div. Assoc. He is semi-retired from farming.

JAMES A. OSMAN, Captain, was born June 14, 1921, at Manchester, OH. He joined the Army, Infantry, Aug. 12, 1940; assigned to Camp Shelby, Ft. Benning, Japan, Korea and Ft. Lewis.

Participated in the invasion of Normandy and Korean Conflict. He received the Purple Heart with cluster and a medical retirement in November 1951. Achieved the rank of captain.

He and his wife, Maggie Dean, have three children: Sandy, Jim and Ferne. Osman is retired from the Arizona School System.

LEROY J. OSMAN, Major, was born Dec. 12, 1900 in Manchester, OH. He joined the service Aug. 9, 1932; and was assigned to Co. E, 147th Inf., 37th Div. Stationed at Schofield Barracks, Military Reservation, HI; Camp Shelby, MS; Indiantown Gap Mil. Res. Fiji Islands, Camp Roberts, CA, Japan, Korea, Ft. Custer, MI, Germany and Ft. Story, VA.

While removing the dead and wounded from the battlefield in Korea, he discovered his son who had been severely wounded.

His awards/medals include the Korean Service Medal with four BSs, Bronze Star Medal, UN Service Ribbon, ROK Presidential Unit Citation, Army Commendation Medal, American Campaign Medal, Asiatic-Pacific Campaign Medal, WWII Victory Medal, OCC Medal (Germany), Combat Infantry Badge, National Defense Service Medal and Armed Forces Reserve Medal.

Released from military on Dec. 2, 1960 as major.

He and his wife Laura have four sons: Lester, James, Bill and Bob.

Leroy J. Osman passed away Dec. 26, 1968.

WILLIAM R. OSMAN, Staff Sergeant, was born Dec. 20, 1922 at Manchester, OH. He joined the service Aug. 3, 1940; assigned to Co. E, 147th Inf., 37th Div.; stationed at Camp Shelby, MS; Indiantown Gap Military Reservation, PA; Fiji Island, Guadalcanal, British Samoa, Wallis Island, New Caledonia, Emirau, Letterman's General Hospital, San Francisco, Finney's General Hospital, GA, Wakeman's General Hospital and Camp Atterbury, IN.

Memorable experience was serving in the military along with his father and brother. They were all sergeants in Co. E, 147th Inf. He was discharged July 3, 1945 as staff sergeant. His awards include the Combat Infantry Badge, Bronze Star Medal, Good Conduct Medal, American Campaign Medal, Asiatic-Pacific Campaign with one cluster and WWII Victory Medal.

After 35 years of teaching, he retired in 1986. He spends much of his time, fishing, hunting, gardening and "Honey Do's." He lives with his wife Patricia and they have three daughters: Gretchen Cardinale, Lisa Sanborn and Pat Osberg.

BERNARD L. PATTERSON, Captain, was born July 12, 1919, Roanoke, VA. He joined the Army on March 26, 1942; Infantry, OCS; Co. F, 145th, 37th Div.; and was stationed at Ft. Benning, GA, New Caledonia, Guadalcanal, Hill 700, Bougainville, Intramuros, Manila, Mt. Pacajuan and North Luzon.

His memorable experience was when torpedoed off Guadalcanal on Oct. 11, 1943. Also memorable was when they were approaching Angeles on the way to Manila and about 150 yards from a wood line they suddenly saw a large Japanese flag being waved. A Japanese officer came out of the woods and Lt. Roegner went toward him. The Japanese began shouting and some one in Patterson's company shot at him but missed. The officer turned and jogged back to his position. About 70 Japanese soldiers had been standing with rifles down in the open in front of the trees, and after the shot they moved back. Lt. Roegne turned and walked back to our lines—not a shot was fired. Lt. Roegne never mentioned this incident in his report. It has haunted Patterson to this day wondering what the Japanese officer wanted.

Was discharged April 21, 1946 as captain. Awards include the American Theater, Asiatic-Pacific (two campaigns), Philippine Liberation Medal, Combat Infantry Badge and Bronze Star.

Patterson is married and the father of three children. Retired M.D., Louisburg, NC.

LLOYD A. PEARTHREE, Master Sergeant, was born Dec. 25, 1919 in Brainerd, MN. He joined the service Nov. 7, 1941; served with HQ Co., 145th Inf. Regt., 37th Div.; stationed at Camp Wheeler, GA; Indiantown Gap, PA; New Zealand, Fiji, Guadalcanal, New Georgia, Bougainville and Luzon.

He participated in action at New Georgia, Bougainville and Luzon. Pearthree was discharged Oct. 7, 1945 as master sergeant. Married to Frances, they have one daughter and three grandsons. He is retired and keeps busy with his hobbies: amateur radio, computers, gardening, wood working and photography.

HAROLD PETERSON (PETE), was born in Stillwater, MN on Dec. 10, 1924. He served from Jan. 7, 1943 to Dec. 24, 1945. He trained at Camp Roberts, CA. In May of 1943, he went to the South Pacific and was assigned to the 37th Div., Co. H, 145th Inf. at Munda, New Georgia.

After a short rest on Guadalcanal, he went to the invasion of Bougainville. He felt some of the fieriest combat was when the Japanese attacked Hill 700 and the rest of the perimeter in March of 1944. He participated in the invasion of Luzon, the battle for Manila, the Mt. Pacawagoa area and the Cagayan Valley in northern Luzon.

His awards include the American Theater Ribbon, Asiatic-Pacific Ribbon with three Battle Stars, Philippine Liberation Ribbon with two stars, Victory Medal, Combat Infantry Badge and the Bronze Star.

He is a retired driver license director for the state of Minnesota and resides with his wife, Evelyn, in Coon Rapids, MN; they have one daughter, Karen.

JOE J. PETRASEK, Tech Sergeant, was born Dec. 20, 1913 in Flatonia, TX. He joined the Army Infantry on July 20, 1942 and trained at Camp Roberts, CA; Fort McDowel and Camp Stoneman.

Participated in action at New Georgia, battle on Hill 700, Lingayen Gulf, Luzon and Manila. Memorable experience was guiding and carrying supplies at Mt. Pacawagoa, antitank and native crews; battle of Ourang Pass; Cagayan blitz; and a patrol on Pinaquian when the war ended.

Discharged Oct. 13, 1945 as tech sergeant. His awards include the Combat Badge, Bronze Star with Golden V for Valor, Purple Heart, Asiatic-Pacific Medal, Victory Medal, Good Conduct Medal and Philippine Liberation Ribbon,

Petrasek is single; he is retired from the Texas Highway Dept.

RICHARD B. PHARE, was born Dec. 23, 1921. He trained at Camp Wolters, TX; shipped to the South Pacific; and joined Co. E, 148th Regt., 37th Div. as a machine gunner. After the battle of Manila, they set up camp at San Juan Heights for R&R. They headed for

Baguio in April where he won the Bronze Star and Purple Heart medals on April 25, 1945.

His write-up is: "For heroic achievement in connection with military operations against the enemy at Luzon, Philippine Islands on April 25, 1945. Private Phare displayed exceptional courage and devotion to duty when he crawled across 40 yards of open terrain exposed to intense enemy fire in order to man a machine gun which had been put out of action by the death of its operator. By delivering accurate machine gun fire against enemy pillbox and forcing its occupants to take cover, Private Phare made it possible for a rocket launcher operator to move forward and destroy the Japanese fortification."

JOHN F. PICKENS, Sergeant, was born in Newport, OH on Oct. 14, 1900. He served in the USMC in 1918; joined Btry. C, 135th, FA ONG, 37th Div. Alliance, OH, June 1940 with the rank of mess sergeant. Btry. C ONG was called to active duty in October 1940 and trained at Camp Shelby, MS and Indiantown Gap, PA. In May 1942, the division went to the South Pacific (New Zealand and Fiji Island).

In Spring of 1943, he and several other men were chosen to form a cadre and returned to Camp Joseph T. Robinson, AR where the 561st FA BN was activated on July 9, 1943. After training, this battalion was sent to Europe. He participated in battles at St. Lo and Brest in France, St. Vith, Namur, Battle of the Bulge in Belgium and on into Germany.

He was awarded the Asiatic-Pacific Ribbon, European Theater Ribbon, Bronze Star Medal and WWII Medal. He was discharged with rank of staff sergeant in July 1945.

Returned to Ohio and pursued his education earning a BS and master degrees in education. Was a teacher, principal and superintendent in the Ohio Public School System until his retirement in 1967. He passed away in March 1976. *Submitted by his son, Robert O. Pickens.*

VERNON PIERCE, born at Mt. Sterling, OH on Nov. 26, 1915, and was reared in the Masonic Home in Springfield, OH. He graduated from SHS in 1935 and was drafted in the Army's Co. K, 147th Inf. at Camp Shelby, MS. The regiment was shipped to the South Pacific in April 1942.

Landed in Tongatabu and sent to Guadalcanal in November 1942 for combat. After six months they were sent to western Samoa for rehabilitation. Later served in New Caledonia and Emirau Island. Rotated to the States after two years, reassigned to Camp Reynolds, PA, then Indiantown Gap, PA. Next was transferred to Carlisle Barracks, PA and assigned to the printing department.

Discharged in July 1945, he moved to Long Beach, CA and worked as a printer. Later, he went to work for the U.S. Postal Service, retiring in October 1981. He is a member of DAV, VFW, Guadalcanal Campaign Veterans Assoc. and Pacific Coast Chapter 37th Div. Vets. Assoc. and enjoys attending military reunions.

DONALD H. PING, Tech-4, was born April 24, 1925 near Indianapolis, IN. He became the fourth generation in his family line to serve in the military.

When drafted he was sent to Ft. Bragg, NC for his training as an artillery gunner. At completion of basic he shipped out of San Francisco on March 18, 1944 as a replacement to the 136th FA BN. Good fortune prevailed with the opportunity to become a surveyor in HQ Btry., a post that he retained to war's end.

After eight months on Bougainville, he participated in the invasion of Luzon; capture of Manila; advance on and capture of Baguio; and finally aided in the rapid, caring drive up the Cagayan Valley where the enemy finally capitulated.

The highlight in his career came after Baguio when he had a brief reunion with his Seabee father who was stationed on Samar Island. His dad persevered in tracking him down, against all odds, near Cabantuan while on a seven day pass.

After the war, he became a chiropractor, wrote his autobiography of military life *The Smoking War*. He lives with his wife, Dorothy, in Warren, IN.

ELTJO POOL, Sergeant, was born May 20, 1921, Kalamazoo, MI. He joined the service April 16, 1942 and was assigned to Co. I, 129th Inf., 37th Div. Stations include: Camp Forrest, TN, Fiji Islands, New Hebrides, Bougainville and Luzon.

Participated in Bougainville Luzon Beachhead, Baguio-Cagayan Valley and Manila.

Pool was recommended for the Distinguished Service Cross Medal for the following action on Luzon, P.I., 1945: "For extraordinary heroism during the 129th Inf. Regt.'s advance in the Cagayan Valley, Luzon on June 2, 1945 near Bone South. The 3rd Plt. of Co. I had been advancing and was preparing for the night and had dug their slit trenches. The officer in charge ordered a search of the immediate front for security purposes. Sgt. Pool was the first scout and investigated a culvert under the road. When he stuck his head in for a clearer view and saw Jap helmets and some men, he immediately yelled 'Japs.' By this time he was joined by the other scout and when the Japs fired at them and threw a grenade, Sgt. Pool threw himself and the other scout on the ground. This action saved their lives. With the enemy being located, Sgt. Pool began to throw grenades into the culvert. The first grenade was thrown back at him so thereafter, he released the handle before throwing and no more were thrown back. When grenades were gone, he threw the smoke grenade and asked for covering rifle fire while he went for more grenades. With the new supply of grenades, Sgt. Pool threw 12 more until no further sounds were made. When action was terminated a count of 21 enemy dead were counted. Pool's action and his display of courage was an inspiration to all. His immediate action saved the lives of several men and provided an example that is worthy of the highest traditions of the military service."

Discharged Dec. 20, 1945 as sergeant. His awards include three Bronze Stars and two Purple Hearts.

Married 54 years and has one son and one daughter. He is retired.

WARD S. PORTER, T-4, was born Oct. 30, 1918 in Cleveland, OH. He enlisted in the 37th Div., 148th

Inf. on Feb. 11, 1941. In May 1942 he was sent overseas and served until June 1944 in the Fiji Islands, New Georgia and Bougainville, Solomon Islands where he was awarded the Bronze Star.

Received the Asiatic-Pacific Theater Ribbon with Bronze Star, American Defense Service Medal and Good Conduct Ribbon.

In June 1944, he returned from the Southwest Pacific and was assigned to Camp Crowder, MO to teach at the Army Signal Center. There he received two commendations for the excellence of his work.

After separation from the Army in September 1945, he returned to Cleveland where he worked for the Atlantic Oil Co. In November 1966 he moved with his family, wife Margaret, sons, Richard and Ward, and daughter Peggy to Lake Worth, FL where he owned and managed apartment buildings and was an active member of the Kiwanis Club serving for nine years as treasurer and also as club secretary and board member.

He passed away Sept. 27, 1991 and is buried in Fort Logan National Cemetery in Denver, CO.

BENNY WILLIAM PRATER, was born March 13, 1925 in Council Bluffs, IA. At the age of two, his family moved to Clearwater, NE where he attended and graduated from Clearwater High School in May 1943. He enlisted in the Army on June 5, 1943 and was sent to Fort McClellan, AL for basic training.

He departed for overseas from Camp Shanks, NY and was sent to the South Pacific and served in New Caledonia, Guadalcanal and Bougainville where he joined the 145th Inf. 37th Div. He participated in the invasion of Luzon and the battles of Manila, Malabon and Pacawagoa.

Awarded the Combat Infantry Badge, Bronze Star, Asiatic-Pacific Theater Ribbon with two Bronze Battle Stars and the Philippine Liberation Ribbon with one Bronze Battle Star.

He was discharged from Fort Logan, CO on Dec. 17, 1945. He is retired after 25 years as fire chief of the Clearwater Volunteer Fire Depart. and is completing his 40th year with the same company as a automobile salesman. He and his wife Ruth are the parents of one daughter and two sons; they have four grandchildren. He is an active member of the Clearwater Legion, Post 267.

WALTER W. RADER, T-Sergeant, was born May 21, 1920 in Chillicote, OH and reared in Manchester, OH. Walter and his two brothers, Charles and Robert, all entered the military on the same day in October 1939.

Walter was stationed at Camp Shelby, MS and joined the 37th Div., Co. E, 147th Inf. He participated in battles in Guadalcanal, New Georgia, Bougainville and New Caledonia. He suffered from malaria. He stayed in the service, retiring in 1963. He served in Korea, Germany and Camp Cumberland, PA After retirement he worked for the U.S. Post Office in Washington, DC. He retired from there to Jacksonville, FL where he passed away from cancer, Jan. 31, 1988, and buried with honors at Arlington National Cemetery Feb. 8, 1988. Married, he had two daughters, Connie and Gail.

Robert was discharged Oct. 17, 1940, Camp Shelby, MS. He finished high school and re-entered the service with the 101st Abn. Div. and fought in battles at Normandy, Holland, Bastogne and Belgium.

Charles spent 44 months in the South Pacific. He was ill with malaria. He participated in battles in Guadalcanal, New Caledonia, Bougainville and New Georgia.

JAMES G. RALLS SR., was born Dec. 8, 1920, Front Royal, VA. He joined the Army Jan. 21, 1941 and was assigned to the 99th FA Pack Artillery, Fort Hoyle, MD.

Was shipped out as special troops to the South Pacific in January 1942 to Bora Bora. He joined in with the first Navy CB ever formed, heavy equipment, in which several large storage tanks were built for oil and fresh water to service the small ships and submarines. The code name was (Bobcats). At an adjoining island, they built a large airport which is still used today. Sometime in 1943 he was reassigned to the 37th Div., 136th FA Btry. at the Guadalcanal to Bougainville.

In May 1944 after two years foreign service was rotated, then to Cadre 2-4-2 Field Artillery, Fort Bragg, NC; the final class. Was discharged Oct. 5, 1945.

He and wife, Barbara, have been married 48 years; they have seven children all on their own. Worked for Sparrows Point Police Dept., until retiring in 1983.

CARL V. RAMMEL, T-5, was born Oct. 5, 1918 in Burkettsville, OH. He trained at Camp Shelby, MS and served from Feb. 1, 1941 to July 31, 1945, with the 37th Div., B Btry., 136th FA.

Initially landing on New Zealand, he was moved to Fiji and then to Guadalcanal where he took part in the end of the fighting there. He and his outfit participated in making the beachheads on New Georgia, Bougainville and Luzon.

He was awarded the Asiatic-Pacific Ribbon with two Bronze Stars, American Defense Service Medal, Philippine Liberation Ribbon with one Bronze Star and a Good Conduct Ribbon.

Rammel is a retired lithographer. He and his wife, Eleanor, now reside in Miamisburg, OH. They have three children and six grandchildren.

RUSSELL A. RAMSEY, Major General, was born in Sandusky, OH on May 11, 1904. Commissioned out of Princeton University's Army ROTC as an artilleryman in 1935, he chose the Officers Reserve Corps while attending Michigan Law School. As a practicing attorney in Sandusky, he found more opportunity for the citizen soldiering that he loved with the Ohio National Guard, which he joined in 1937.

Ramsey led Btry. E, 135th FA overland to Camp Shelby, MS in October 1940. He shipped out to the Fiji Islands aboard the *SS President McKinley* with the 37th Div. in 1942. He then went on to New Georgia and Bougainville Campaigns in the Solomon Islands as a lieutenant colonel commanding the 3rd Bn., 145th Inf. Regt.

He was Division G-3 for the Lingayen Gulf amphibious landing on Luzon in January 1945. When Manila was liberated, Russell was promoted to colonel and served as chief of staff, 37th Div. until demobilization. His WWII service won him the Silver Star, Legion of Merit, Bronze Star with V, and his first

OLC, Purple Heart, Combat Infantry Badge and three Battle Stars plus an Arrowhead on his Theater Campaign Ribbon.

In 1946 Russell was transferred back to the Army Reserve, this time as commanding general of the Ohio 83rd Inf. Div. until its conversion to a training unit in 1960, when he retired with 35 years of combined Reserve, National Guard, and AUS service.

A career lawyer in civilian life, Ramsey was a strong champion of citizen readiness for military mobilization. He was also a lay leader in the Episcopal Church. He died at age 86 on Feb. 20, 1991, under his son's care in Albany, GA. His last outing was to watch the Georgia National Guard march off to mobilization for Operation Desert Shield/Storm, it was 50 years to the day from his own National Guard mobilization for WWII. His biography *On Law and Country;* the biography and speeches of Russell A. Ramsey was written and edited by his son, Dr. Russell W. Ramsey. *Submitted by Russell W. Ramsey*

ERNEST F. RANSDELL, Private First Class, was born March 21, 1925 at Washington, DC. He joined the service in December 1942; Schofield and was assigned to Infantry, 610, 748th, 37th Div. Stationed at Schofield Barracks, HI; Bougainville, S.I. and Luzon.

He was wounded 25 miles east of Manila on May 8, 1945. Discharged in December 1945 as private first class. He received the Combat Infantry Badge and Purple Heart.

Divorced, he has three children. He retired after 32 years service at Long Beach Post Office.

RALPH RECHER, born July 4, 1918 in Montgomery County, OH. He was inducted into the 37th Div., 147th Inf., Service Co. Feb. 1, 1941. Went overseas on April 7, 1942 and served for 33 months in the South Pacific: Tonga, Guadalcanal, British Samoa, New Caledonia, Emirau and New Caledonia again.

His most memorable experience occurred on Christmas Day 1943 on British Samoa. During a test ride in a Ventura bomber with a new engine, the pilot at 4,000 feet altitude, put the plane into a dive and pulled out at wave-top height between two ships anchored parallel to each other in the harbor. Medals and awards include the Asiatic-Pacific Ribbon with three Bronze Campaign Stars, Bronze Star Medal, Combat Infantry Badge, Good Conduct Medal, American Defense Service Medal, WWII Victory Medal and he is entitled to wear the Solomon Islands Campaign 50th Anniversary Medal.

Discharged May 30, 1945

EARL WILLIAM RASMUSSEN, 1st Sergeant, was born June 29, 1919 in Woodstock, IL. He joined the Army March 5, 1941 and served with Co. I, 129th Inf., 37th Div. and was stationed at Clark Field, Fiji Islands, Solomon Islands, Lingayen Gulf, Manila, New Hebrides, Bougainville, Ft. Stotsenburg, Baguio, Cagayan Valley, Aparri and Camp Forrest, TN.

He participated in the Asiatic-Pacific Theater and earned the Asiatic-Pacific Theater Ribbon with two Bronze Battle Stars, Philippine Liberation Ribbon, Purple Heart, Good Conduct Ribbon, American Defense Service Ribbon, one service stripe and five Overseas Service Bars. He was discharged July 27, 1945 as first sergeant.

He and his wife, Lucille, have a daughter, Ella, and sons: Joseph, Frank, Philip, David and one infant son deceased. They live in Cherokee Village, AR. Rasmussen organized many reunions, the first in 1961 and the last in 1990.

FREDERICK J. REICHELDERFER, Staff Sergeant, was born Sept. 19, 1924, at Cridersville, OH. He graduated from high school in 1942 and joined the 37th Div., Co. L, 3rd Plt. on Guadalcanal in 1943. He made landings on Bougainville and Luzon where he was wounded in the shoulder in June of 1945 after the battle for Manila.

He was shipped home when the war ended, arriving at San Francisco with the Division and actually arrived in Cridersville the day before Christmas in 1945. His awards include the Purple Heart, Bronze Star and one OLC, two theater and service pins, Combat Infantry Badge, Good Conduct Medal and Philippine Liberation Medal.

Reichelderfer is retired from BP Oil Co. He lives with his wife Betty in the village of Cridersville. They have two grown children, Cathy and David. They keep busy in their church and many civic affairs and have traveled many places, including a trip back to Luzon in 1985.

RAYMOND S. REYNOLDS, was born Nov. 26, 1924, at Tampa, FL. He joined the military service July 17, 1942; went to Camp Robinson, AR for basic training; and Angel Island, San Francisco.

Assigned to the 37th Div., 145th Inf., HQ Co., Bn. 2, he participated in action at Guadalcanal, New Georgia, Bougainville, Luzon, Manila, Cagayen, etc.

Reynolds was discharged Dec. 17, 1945. His awards/medals include the Bronze Star, Bronze Star Cluster, Infantry Badge and Liberation.

He and his wife, Beverly, have three daughters. He is retired and enjoys woodworking for a hobby.

CHARLES G. RIMMEL, T-5, was born in St. Louis, MO on May 12, 1919. He served in the Army from June 1, 1944 to Feb. 23, 1946, and trained at Camp Wolters, TX.

In January 1945, he went to the South Pacific and was assigned to the 37th Div., Co. A, 129th Inf. in time to start the trek for the battle of Baguio. He also participated in the drive up the Cagayan Valley to Aparri.

He was awarded the Combat Infantry Badge, WWII Victory Ribbon, Asiatic-Pacific Ribbon with two Bronze Stars and Philippine Liberation Ribbon with one Bronze Star.

Rimmel retired in 1981 after 34 years as a machine shop foreman. He and his wife, Dorothy, have been married 52 years and have a son and a daughter. They still reside in St. Louis, MO.

JOHN N. RIZZUTO, Staff Sergeant, was born July 2, 1921 at Brooklyn, NY. He joined the service Feb. 12, 1943 and served in the Medical Detachment, 37th Div., 148th Inf. Regt. He was stationed at Guadalcanal, Bougainville and Luzon and participated from the landing on Nov. 9, 1943 until the end of the war in the Philippines.

All of his time overseas was memorable. He earned the Combat Medical Badge, Bronze Star, Purple Heart, Presidential Citation, Meritorious Unit Emblem, Asiatic Campaign Medal with Arrowhead and two Bronze Stars, WWII Victory Medal, Good Conduct Medal, Philippine Unit Citation Badge, Philippine Liberation Medal and Philippine Independence. Discharged Dec. 31, 1945 as staff sergeant.

Retired after 42 years of teaching. He has been married 45 years and has one son Christopher.

MACARIO H. RODRIGUEZ, Private First Class, was born Dec. 22, 1924 in Staples, TX. He joined the Army June 23, 1943, with basic training at Camp Roberts, CA. Assigned to Btry. C, 135th FA BN with the duty of loading the 105 gun; he participated in the invasion of Luzon.

Overseas duty in South Pacific, New Caledonia, Guadalcanal, Bougainville, Philippine Islands, Luzon and Manila. His memorable experience was New Caledonia and unloading war and food supplies. Discharged Jan. 20, 1946 as private first class. He earned the Asiatic-Pacific Campaign Medal with two Bronze Stars, WWII Victory Medal, Philippine Liberation Ribbon with one Bronze Star and the Good Conduct Medal.

Still working as a barber, he lives in Edinburg, TX with his wife, Maria. They have daughter, Estela, and two grandchildren, Jessica and Christopher.

WILLIAM F. RODGERS, Private First Class, was born April 3, 1919 at Spartanburg, SC. He joined the Army Nov. 11, 1941; assigned to Co. G, 145th, 37th Div., AA gunner on ships; stationed at Ft. Jackson and Indiantown Gap, PA. Served 37 months overseas at Fiji Islands, Guadalcanal, New Georgia, Bougainville and Luzon.

Memorable experiences include Walled City, Manila, Mt. Pacawagon and Hill 700.

Awards include Combat Infantry Badge, Asiatic-Pacific Ribbon with two Bronze Service Stars, Bronze Star, Purple Heart, Philippine Liberation Ribbon with one Bronze Service Star, Good Conduct, American Defense Ribbon, WWII Victory and six Overseas Bars. He was discharged Oct. 19, 1945 as private first class.

Retired, he lives with his wife, Delma, at Del Rio, TN.

REXFORD W. ROGERS, Major, was born Aug. 7, 1918 at Gouveneur, NY. He joined the service March 12, 1942 and served in the Signal Corps. Stations: 77th Sig. Co., 77th Inf. Div.; OSC Ft. Monmouth, Ft. Kilmer and Ft. Dix, NJ; Columbia, SC; Lexington Signal Depot, KY; Camp Reynolds, PA and Camp Beale, CA.

Overseas duty with 37th Sig. Corps, 37th Inf. Div. at Bougainville; Yokohama Sig. Svc. Det. Participated in action at Lingayen, battle of Manila, Baguio and Cagayan Valley. His memorable experience was being indoctrinated into the combat zone at Bougainville. Had many exciting experiences while installing telephone communications in and around the Presidential Palace during the battle of Manila with lots of incoming mortar fire.

Earned the Bronze Star, American Campaign Medal, Philippine Liberation Ribbon, WWII Victory Medal, Philippine Presidential Unit Citation, Meritorious Unit Citation, Army of Occupation (Japan), three Overseas Bars, two Battle Stars and one Arrowhead. Discharged from WWII March 31, 1946 and from the Korean Conflict Oct. 10, 1952. He achieved the rank of major.

Retired in 1979 from New York Telephone Co. after 40 years service. He lives with his wife, Hope, in Clearwater, FL. They have a daughter, Holly, living in Ontario, CA. He enjoys golf, bridge and travel and has been the leader of a dance band for the last 13 years.

WILLIAM S. ROTHE, Captain, was born Feb. 25, 1920 in Weston, OH. He joined the service in April

1943 and served in the Medical Corps, 37th Div., 1st Bn., 148th Inf. Stationed at 315th Gen. Hosp., 165th Station Hosp., 153rd Station Hosp., Philippines and Cagayan Valley.

Discharged in December 1946 as captain. His awards include the Combat Medical Badge, Bronze Star, Purple Heart, American Theater, Pacific Theater and star, Philippine Liberation and star, Philippine Independence, WWII Victory Medal and Philippine Distinguished Unit Citation.

A retired physician, he lives with his wife at Thousand Palms, CA. They have five sons.

S. FRANK RUGGIO, Sergeant, was born Feb. 7, 1922 in Chicago, IL. He entered the service in December of 1942; had basic training at Camp Wolters, TX and left there for the PTD. Trained in jungle warfare in the New Hebrides. Made beachhead on the island of Bougainville, Solomon Island. Saw action in the battle of Northern Solomons from Lingayen Gulf to the streets of Manila up the Cagayan Valley to Appari where Truman saved them with his decision to drop the A bomb.

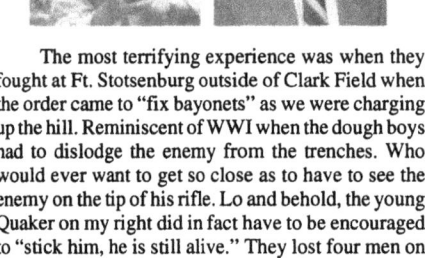

The most terrifying experience was when they fought at Ft. Stotsenburg outside of Clark Field when the order came to "fix bayonets" as we were charging up the hill. Reminiscent of WWI when the dough boys had to dislodge the enemy from the trenches. Who would ever want to get so close as to have to see the enemy on the tip of his rifle. Lo and behold, the young Quaker on my right did in fact have to be encouraged to "stick him, he is still alive." They lost four men on that skirmish. They did survive on "the Top of the World," the name they gave the high ground for which they paid so dearly.

When in combat with direct enemy contact each and every fight is sudden and ends quickly. Everyone engaged in direct combat has his own "little war," directed in his own field of fire. You have to have him in your own sights in order to kill. Or, as in Ft. Stotsenburg, you have to be very, very close to kill.

But, that is all part of another life. From the city bred boy scout, salesman to the quasi retired insurance broker, he is glad to have lived through it all. He would never wish the horror on anyone. "The camaraderie that exists with the men of an outfit is something of an inward pride and fondness for one another that is an absolute part of 'your other life' that exists and comes alive when you meet at a reunion and you reminisce. How vivid the memories are after 52 years."

Discharged Jan. 10, 1946 as sergeant. He earned the Purple Heart with cluster, Bronze Star with cluster, Philippine Liberation Ribbon with one Bronze Star, Philippine Unit Citation, Asiatic-Pacific Theater Ribbon with two Bronze Battle Stars and Bronze Arrowhead, WWII Victory Medal, Combat Infantry Badge and one Service Stripe and five Overseas Service Bars.

He has a charming wife who has mothered two sons, both of whom are married. The eldest has taken over his dad's insurance agency and the other son is a doctor of dentistry.

MAX N. RUHL, Colonel, was born in Franklin, PA in 1915 and grew up in Warren, OH. He received a bachelor of industrial engineering degree from Ohio State in 1939 and was drafted in 1941. He was sent with the 148th Inf. Regt. to Fiji, Guadalcanal and New Georgia. Engineer OCS followed in 1944.

He later served in Guam, Korea and Germany with assignments at MIT, Command and General Staff College, Army Logistics Management Center, ODCSLOG and Artillery School interspersed.

After 27 years of service, he was retired at Ft. Sill, OK in 1968. He received the Silver Star, Legion of Merit, Bronze Star, Defense and Army Commendation Medals and Combat Medic Badge.

He moved to a hill farm near Woodbury, TN and worked in the Woodbury Post Office until 1982. He and his wife, Barbara, have four children, six grandchildren and one great-grandchild.

JAMES RYAN, was born on March 22, 1920. He was drafted into the service in January 1942 and served until March 13, 1946. Initially, he asked to be assigned to the Air Corps, but was rejected and ended up at Camp Croft, SC for basic infantry training. After 13 weeks of training, he was assigned to the cadre as an instructor. The following year, as a sergeant, he attended OCS at Ft. Benning, GA.

On July 14, 1943, he graduated as a 2nd lieutenant. On Aug. 14, 1943, he was married to Marie E. Scouten and in March 1944, he went to the South Pacific. There he joined Co. F, 145th Inf. on Bougainville and was assigned to the 2nd Plt. of F Co. He served with this same platoon until he was shipped back to the States in November 1945. During this time he participated in all the company's activities on Bougainville, the Luzon Invasion, the battle for Manila, the breaching of the Walled City, the assault on Mt. Pacawagon and the subsequent cleaning up operations until leaving Luzon to return home.

He was awarded the Combat Infantry Badge, Silver Star, Bronze Star Medal with OLC, Purple Heart, American Campaign Medal, Asiatic-Pacific Campaign Medal, WWII Victory Medal and the Philippine Liberation Ribbon.

After being discharged in 1946, he attended college and in 1951 received a chemical engineering degree from the Massachusetts Institute of Technology. He worked for the Colgate Palmolive Co. for 33 years in a management capacity until retiring in 1983.

He lives in Pompton Plains, NJ with his wife of 50 years, Marie; they have two sons, one daughter and six grandchildren.

WALTER S. SAMEK, Sergeant, was born March 25, 1914 in Cleveland, OH. He joined the service Jan. 31, 1941 and served with Co. D, 145th Inf., 37th Div. He was stationed at Camp Shelby, MS; Indiantown Gap, PA; Fiji and Guadalcanal.

He participated in action at New Georgia, Munda, Bougainville, Luzon and Philippines. Memorable experience was battle on Hill 700, Bougainville and Manila.

Discharged July 27, 1945 as sergeant, Signal

NCO 542. He earned the Combat Infantry Badge, Philippine Liberation Ribbon with one Bronze Star, Asiatic Pacific Ribbon with two Bronze Stars, American Defense Service and Good Conduct Ribbon.

Married 48 years and has son, Steven, and daughter, Rita. He is semi-retired from real estate business.

DONALD L. SANFREY SR., Sergeant, was born and raised in Warren, OH. He enlisted in Co. F, 145th Inf. in October 1939 and remained with the 37th Div. throughout all his service time. He went to Camp Shelby, MS in November 1940 for further training and while there attained the rank of sergeant.

Was shipped out to the South Pacific in May of 1942. Stopped in New Zealand for a short time, then on to the Fiji Islands, Guadalcanal, New Georgia, and Bougainville in the Solomon Islands. While at Guadalcanal he transferred into the 37th Div., MP Co. and participated in the battle for the Philippines.

Returned to the States and was discharged in October 1945. Upon returning home, he went to work for General Motors, leaving in 1955 to become Ohio State Hwy. patrolman, then back to General Motors in 1966 until he retired in 1985.

He is a member of the American Legion, a life member of the DAV, VFW and the 37th Div. Veterans Assoc. He and his wife reside in Warren, OH; they have four children.

EUGENE SCHMID, Staff Sergeant, was born Oct. 15, 1922 in Germany. He joined the service in October 1942 and served with Army Clearing Co., 112th Med. Bn., 37th Div. He was stationed at Camp Barkeley, TX; Fitzsimmons Gen. Hosp., Denver, CO; and California

Overseas duty at New Caledonia, Bougainville, Solomon Islands, Luzon and Philippines. Participated in action at Luzon, Lingayen Invasion, battle for Manila. His memorable experience was treating Rodriques (Medal of Honor recipient) just prior to his going home.

Awards include the Asiatic-Pacific Theater Ribbon with two Bronze Stars and the Philippine Liberation Medal with one Bronze Star.

He married his college sweetheart, Helen Ault, and they have four children: Theodore, Diana, Eugenie, Barbara, and five grandchildren.

CHARLES F. SCHMIDT, Tech Sergeant, was born June 6, 1919 at Donora, PA. He joined the Army

on Jan. 23, 1941 and served in the Infantry, Co. D, 145th Inf., 37th Div. and was stationed at Camp Shelby.

Overseas duty was in the Philippines, New Georgia, Luzon, Northern Solomons and Bougainville. Memorable experiences are friendships of Army buddies and of the friends lost.

Discharged Sept. 5, 1945 as tech sergeant. He earned the Purple Heart with cluster, Bronze Star, Silver Star, Combat Infantry Badge and Philippine Liberation Ribbon.

Retired, he enjoys golf, travel and life. Married Carol on Aug. 23, 1947; they have a daughter and a son.

HAROLD E. SEARS, was born Aug. 14, 1920 in Morrow, OH. On Oct. 14, 1940, he joined the Army National Guard in Ohio, then transferred to regular Army. He was stationed at Camp Shelby, MS; Indiantown Gap, PA; Guadalcanal; Bougainville; and Bismarck.

Discharged in July 1945 (WWII) and in 1954 (Korea). He earned the Combat Infantry Badge, Good Conduct Medal, APTO Ribbon and American Defense Service Medal. Married 49 years to Eleanor Fennell. Harold Sears suffered a cardiac arrest.

CHRIS SEIBERT, was born in Cincinnati, OH on July 5, 1915. He served in Co. B, Rifle Co., 147th Inf. for six months. Transferred to Service Co., 147th Inf., Camp Shelby, where he served as a welder.

Was sent overseas on April 7, 1942, and served for 33 months in the South Pacific; island hopped for 33 months: Tonga, Guadalcanal, British Samoa, New Caledonia, Emirau, then back to New Caledonia.

He remembers the still as his unforgettable experience. It was fabricated on Tonga and used extensively on the islands, producing "fine spirits" which quite a number of troops enjoyed. Whenever the order came to move to another island, the order came, "Crate the still first." It was sold to the Air Force on Emirau and it may still be producing good old "Jungle Juice" today for the natives.

He was discharged July 5, 1945. His awards include the Asiatic-Pacific Ribbon with three Bronze Campaign Stars, Bronze Star Medal, Combat Infantry Badge, Good Conduct Medal, American Defense Service Medal, WWII Victory Medal and he is entitled to wear the Solomon Island Campaign 50th Anniversary Medal, authorized by the Solomon Islands Government on Aug. 7, 1992. His company was the only company in the 147th Inf. RCT, USA to be awarded a Presidential Unit Citation.

LOWELL SENEFELD, T-5, was born in Franklin County, IN on Aug. 7, 1915. He served from Oct. 8, 1941 to July 27, 1945. He was inducted at Fort Harrison, IN and took basic training at Fort Sill, OK. In January 1942 he was assigned to the 135FA BN, 37th Div. at Camp Shelby, MS. He then moved to

Indiantown Gap, PA and on to Oakland, CA. On May 26, 1942, he sailed from San Francisco to the South Pacific to New Zealand, then Fiji Island Guadalcanal. He then took part in the invasion of the New Georgian Island. Then he went back to Guadalcanal before going on the invasion of Bougainville Island. Next was invasion of Luzon Island in the Philippine Islands, landing at Lingayen Gulf and driving south to Manila.

From Manila he returned to the States and was discharged on July 27, 1945, and was awarded the Asiatic-Pacific Theater Ribbon with two Bronze Stars, American Defense Service Medal, Philippine Liberation Ribbon with one Bronze Star and the Good Conduct Ribbon.

Retired from farming, he lives with his wife, Clarannella, in the town of Brookville, IN.

DONALD W. SHEETS, Private First Class, served on New Caledonia, Guadalcanal, Bougainville, Luzon and was wounded Feb. 23, 1945 while serving with Co. G, 145th Inf. at Wall City, Manila. He was hospitalized for 14 months at various locations and was discharged at Borden General Hospital, Chickasha, OK on April 26, 1946.

Awards include the Asiatic-Pacific Ribbon and two Bronze Stars, Purple Heart, Bronze Arrowhead, Philippine Liberation Ribbon and one Bronze Star, Good Conduct Medal, American Theater Ribbon and Victory Medal.

STEPHEN SHEPAS, Major, was born July 13, 1917 at Campbell, OH. He joined the Army National Guard on July 15, 1940 and served with the 37th Div. He was stationed at Camp Shelby, MS and overseas duty at Munda, New Georgia, Bougainville, Philippine Islands and Manila.

Participated in Battle for Hill 700, Manila and Munda Airfield. After the battle of Hill 700, he was amazed at the thousands of Japanese bodies piled everywhere. Hundreds of Navy, Marine, Airmen, CBs and support personnel scrounged for souvenirs. Their units were relieved and rotated to Guadalcanal for R&R, but the 37th was never relieved. They were on combat status from their first day to the end of the war in the Philippines.

Retired July 15, 1987, AUS, major. His awards/medals include the Silver Star, Bronze Star (2), Commendation Medal, Combat Infantry Badge, Philippine Presidential Unit Citation, American Defense, National Defense, Armed Forces Reserve Medal, American Campaign, Asiatic-Pacific, WWII Victory Medal, Good Conduct Medal and Philippine Liberation Ribbon.

He resides with his wife, Sophia, in Poland, OH; they have a son Richard and daughter Donna. He retired from the post office after 33 years.

THOMAS C. SIKES, Private First Class, was born Nov. 3, 1914 in Bannockburn, Berrien County, GA. He joined the service Jan. 13, 1942 and served with Co. G, 2nd Bn. and also with Co. L, 147th Inf., 37th Div.

Was a sniper and worked with CBs, Marines and Engineers, helping to build roads and airstrips. He drove a jeep named *Miss Ethyl* and hauled personnel, supplies, mail and ammunition. Drove under fire and during bombing raids. Served in Guadalcanal and Solomon Islands.

Discharged Oct. 7, 1945, at Camp Livingston, LA. His awards include the Asiatic-Pacific Theater Ribbon, Expert Infantry Badge, Good Conduct Medal and two Bronze Stars.

Thomas C. Sikes is deceased. *Submitted by his widow, Ethyl V. Sikes.*

BURT E. SILVERTHORN, was born Jan. 24, 1915, at Bradford, PA. He joined the service and served with B Btry., 135th FA BN, 37th Div. and was stationed at Camp Shelby, Camp Indiantown Gap, PA. Rest

Overseas duty at Munda, Hill 700, Angeles, Manila, Mt. Pacwagon and Lingayen Valley.

Discharged Aug. 16, 1945. His awards include the Philippine Presidential Distinguished Unit Citation, WWII Victory, Bronze Star with V device, Asiatic-Pacific, Good Conduct and Philippine Liberation Ribbon.

A retired railroad worker, he makes his home in Port Richey, FL. He has no family.

JOSEPH F. SIMONE, Private First Class, was born Oct. 18, 1922 in Southington, CT. He joined the service Jan. 28, 1943 and served with HQ Btry. 140th FA as field lineman, 641, 37th Div. He was stationed at Ft. Sill, New Caledonia, Guadalcanal, Ft. Devens, Northern Solomons, Western Pacific and Luzon.

Discharged Jan. 27, 1946 as private first class. His awards/medals include the Asiatic-Pacific Theater Ribbon, Philippine Liberation Ribbon with Bronze Service Star, Good Conduct Medal and Victory Medal.

Worked 50 years with Ideal Forge and retired as vice president. He lives with his wife, Lillian, in Southington, CT; they have three daughters: Susan, Barbara and Johanna, and a son, Joe Jr.

LYNN L. SIMPSON, Sergeant, was born Dec. 20, 1924 at Bloomington, IL. He joined the service March 12, 1943; trained at Camp Roberts, CA and joined the 37th Div., 148th Inf., Co. L at Guadalcanal in August 1943.

Memorable Experiences: beachhead landing on Jan. 9, 1945 at Luzon; Co. L, 148th Inf. on point when entering Manila during the night of Feb. 3 and 4, 1945 at the Caloocan Railroad Station; crossing the Tulia Han River; and later crossing the Pasig River.

Discharged Dec. 15, 1944 as sergeant, communications. His awards include the Combat Infantry Badge, Bronze Star and Presidential Unit Citation.

Retired from 40 years with Caterpillar Tractor Co. in Quality Control Div. He and his wife, Bertha Lanham, and six children lived in Glasgow, Scotland for five years (1962-66) and later in France (40 miles from Paris) for two years, 1980-82. Retired in December 1984 and now lives in their home town of Bloomington, IL.

He does volunteer work with local historical society and attends the 148th Inf. reunions each year held at Camp Perry, OH.

CARL M. SMITH, Staff Sergeant, was born April 30, 1919 in Upper Sandusky, OH. He joined the service on Jan. 24, 1941 and served with Co. F, 148th Inf., 37th Div. He was stationed at Camp Shelby, MS, Indiantown Gap, PA, Fiji and South Pacific.

Participated in action at New Georgia, Bougainville and Luzon. His memorable experience was going home after 40 months overseas. He was discharged Oct. 3, 1945 as staff sergeant. His awards include the Combat Infantry Badge, Silver Star, Asiatic-Pacific Ribbon, two Bronze Stars, American Defense Medal, Philippine Liberation with one star, Good Conduct and Distinguished Unit Citation.

Married 48 years and lives in Tiffin, OH. He has four children and nine grandchildren. Stays busy traveling, camping and golfing.

RALPH G. SMITH, Colonel, was born Sept. 13, 1910 at Charleston, WV. He was drafted Dec. 19, 1943 and served in the JAG.

His memorable experience was WWII and the Korean Conflict. Col. Smith received many awards, but his highest was the Legion of Merit.

Retired, he lives with his wife, Frances, in Columbus, OH; they have three adult children.

CHARLES SOHAR, Tech 5, was born May 7, 1916 at Akron, OH. He joined the service Jan. 22, 1941 and served with Btry. A, 140th FA BN, 37th Div.

Overseas duty at Fiji, Guadalcanal, Bougainville, invasion of Philippines, battle of Luzon and battle of Northern Solomons. His memorable experience was being wounded June 16, 1945.

Discharged Oct. 3, 1945 as Tech 5, He received the Purple Heart, two Bronze Stars, American Defense Medal, Asiatic-Pacific Theater, Philippine Liberation Ribbon and Good Conduct Ribbon.

Retired since 1978, he makes his home in Kidron, OH. He has four sons, one daughter and 14 grandchildren.

CLARENCE JAMES SOTERA (C.J.), Staff Sergeant, was born Aug. 17, 1915 in Cleveland, OH. He enlisted in the 37th Div. in 1938 (Reserves) and stayed with the unit until 1944.

Was sent to the South Pacific in April 1942 as a member of the Forward Echelon, Advance Detachment, 37th Div. They traveled first to Australia and then to New Zealand. Sent back to the States in 1944 to Ft. Belvoir, VA and became an instructor in the Engineering School in surveying course.

Was discharged Sept. 6, 1945 with the rank of staff sergeant. After leaving the service, he went to work for the Department of Defense at Ft. Belvoir. Worked for ERDL, Engineer Research and Development Laboratory. He retired June 29, 1979 with 40 years of service.

Resides in Alexandria, VA with his wife, Corinne; they have three daughters, one son and six grandchildren. He is a member of the 24 Post of the American Legion.

RAYMAN C. SPALSBURY, Colonel (RET), was born in Mount Pleasant, MI on April 6, 1915. He enlisted April 23, 1941, assigned to AT Co., 126th Inf., 32nd Inf. Division, Camp Livingston, LA. Promoted to corporal, then sergeant. Attended OCS Fort Benning, GA and commissioned July 9, 1942. Served at IRTC Camp Wheeler, GA; Camp Butner, NC; Camp Phillips, KS; Camp Lugana, AZ (80th Div.); Fort McClellan, AL and Ft. Lewis, WA.

He went to the South Pacific in March 1944, landing at New Caledonia. Went to Guadalcanal and Bougainville and was assigned to the C Co., 145th Inf., 37th Div. He participated in landing on Luzon, battle of Manila as platoon leader and company commander, and was at Tuguegarao, Luzon on V-J Day. He served with 21st Inf., 24th Div. in Army of Occupation in Kyushu, Japan, 1947-48. Was wounded twice: Feb. 28, 1945 at Intramuros, Manila and May 7, 1945 at Mt. Pacwagon, Luzon.

He was awarded the Combat Infantry Badge, Bronze Star Medal with OLC, Purple Heart Medal with OLC, Good Conduct Medal, Army Reserve Achievement Medal, and the following service medals: American Defense, American Theater, Asiatic-Pacific Theater with two Bronze Service Stars, WWII Victory, Army of Occupation (Japan), Army Reserve with two Hour Glasses, Philippine Liberation with one Bronze Service Star, Philippine Independence and Philippine Presidential Unit Award.

He retired April 12, 1975 as Colonel, AUS. Also retired as assistant postmaster, Lansing, MI. He has two daughters, two granddaughters, a grandson, and one great-granddaughter.

He and his wife reside in Lansing, MI.

RALPH W. SPEARS, Sergeant, was born May 29, 1926 in Pittsburgh, PA. He joined the Army in 1944 and served as rifleman with Co. I, 145th Inf. 37th Div. He was stationed in the States and overseas at New Guinea and Philippine Islands.

Memorable experiences include Balete Pass, Orong Pass, Cagayan Valley, Luzon Island and when peace was declared.

Discharged in November 1946 as sergeant. He received the Bronze Star, Combat Infantry Badge, Meritorious Unit Citation and Philippine Victory Medal. Retired, he lives with his wife, Nadine, in New Castle, PA; they have two sons, Edwin and David; daughter, Lana; and six grandchildren.

GEORGE A. SPEES, Staff Sergeant, was born Jan. 4, 1919 at Green Bay, WI. He joined the service in 1940 and served in the Infantry. Basic training was at Camp Wolters, TX, then overseas to South Pacific.

Participated in action at Solomons and Philippine Island Beachhead.

His memorable experiences include: out-running a grenade; street fighting, Manila and many that should be forgotten.

Discharged in August 1945 as staff sergeant. He received the Bronze Star and refused battlefield commission.

Married 47 years, he has three daughters, four granddaughters, one grandson and one great-granddaughter. Retired 12 years ago and lives in Carmichael, CA.

CARL B. SPONSELLER, T-4, was born Sept. 14, 1910 in Plymouth, OH. Graduated in 1929, worked as machinist four years before being drafted in the Army in January 1941. He trained at Camp Shelby, MS with the 37th Div. ASN. Received temporary discharge in October and was recalled in December 1941 to Camp Shelby, 140th FA BN.

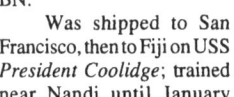

Was shipped to San Francisco, then to Fiji on USS *President Coolidge*; trained near Nandi until January 1943; then combat duty at Guadalcanal, Russell Island, New Georgia Campaign and Bougainville Campaign.

Memorable Experience: Their radio had a 13 foot high antenna and it drew enemy fire thus endangering the operator and men nearby. He and another radio-operator, Bill M., decided to make an improvement to the equipment. After trying it at base camp, they put it to the test on the front line and the operator thought it was great. He could be obscure and out of danger and the communications were better than ever. When the battalion communications officer heard of it, he ordered Sponseller to dismantle the unit since it was not approved by the U.S. Sig. Corps; but since the captain was due for rotation and Sponseller had enough points to return to the States, he didn't dismantle it. He learned later that the captain's replacement understood the unit's advantage and kept using it, and that Bill M. was awarded a commendation for the improvement.

Returned to the States and was discharged in October 1945. Awards/Medals: was elected for the Philippine Campaign, Manila Liberation, Baguio Campaign, Cagayan Valley Campaign and earned the American Defense, Asiatic-Pacific, Combat Action and Good Conduct Medals.

Married and moved to California; they have two boys. He attended UC Berkeley, followed by machinist and electric trades. He retired in 1985 and is living in El Cerrito, CA. He is on the maintenance staff of Mt. Diablo-Silverado Council, Boy Scouts of America.

ROBERT W. STEFFY (BOB), T-5, was born Aug. 6, 1918 in Hartville, OH. He was inducted Feb. 11, 1941 at Cleveland, OH. He remembers that there were moments of boredom, moments of terror and times when laughter ruled. He made friends that have lasted a lifetime. Also memorable was the travel involved and the people he met, especially in New Zealand and the Philippines. He served in Korea with an ONG FA unit.

Discharged June 24, 1945 at Camp Atterbury, IN. His battalion received a Commendation for Bougainville.

Steffy is retired, reads a lot and collects military history. He lives alone, mows a lot of grass and sometimes set up a flea market stand. He likes to tinker and restore discarded items for resale. He has two daughters, one granddaughter, four grandsons and great-grandson. His youngest daughter served with her Army Reserve unit in the Persian Gulf War.

Belongs to several veterans organizations and twice has been commander of American Legion Post #44 and past Stark County Commander of the Legion. He is president of the Stark County Chapter of the 37th Div. Veterans Assoc.

ROBERT R. STEPUTIS, T/Sergeant, was born in Seattle, WA on May 11, 1921. He was inducted at Fort Lewis, WA on March 23, 1943, and had basic training at Fort Leonard Wood, MO with 75th Inf. Div.

On Sept. 21, 1943 he departed from San Francisco aboard Matson Line luxury liner the *Lurline*, arriving Noumea, New Caledonia on October 3; later shipped to Guadalcanal via hospital ship USS *Pinkney* joining 37th Div. H Co. on October 29 and greeted by the charming company commander, Capt. Martin Haug. Although he was trained in a mortar platoon, he shortly was assigned to Co. HQ as a runner in preparation for action.

On to Bougainville landing November 13, called to 129th Inf. Band by WO Lee Douglas on Jan. 31, 1944 (playing French horn) but shortly thereafter called to Division HQ by Lt. Col. Demas Sears for assignment in G-2 Section, in which he served the balance of the war. He landed with the division on Luzon's Lingayen Gulf Jan. 10, 1945 participating in the campaign to liberate Luzon and the entire Philippine Islands and formulated the Japanese surrender document for Northern Luzon.

Returned to the U.S. Dec. 11, 1945 and was honorably discharged December 21. Married Betty on Jan. 10, 1946; they have two children and three grandchildren. Their son Kirk and family are serving as missionaries at Faith Academy in Manila where Bob and Betty visit at least twice a year. Retired from United Airlines after 35 and a half years service and now resides in Kauai, HI.

EARL C. STEWART, was born at Charleston, WV on March 3, 1925. He served from June 15, 1944 to Dec. 27, 1945. Basic training was at Camp Croft, SC in November 1944; assigned to South Pacific Theater first arriving in Philippines, Leyte Island and later assigned to Co. A, 129th Inf. Regt. of 37th Div. in January 1945. He served as rifleman, loaded, aimed and fired a rifle to destroy enemy personnel and assisted in capturing and holding enemy positions.

He participated in following battles: Clark Field, Fort Stotsenburg, Manila, Baguio and Cagayan Valley. He was awarded the Marksman Badge with Rifle Bar, Combat Infantry Badge, Good Conduct Medal, Asiatic-Pacific Campaign Medal with two Bronze Stars, WWII Victory Medal, Philippine Liberation Medal with one Bronze Star, Presidential Unit Citation Badge and Bronze Star Medal.

He is retired from West Virginia Dept. of Health and resides in Hurricane, WV with his wife Dee. He is a member of the First Baptist Church of Hurricane, 32° Mason, Shriner, Odd Fellow, Knights Pythias, life member of VFW, American Legion, 37th Div. Assoc. and charter member of Co. A Assoc. and Co. A Chapter 129th Inf. 37th Div. Assoc.

He has two daughters, Dorinda Stutts of Lexington, NC and Laberta Lucas of Hurricane, WV; two step-children, William Davis of Savannah, GA and Debra Fedd of Huntington, VA; one grandson; five step-granddaughters and one step-grandson. He enjoys gardening, hunting, fishing, golfing, bowling, attending Army reunions and traveling in his motorhome.

ROBERT W. STOLL, was born Feb. 24, 1922 and educated in Rochester, NY. He was drafted into active service at Fort Dix, NJ on Sept. 7, 1943. Went to Fort McClellan, AL for basic training. After a month at Fort Ord, CA, he was shipped to Camp Stoneman, New Caledonia Island.

He joined the 37th Div. on Bougainville, Solomon Islands in March 1944. Company L fought the Japanese in Luzon, Philippines and later became HQ Company Clerk. Received the Combat Infantryman Badge, Asiatic-Pacific and Purple Heart Ribbons, Bronze Star Medal, WWII Victory Medal, Philippine Liberation Ribbon with one star. Was discharged on Dec. 28, 1945 at Fort Dix.

Went to University of Buffalo and worked at Dupont for 32 years. Married Elizabeth and they reside in Niagara Falls, NY. He does garden work, plays golf and bowls. They enjoy traveling to Hawaii, Alaska, Europe, Panama Canal and cruising the Caribbean Islands.

W. WALLACE STOVER (SMOKY), Lieutenant Colonel, was born Feb. 20, 1917 in Columbus, OH. He was called to active duty in May 1941 as a 2nd lieutenant. Served with several companies in 145th and 129th Inf. in 37th Div.

Stationed at Camp Shelby, Ft. Benning,

37th Infantry Division—91

Indiantown Gap, New Zealand, Fiji, New Hebrides, Guadalcanal and Bougainville. Memorable experience was leading a combat patrol with Fijian scouts and 100 native carriers up Laruma River and met advance party of Japs on way to attack our lines.

Retired in October 1966. He received the Distinguished Service Cross, Bronze Star with stars and arrow and all the usual ribbons.

A retired college administrator, he lives in Ohio and Florida with Virginia.

ALFRED F. STRECK, Colonel, was born Jan. 5, 1926 in Hilo, T.H. He graduated Armored OCS, Ft. Knox, KY; assigned to the 37th Inf. Div., 137th TK BN, Camp Polk, LA; served as the tank battalion personnel officer, 2nd lieutenant and assistant adjutant; eight weeks training at Camp Irwin, CA. During WWII he was PFC aerial gunner B-24 Liberator aircraft, supply clerk and personnel clerk CONUS April 1944-May 1946.

Separated Sept. 30, 1953. Assigned USA Ready Reserve 1952 through 1970. Civil affairs/military government officer, finance officer, military intelligence officer. He transferred to the USAF Ready Reserve, HQ PACAF, Hickam AFB, HI, 1970, lieutenant colonel Security Police.

From 1972-1980, additional USAFR duty USAF Academy, liaison officer. Reassigned to HQ North American Air Defense Command, Colorado Springs 1981-84. Retired as colonel, Logistics Plans & Program Staff Officer. Highest award received was the Defense Meritorious Service Medal.

He is a contract investigator for Honolulu Police Commission, city and county of Honolulu, HI (civil service) and retired from Federal Civil Service after 29 years. Married and has four children and nine grandchildren. He is a permanent resident of Hawaii.

WILLIAM F. SULLIVAN, Lieutenant Colonel, enlisted in B Btry. of the 135th FA in September 1938. He went overseas with the d ivision and was selected for OCS on Fiji and was commissioned as a 2nd lieutenant in January of 1943. He served with the 135th FA BN throughout the war and returned to the States with the division in December 1945 as XO of Btry. B, 135th FA BN.

One of his most memorable experiences of the war was the time while in support of the 145th Inf. on Mt. Pacwagon, a Jap demolition team infiltrated the battery area and blew up one of the howitzers.

When the division was re-activated in 1946, he again joined the 135th FA as A Btry. commander. He went on active duty with the division in 1952. He spent that tour of duty at Camp Polk. He transferred from the National Guard to the Army Reserve in 1961 and served in the Reserve until retirement in 1971 as lieutenant colonel.

Retired from Ford Motor Co. in 1979 and resides in the Cleveland and Ohio area.

ALLAN J. SUSOEFF, Tech 5, was born March 23, 1925 at Sheridan, CA. He joined the military service July 15, 1943 and served in the Army Technical Corps 5, 37th Div. Recon Trp. He was stationed at Camp Fannin, TX; Fort Ord, CA; Camp Stoneman, CA; and Camp Beale, CA.

Participated in battles in the Solomon Islands, South Pacific, Luzon and Philippine Islands. His memorable experience was being one of the first in the invasion of Luzon, Philippines. He was wounded in northern Luzon. Discharged Dec. 23, 1945. His medals/awards include the Asiatic-Pacific Ribbon with two stars, Victory Medal, Purple Heart, Distinguished Unit Badge and Philippine Liberation Ribbon.

A retired truck driver, he lives in San Mateo, CA. He has two granddaughters.

GEORGE H. SWEIGERT, Staff Sergeant, was born Feb. 7, 1920 in Akron, OH. He joined the service in April 1940 and served with HQ Co., 145th Inf., 37th Div. He was stationed at Camp Shelby, Fiji Island, Guadalcanal, New Georgia, Camp Blanding, Bougainville and Rendova.

His memorable experiences include the landings at Bougainville and New Georgia.

Discharged in July 1945 as staff sergeant. He received the Combat Infantry Badge, Good Conduct and Meritorious Service.

Retired, he lives with his wife, Kay, in Fort Wayne, IN; they have five children. His hobby is amateur radio, computers and reading.

DONALD B. THOMSON, Lieutenant Colonel, was born April 16, 1913, Edmonton, Alberta, Canada. He joined the USN on Jan. 10, 1930 and the USA Oct. 10, 1938. Served with the USA, Artillery, 37th Inf. Div., 25th Inf. Div. in Korea.

Military locations/stations include Camp Stewart, GA; Camp Davis, NC; Bougainville; Luzon; KSNG as advisor; Korea; Japan, and Ft. Rucker, AL. He participated in action at Bougainville, Lingayen Gulf to Manila, Baguio, Cagayan Valley and in Korea (1950-52).

Memorable Experiences: making the gulf landing with his aviation section in DUKW; observing final assault of the Intramuros in Manila; flying observation missions over and behind Japanese lines to guide infantry away from ambushes; and helping to burn North Koreans out of buildings in Seoul.

Discharged May 1, 1962 as lieutenant colonel. His awards and medals include the Silver Star, three Bronze Stars, five Air Medals and two Commendation Ribbons.

Retired and has a home in Boulder City, NV and one in Seal Beach, CA. His wife, Mimi, passed away of cancer in 1987. He has three daughters: one is a chief petty officer in the USN, one in the computer business in North Carolina and one is a school teacher in North Carolina.

WILMOT B. THOMPSON, Private First Class, was born in Virgil, SD on Dec. 2, 1910. He served Dec. 26, 1943 to Nov. 3, 1945; trained at Camp Wolters, TX until April 1943; departed San Francisco the last of April 1943 for New Hebrides Islands for more training in jungle warfare with D Co., 129th Inf., 37th Div.

He was in Guadalcanal for a few days then on to Bougainville in November 1943. Participated in the Battle for Bougainville until March 27, 1944 when he was wounded; transferred to 9th Station Hospital on Guadalcanal; then on to 8th General Hospital, New Caledonia April 8.

Returned to Letterman General Hospital May 18, 1944. Then on to O'Reilly General Hospital on June 3, 1944 until December 1944. Was attached to MP duty at Algona, IA; Montgomery, MN; and Greely, CO.

Discharged Nov. 3, 1945. His awards include the Good Conduct Medal, Asiatic-Pacific Ribbon, Purple Heart and Silver Star.

He has been retired since 1976 doing part-time marketing and public relations.

REX F. TILLOTSON, Sergeant T/4, was born Dec. 20, 1920 in Mt. Airy, NC. He joined the military service in October 1942 and served in the Medical Detachment, 145th Inf., 37th Div. Some of his stations were Camp Grant, IL; Camp Beale, CA; New Guinea, Bougainville, Luzon and Leyte, Philippines and others. His memorable experiences are to many to list.

Was discharged Dec. 22, 1945 as sergeant T/4 (surgical technician). His awards include the Medical Combat Badge, Silver Star Medal, two Bronze Stars, Asiatic-Pacific Campaign Medal with three Bronze Service Stars, Philippine Liberation Medal with Bronze Service Star and others.

His last position was as associate dean of admissions at the College of William and Mary. Retired, he is currently serving as director of the American Legion. He has four daughters: Susan, Beth, Nita and Patricia.

HARRY C. TKACH, Tech Sergeant, was born Sept. 5, 1918 in Struthers, OH. He joined the military service Jan. 27, 1941 and served in the Infantry, 145th Regt., 37th Div. Was stationed at Camp Shelby, Indiantown Gap, Fiji Islands, New Georgia, Guadalcanal, New Zealand, Solomon Island and Bougainville.

Memorable Experiences: when a friendly shell fell five feet above their pillbox on Bougainville; and when he was in the 142nd General Hospital in Fiji and Mrs. Roosevelt came to visit.

Discharged Aug. 8, 1945 as tech sergeant. His awards include the Combat Infantry Badge, Good Conduct and Bronze Star.

Tkach is single and lives in Struthers, OH; he is retired from civil service and has four sisters.

PAUL R. TOTTEN, Staff Sergeant, was born in Greenwood, IN on Aug. 29, 1924. He served from July 2, 1942 to December 29, 1945. He had basic training at Camp Roberts, CA; served two and a half years in the South Pacific with combat experience in Bougainville with Canon Co. 145th Regt., 37th Div. He participated in the invasion of Luzon and fought in the battle of Manila with Antitank Co., 145th Regt.

One of his most memorable experiences was the room to room, floor to floor battle with the Japanese soldiers holed up in the post office and city hall buildings inside the Walled City. He was awarded the Asiatic-Pacific Ribbon with two Bronze Stars, Philippine Liberation Medal, Bronze Star Medal, Victory Medal and Distinguished Service Cross.

A commercial real estate appraiser, he and his wife, Carla, reside in Greenwood, IN.

CLELL TOY JR., Sergeant T/4, was born June 21, 1920. He joined the Army Nov. 13, 1941 and after basic training was assigned to Co. B, 147th Inf., 37th Div. at Indiantown Gap, PA. The 147th Inf. (less 2nd Bn.) and the 134th FA BN were combined into the 147th Combat Team and shipped to the Tongan Islands via the Panama Canal on April 7, 1942.

Shortly after joining the 147th Inf. Co. B, he transferred from a rifle platoon squad to the kitchen and eventually was promoted to a first cook. In October 1942 the 147th started moving to Guadalcanal, and on Jan. 30, 1943 fought the last full-scale battle of the Guadalcanal Campaign at the Bonegi River. The 147th went to British Samoa, New Caledonia, Emirau Island, participated in the Iwo Jima Campaign, Tinian and Okinawa.

Discharged Aug. 20, 1945 as T-4. His awards include the Bronze Star Medal, Good Conduct Medal, American Defense Service Medal, Asiatic-Pacific Theater Medal with three Bronze Campaign Stars, WWII Victory Medal, and he is authorized to wear the Guadalcanal/Solomon Islands 50th Anniversary Campaign Ribbons.

A retired dairy/tobacco farmer, his wife is deceased. He has a daughter, son and three grandchildren.

SUSUMU TOYODA, Major, was born Oct. 3, 1919 in San Gabriel, CA. He entered the military service on March 11, 1941. In December 1943, he and his six-member Japanese language team were assigned to the 37th Inf. Div., Bougainville. In support of the division's operations, there and in the Philippines, the team chalked up a number of intelligence successes.

Gathering intelligence about Japanese military activities on Bougainville was a difficult job and capturing a Japanese PW was a rare event indeed. One of their first was captured in late February 1944. Quite surprisingly, this member of the 45th Inf. Regt. of the infamous 6th Div. (known for the rape of Nanking) divulged much valuable information and helped to bring an end to the enemy attacks against the Torokina perimeter.

At the end of WWII, while assigned to the Army Language School (Ft. Snelling, MN), he served as battalion adjutant and later as instructor, and continued in that capacity when the school moved to Monterey, CA. His next assignment in November 1949 was to the Allied Translation and Interpreters Service, Tokyo, interrogating repatriated Japanese soldiers from Siberia.

As the Korean Conflict was winding down, he was assigned to South Korea to interrogate Chinese and North Korean POWs. He was recalled to Tokyo in 1952 to become interpreter-aide to Gen. Matthew B. Ridgway and later to Gens. Mark W. Clark, John E. Hull and Maxwell D. Taylor. Subsequent assignments were at the Pentagon, Advanced Intelligence School and Okinawa.

He received a battlefield commission in the Philippines, May 9, 1945. He was a recipient of the Soldiers Medal, Bronze Star and Oak Leaf Cluster, Good Conduct Medal and 11 campaign and service medals. Maj. Toyoda was discharged Nov. 30, 1962.

Retired to Mesa, AZ for nearly nine years before settling in Carlsbad, CA in 1985.

ROBERT C. TURNER, Staff Sergeant, was born in Washington, DC on Oct. 3, 1920. He served in the National Guard and his engineer regiment was called into federal service on Feb. 3, 1941. He trained at Ft. George Meade, MD and at the Ft. Belvoir, VA Engineering School for Combat Engineers.

Turner's unit joined the 37th Inf. Div. at Indiantown Gap, PA. The division was shipped overseas in the spring of 1942 to the Fiji Islands. Next, moving forward to Guadalcanal, New Georgia and Bougainville, engaging in a number of operations of trail blazing, bridge building and often times, fire fights with the enemy when operating with the 148th Inf. Combat Team.

He was awarded the Silver Star for gallantry in action on the island of New Georgia. He was discharged on Aug. 16, 1945, and was married Dec. 7, 1946, to a grand lady from Texas who passed away Dec. 21, 1990. They had two fine sons. His home is Kensington, MD and he is retired from the Bell Telephone Co.

RICHARD L. VOSBURGH, Private First Class, of Elyria, OH was born Oct. 20, 1921 and enlisted in OHNG, November 1939. He later transferred to Berea, OH, Co. D, 145th Inf. and was with the 1st Med. Detach. at Guadalcanal. He trained at Camp Perry, OH and Camp Shelby, MS. He was stationed at Suva Fiji, fighting in battles at Guadalcanal, Munda Island, Bougainville and the Philippines.

He was discharged October 1945 as a private first class and received the Medical Combat Badge, Good Conduct Medal, American Defense Ribbon, Asiatic-Pacific Ribbon with two Bronze Stars and the Philippine Liberation Ribbon with one Bronze Star.

Vosburgh retired from E+L Transport and is taking life easy. He has been married to Rebecca for 45 years and has three married daughters: Judith Evans, Rebecca Scheutzow and Bonnie Stokely. There are six grandchildren and two great-grandchildren.

DOYLE MAYLON WALKER, Staff Sergeant, was born April 16, 1923 in Snyder, TX. He joined the military service in 1942 and was assigned to Co. B, 129th Inf., attached to the 37th Div. He trained at Camp Wolters, TX, Luzon, Philippines, New Hebrides, Bougainville, Solomon Islands and Guadalcanal.

He was discharged Sept. 18, 1945, as staff sergeant. His awards/medals include the Purple Heart with second OLC, Bronze Star, Philippine Liberation, Good Conduct and APO Ribbon. Retired from CE, NATCO and lives in Electra, TX with his wife, Bernice. They have three children, seven grandchildren and one great-grandchild. His hobbies are fishing, camping and traveling.

JAMES C. WALKER, T-5, was born May 2, 1917 in Smithville, TN. He joined the military service Oct. 22, 1941 and was assigned to the 145th Inf. Co. E, then transferred to 737th Ord. Co. in 1943 to the end of the war.

Stationed at Camp Shelby and various locations in the Philippines, where he participated in all the battles and invasions of the 37th Div. His memorable experience was repairing all types of instruments for the Army and sometimes for the Air Force.

Discharged Oct. 20, 1945 as tech 5. He received all the usual medals and awards.

A jeweler from 1945-1977 when he retired. He resides with his wife in West Palm Beach, FL; they have two sons, James and Robert.

JACK C. WANDER, Private First Class, was born July 15, 1921 at Columbus, OH. He joined the military service in 1941 and served with the Army, HQ Btry., 134th FA in the South Pacific.

Wander was discharged in 1945. Following the service he worked in the printing industry and also at the Association's HQ office. He passed away May 23, 1985, leaving his wife, Doris; son, Stephen; daughter, Robin; and four grandchildren.

STEPHEN J. WARGO, Tech Sergeant, was born in Campbell, OH on July 22, 1922. He enlisted in Co.

H, 145th Inf. Regt., 37th Div. OHNG in August 1940; federalized in October 1940; trained at Camp Shelby, MS and was shipped to the South Pacific in May 1942.

Landed in Auckland, New Zealand, Fiji Islands, Guadalcanal and Solomon Islands. He participated in the invasion of New Georgia; taking of Munda Air-

37th Infantry Division—93

field; Bougainville, was twice wounded on Hill 700; landed at Lingayen Gulf, Luzon, Philippine Islands, January 1945. He took part in the battle for Manila and Mount Pacwagon.

Rotated during the divisions race up the Cagayan Valley; discharged at Camp Atterbury, IN; and arrived home on V-J Day. His awards include the Silver Star, Bronze Star for Valor, Purple Heart with cluster, Combat Infantry Badge, CBI American Theater Ribbon, Asiatic-Pacific Ribbon with two Bronze Service Stars, Philippine Liberation Ribbon with one Bronze Star and the Victory Medal.

Wargo re-enlisted for the Korean Conflict; retired Regular Army in December 1965; civilian intelligence officer, USAF; retired June 1983, GS-13. He and his wife, Rita, reside in Fairborn, OH

ERWIN O. WESTERMERER, Tech Sergeant, was born June 26, 1917. He joined the military service Feb. 2, 1942 and served with the 37th Div. as Army Scout. Stationed at Camp Forrest, TN; Fiji Islands; New Hebrides; Northern Solomons; and Philippine Islands.

Participated in action in the southern Philippines, northern Solomons and Luzon. One of his memorable experiences was meeting Gen. MacArthur at Pasig River near Manila.

Discharged Oct. 13, 1945 as tech sergeant. He received three Bronze Stars, Purple Heart, Good Conduct, Philippine Liberation Ribbon with Bronze Star and Asiatic-Pacific Campaign Ribbon.

A retired contractor, he lives with his wife, Felice, in Boise, ID. They have four sons, three daughters and seven grandchildren.

LAWRENCE K. WHITE (RED), Colonel, was born in Union City, TN on June 10, 1912. He graduated from West Point in 1933; served as battalion commander and executive, 129th Inf. in the Fijis and New Hebrides; as assistant G-3 on Guadalcanal and New Georgia; and as Chief of Staff Vella LaVella Task Force and regimental commander of the 148th Inf. during the Bougainville and Philippine campaigns.

Severely wounded April 17, 1945 near Baguio, he was retired for combat disability March 31, 1947. Thereafter, he served the Central Intelligence Agency for 25 years in senior positions including Chief Foreign Broadcast Information Service, Deputy Director (Administration) and Executive Director.

He retired in 1972 and resides in Vero Beach, FL. His decorations include the Distinguished Service Cross, Silver Star, Legion of Merit with OLC, Bronze Star Medal for Valor with two OLCs, Navy Commendation Ribbon, Combat Infantry Badge, Purple Heart, Presidential Unit Citation and the Distinguished Intelligence Medal.

HOMER F. WINEGARDNER, Private First Class, was born Jan. 30, 1921 at Thornville, OH. He joined the military and served in the Army Infantry. He was stationed at Ft. McClellan, AL.

He participated in the Luzon Campaign and Pacific Theater with the 37th Div. as a heavy machine gunner.

Winegardner received the WWII Victory Medal and the Purple Heart for wounds received in the Pacific Theater. Was discharged Dec. 18, 1945 as private first class.

Retired, he lives with his wife, Hannah, in Thornville, OH; they have two children, Charles and Cynthia.

FRED WINTRICH, Tech Sergeant, was born in Cleveland, OH on Aug. 6, 1917. He enlisted in the Ohio National Guard in 1937 and was mobilized to federal service in September 1940. He trained with Co. C, 112th Engr. Regt. (combat). This training included the famous Louisiana Maneuvers where he participated with the 37th Div. at Camp Shelby, MS. T/SGT Wintrich was the division water supply NCO.

After completing training with the 112th, he was selected as part of the divisional advance detachment and shipped out through San Francisco to Melbourne Australia. During his two years of combat service overseas, he participated in the fortification of the Fiji Islands and the operations at Guadalcanal, New Georgia (combat landing) and Bougainville. Wintrich was discharged from Ft. Dix, NJ on Aug. 31, 1945.

He is a lifetime member of the VFW and the 37th Div. Assoc. He is retired and lives in Cleveland, OH.

BENJAMIN TAPPAN WRIGHT, Lieutenant Colonel, was born Aug. 24, 1922 at Berkeley, CA. He joined the military service in 1940 and served in the Army, HQ Btry., 136th FA BN, 37th Div. He was stationed at Ft. Sill, OK; Camp Gruber, OK; Ft. Bragg, NC; Ft. Ord, CA; and Luzon, Philippine Islands.

He attended OCS Class 88, Ft. Sill, OK in 1943. Participated in action at Luzon Campaign in 1945 and at Cagayan Valley.

His awards include the Philippine Distinguished Unit Citation, Philippine Liberation, Independence Medals, American Theater, Asiatic-Pacific, WWII Victory Medals and the Armed Forces Reserve Medal with Hourglass (20 years).

Retired Reserve 1965 and AUS 1982 as lieutenant colonel.

Has a BS from Harvard College (1943) and JD from Boston University School of Law (1950). Retired, he was former senior VP, secretary, general counsel of The Badger Co. Inc. He is world championship referee, International Skating Union, Chairman Figure Skating Technical Committee, ISU and past president of U.S. Figure Skating Technical Committee.

He lives with his wife, former Mary Louise Premer, in Belmont, MA; there are no children.

MELVIN F. YOST, Private First Class, was born June 18, 1924 in Fairmont, WV. He joined the Army on Sept. 18, 1943, served with the 37th Ohio Div.; stationed at Camp Wolters, TX.

He left San Francisco harbor on the USS *General J.R. Brooks* and landed in New Caledonia. From there went to Guadalcanal, Bougainville then joined the 37th Div., Co. K of the 148th  Regt. He made the invasion of the Philippines on the island of Luzon on Jan. 9, 1945. His memorable experience occurred when he left the landing boat and landed in water up to his arm pits and had to be pulled out by one of his buddies. Another memorable experience occurred when he was in China crossing a bridge that was wired up with bombs. He tripped over the wires, but was lucky and the bombs never went off. He experienced many other close calls to numerous too mention. The happiest moment of his life was when the war ended and he headed for home.

Awards include the Asiatic-Pacific Theater Ribbon with three Bronze Service Stars, Philippine Liberation Ribbon with one Bronze Service Star, WWII Victory Medal, Bronze Star Medal, Purple Heart, Good Conduct Medal and Bronze Arrowhead Medal. Discharged Jan. 5, 1946 as private first class.

Retired from Westinghouse Electric Corp. He has a son, two daughters and three grandchildren.

JACK YOUNG, Staff Sergeant, was born in Mentor, OH on Oct. 30, 1920. He was the 15th person to volunteer for the draft in Lake County, OH and joined the 37th Inf. Div. at Camp Shelby, MS on Feb. 1, 1941.

He went overseas with the 37th on May 26, 1942 and returned with the main body of the division on Sept. 26, 1945. He participated in all of the 37th's campaigns in the Pacific theater (Northern Solomons, Luzon) serving with HQ Co., 148th Inf. as radio chief and at various times in the same capacity with HQ Co., 1st and 2nd Bns.

His service awards include Good Conduct Medal, Combat Infantry Badge, Asiatic-Pacific Ribbon with two Bronze Stars, American Defense Service Medal, Philippine Liberation Ribbon with one Bronze Star, Unit Citation Award and the Bronze Star Medal.

Jack is a widower and retired, having spent 40 years in the mail-order nursery business.

A salute to "Old Glory" as it is raised above the American Embassy in Tokyo, Japan, Sept. 8, 1945. L to R: Maj. Gen. Will C. Chase C/CG 1st Cav. Div.; Admiral William Halsey; Lt. Gen. Robert L. Eichelberger and General of the Army Douglas MacArthur. (U.S. Army Photo)

Index

This Index includes surnames, placenames, ship's names and significant terms in the general history text section of this book. Photos and the veteran's section are not indexed.

A

Ahern 39, 51
Alcoa Polaris 31
Alexander 37
Allison 48
American Legion 26
Aola 37
Aparri 11
Aquarius 30
Arundel 39
Asai 55
Ayers 31, 32
Ayres 55

B

Bach 55
Baesel 12
Baguio 11, 17, 54
Bailey 30
Bairoko 39
Balintawak 11, 33
Ballette 11
Beach 37, 49
Beaufort Bay 27
Beightler 12, 22, 26, 31, 43
Bell 48
Bilibid 11
Blount 19, 31
Boanos 48
Bonegi 38
Bougainville
   8, 9, 16, 17, 29, 30, 33, 55
Bourmont 13, 14
Boyd 30
Braden 32
Brest 14
British Somoa 38
Buescher 38
Buesher 27
Buschard 48

C

Cabanatuan 12
Cagayan 11, 17, 34, 46
Calhoun 48
Camp Knox 9
Camp Lee 13
Camp Perry 9, 13
Camp Polk 12
Camp Shelby
   9, 19, 20, 21, 22, 23, 26, 40, 46, 49
Camp Sheridan 8, 13, 14
Camp Upton 14

Camp Wheeler 32
Camp Wolters 22
Cape Esperance 38
Carlson 26
Carney Field 27
Carr 48
Caserta 13
Casualties 18, 60
Cervantes 33
Chadwick 19
Chaney 26, 29, 36, 46, 48, 53
Ciccetti 12
Clark 32, 33
Collins 37
Correages 34
Cory 48
Cox 8
Crescent City 30
Crosby 33
Cruyshauten 15

D

Daniels 19
Davies 31, 32, 53
Davis 55
De Peyster 20
DeCarre 38
DeHaven 27, 38
Dupage 30
Duport 14

E

Elmore 30
Emery 48
Emirau 27, 30, 38
Eniwetok 51
Erskine 52

F

Farber 55
Farnsworth 13
Fiji 9, 27
Fisher 48
Fiske 20
Fogle 48
Folk 54
Folz 48
Fort Bragg 22
Fort Lewis 27, 38
Fort Meigs 13
Frankel 8, 11, 12
Fujii 55

G

George Clymer 38, 49
Gibbons 55
Gittinger 48
Glass 48
Glore 19, 31
Goshorn 48
Graf 13
Gregg 48
Guadalcanal
   8, 9, 10, 16, 26, 27, 29, 30, 37, 38, 55
Guam 26
Guyer 54

H

Halsey 30
Hammond 48
Hanes 27, 38
Harper 32
Harris 48
Harrison 8, 13
Hasenbein 48
Hass 48
Hathorn Sound 39
Henne 39
Heubel 16
Hill 700 10
Hiroshima 11, 51
Hokama 55
Holtmann 48
Hororatia 14
Huff 48
Hughes 27, 38
Hull 13
Hunter Liggett 26

I

Indiantown 9, 23, 26
Intrepid 54
Ishida 55
Iwo Jima 27, 38, 51, 52, 54

J

Johnson 51, 53

K

Kadrmas 55
Kanda 55
Kattine 48
Kawamoto 55
Kelley 48
Kirker 19, 50

Kistner 48
Kokumbona 37, 38
Komoto 55
Kreber 12
Kreco 48
Krotiak 12
Kuribayashi 51

L

Lacy 54
Lay 48
Leckie 27
Lingayen 17, 54, 55
Lockhart 31
Lombardi 48
Losito 48
Lovko 32
Lunsford 48
Luzon 10, 11, 17, 32, 33, 34

M

MacArthur 34, 54
Macdonald 17
Mains 48
Manila 11, 17, 33, 34, 54
Mason 48
Mathias 32, 33
McCann 48
McGuffin 37
Merritt 48
Meuse-Argonne 8, 13, 15
Middleton 48
Missouri 55
Moen 49
Monterrey 32
Moody 32
Moore 30, 48
Morison 27
Morrison 32
Moss 48
Munda 10, 39
Murley 48

N

Nagasaki 11, 51
Navy Unit Commendation 52
Nestor 14
Neville 26, 36
New Caledonia 26, 27, 31, 38
New Georgia 8, 10, 16, 40
New Guinea 32
New Hebrides 26
Nichols 48
Nimmo 19
Nisei 54, 55
Nolan 48

O

Oconto 32
Ogata 55
Okinawa 27, 31, 38
Ota 55
Outland 40

P

Panol 33
Patch 27
Patterson 48
Pearl Harbor 23, 26, 49
Penet 15
Petrarca 12
Petty 48
Phesus 14
Plassy 14
Pocahontas 13
Potter 48
President Hayes 37
Presidents 62, 63

R

Rape of Nanking 16
Ratterman 19
Rattermann 48
Reese 12
Reichelderfer 34
Rettig 48
Robbins 48
Roberts 32
Robinson 48
Rodriquez 12
Roosevelt 26, 33
Roush 38
Rowin 48
Russell 48

S

Sakamoto 55
Sargent 48
Sasaki 40
Savo 27
Saxton 14
Schwarb 48
Schwing 27, 38, 48
Scott 48
Senter 32
Shields 31
Shropshire 31
Shroyer 48
Sizemore 48
Sloan 48
Smith 48
Snow 48

Snyder 54
Solomon 10
Spalsbury 55
St. Mihiel one. 15
Steele 32
Susquehanna 13
Synghem 9

T

Tinian 27, 31, 38
Titan 14
Tonga 26
Tonga Tabu 26
Tongatabu 36
Toyoda 55
Treat 13
Truman 50, 51
Tumauini 34
Turner 27, 37
Tuttle 36, 38, 46

U

Uriu 55
Uyeda 54

V

Vandegrift 27, 37
Veilleus 32, 34
Verdun 9
Viale 12
Victoria 14
Vila 39

W

Wake 26
Wall 48
Walton 48
Wayne 30
West Virginia. 33
Wheeler 27
White 11
Whiteford 48
Wilcox 48
Williams 32
Willoughby 54
Wilson 8
Woellner 19, 31
Wright 27, 38

Y

Yoshiwara 55
Young 12, 54

Z

Zieta 39

www.ingramcontent.com/pod-product-compliance
Lightning Source LLC
Chambersburg PA
CBHW081827170426
43202CB00019B/2977